RELUCTANT UNION

RELUCTANT UNION

Alsace-Lorraine and
Imperial Germany
1871–1918

Dan P. Silverman

THE PENNSYLVANIA STATE
UNIVERSITY PRESS
University Park and London

Library of Congress Cataloging in Publication Data

Silverman, Dan P.   1935–
  Reluctant union; Alsace-Lorraine and Imperial
Germany, 1871–1918.

  A revision of the author's thesis, Yale, 1963.
  Bibliography: p.
  1. Alsace-Lorraine—Politics and government.
2. Germany—Politics and government—1871–1918.
3. Bismarck, Otto, Fürst von, 1815–1898. 4. Saverne,
Alsace. I. Title.
DD801.A56S53 1972   320.9'44'383081   73–180693
ISBN 0–271–01111–4

Library of Congress Catalog Card Number 73–180693
International Standard Book Number 0–271–01111–4

Designed by Marilyn Shobaken

FOR MY MOTHER AND FATHER

Contents

Preface

> All French territory should be freed and the in-
> vaded portions restored, and the wrong done to
> France by Prussia in 1871 in the matter of Alsace-
> Lorraine, which has unsettled the peace of the
> world for nearly fifty years, should be made secure
> in the interest of all.
>
> WOODROW WILSON

Woodrow Wilson's formula for lasting peace, out-
lined in his "Fourteen Points" speech to Congress, 8 January 1918,
looked both to the past and the future. Like most non-Germans,
Wilson assumed the annexation of Alsace-Lorraine by Germany in
1871 had been "wrong," and that returning the territory to France
in 1918 was "right." Neither Wilson nor the general public, however, had any clear idea of what had happened in Alsace-Lorraine
during the years of German rule. Even today, Alsace-Lorraine is
known to most students of history as an historic source of tension
between France and Germany. Very little is known of the internal
development of the territory under the German regime between 1871
and 1918.

My interest in Alsace-Lorraine dates from 1960, when I completed a seminar paper on Alsace-Lorraine's 1911 constitution. I
was struck by the scarcity of information concerning the development of the Reichsland between 1871 and 1918. There was no lack
of literature dealing with Alsace-Lorraine as an object of international tension, but very little had been written about the internal
history of the territory between 1871 and 1918, and its relationship
to imperial Germany. Indeed, some works created the unmistakable
implication that Alsace-Lorraine had no history between 1871 and

1918; at least one historian, Gaston Zeller, treated the period as a "parenthesis."

It is still generally believed that the Alsace-Lorrainers greeted the German regime in 1871 with universal hatred, and had not appreciably changed their attitude by 1914. Equally common is the belief that the Germans encouraged local hostility by forcing the people to endure severe physical, economic, political, spiritual, and psychological hardships. In short, the Alsace-Lorrainers loved France and hated Germany in 1871, and the Germans used the intervening years before the First World War to prove exactly how justified this popular hatred was.

As I examined each facet of the history of Alsace-Lorraine under German rule, the inadequacies of existing interpretations became ever more apparent. I encountered increasing difficulty in defining the reaction of the Alsace-Lorrainers to German policy in the Reichsland after 1871. After ten years of research and contemplation, I finally discovered the key to understanding Alsace-Lorraine under the German regime; one must discard even the most basic preconceived notions.

The first concept we must shelve is the idea of "the Alsace-Lorrainer." "The Alsace-Lorrainer" is a figment of the imagination; it is a term which implies a real community of interests which in fact did not exist. (I shall use the term in this work, but only as a matter of convenience.) Significant historical, linguistic, political, and economic differences separated Alsatians and Lorrainers, both before and after 1871. Within Alsace-Lorraine, conflicting interests separated Catholics and Protestants, natives and Germans, rural and urban areas, capitalists and socialists, liberals and democrats, free-traders and protectionists; the Alsatian textile industry itself exhibited disharmony among spinners, weavers, dyers, printers, and finishers. We are dealing with a highly pluralistic society, a far cry from the monolithic anti-German phalanx commonly described in the existing literature. The supposedly universal nationalistic hatred of the Germans dissolves in a myriad of political and economic considerations which took precedence over nationalistic sentiment. Some segments of the territorial population opposed the new regime not simply because it was German, but because it suppressed their political and economic aspirations.

The second notion destined for the scrap heap is the idea that the Germans consciously applied a uniformly repressive program of coercion in the Reichsland. The notion of universal repression implies a far greater degree of administrative continuity and fixity of purpose than the Germans were actually able to muster. A continuing struggle between civilian and military authorities, and a basic contradiction in aims between "national military security" and "Germanization" resulted in a great deal of confusion, vacillation, and ineffectiveness in German programs in the Reichsland. Coercion or conciliation? The final choice was never made. Under close scrutiny, the traditional view of effective administration under the combined talents of Prussian bureaucracy and Prussian militarism breaks down completely in Alsace-Lorraine. It is indeed a rather pathetic spectacle. While the highest civilian officials of the territorial administration sought to integrate the Reichsland into the Reich, the highest military officers sought to impose a military dictatorship; and on the sidelines, powerful German textile, tobacco, and iron and steel interests hoped to escape competition from the Reichsland by sabotaging all government efforts at conciliation and integration.

Given the complexity of the situation, it is improper to speak of the "failure" of "German policy" in Alsace-Lorraine. Until the famous Zabern affair of 1913–14, there was at least an even chance that Alsace-Lorraine might be integrated successfully into imperial Germany. Between 1871 and 1914, a continuing process of politicization pointed to some form of representative government within the framework of the German empire as the logical conclusion of the territory's historical development since 1871. By 1914, most Alsace-Lorrainers were willing to become German citizens in the full sense of the word. The triumph of the military in the Zabern affair, followed so closely by the failure of the German military in the First World War, meant that once again Alsace-Lorraine's historical course would be determined by alien forces from without.

D. P. S.

Acknowledgments

To the late Professor Hajo Holborn, who directed this work in its early stages as a doctoral dissertation at Yale University, the writer owes his deepest appreciation for the considerable aid, advice, and encouragement furnished over a period of years. Leonard Krieger and Stanley Mellon helped to define the original scope and objectives of the work; these early objectives have since been broadened. Carl E. Schorske provided needed encouragement through this study's darkest days, and Ari Hoogenboom assisted in correcting some of the stylistic deficiencies of the manuscript.

Financial assistance for the completion of this study was provided at various stages by the Yale University Graduate School, Southern Illinois University, and the American Philosophical Society. Many thanks are due the staffs of the Yale University Library, the Harvard College Library, the New York Public Library, Library of Congress, New England Deposit Library, and the interlibrary loan service of The Pennsylvania State University Library. The writer is particularly indebted to the directors and staffs of the Archives départmentales du Bas-Rhin, the Bibliothèque Nationale et Universitaire de Strasbourg, and the Société Industrielle de Mulhouse. My wife, Suzanne, typed the final draft, for which I am grateful. The greatest debt of all is owed to my parents, who offered more encouragement, understanding, and financial aid than anyone has a right to expect from anyone else.

ALSACE-LORRAINE, 1871-1918

Luxemburg

Rhine Province

PALATINATE

Moselle River

Dieden-hofen

Metz

LORRAINE

Château-Salins

Nancy

FRANCE

St.Dié

Epinal

VOSGES

Wissembourg

LOWER ALSACE

Hagenau

Zabern

Strasbourg

Erstein

Schlestadt

Colmar

UPPER ALSACE

Gueb-willer

Thann

Mulhouse

Altkirch

Belfort

Rhine River

Baden

Kehl

BADEN

Rhine River

Freiburg

Basel

SWITZERLAND

STATUTE MILES
0 5 10   20   30   40

1
BEFORE 1871:
PROVINCES OF FRANCE

Otto von Bismarck embellished his claim to creative genius by bringing into the world a new entity called Alsace-Lorraine, a German Reichsland. As discrete geographical expressions, Alsace and Lorraine claimed centuries-long historical traditions. While the rest of the world deplored the injustice of tearing a people away from its French homeland, the people of Alsace and Lorraine found equally objectionable the forcible compression of two historically, culturally, and linguistically different regions into a single administrative unit. Before 1871, Alsace and Lorraine lacked a community of interests, and demonstrated a rather wide diversity of political viewpoints.

There is no need to repeat the futile attempts to establish whether Alsace and the annexed portion of Lorraine were "French" or "German" in 1871. At the time of the annexation, political and economic considerations outweighed the national question in shaping the mentality of the territory's population. This work as a whole focuses on the internal political, economic, social, and religious development of the Reichsland after 1871; the present chapter performs the same function for the period before 1871. Stressing continuity rather than change after 1871, I shall here attempt to establish the analytic categories within which the history of Alsace and Lorraine can be understood both before and after the annexation.

The history of Alsace and Lorraine is marked by a number of abrupt national and political transitions; but certain categories of understanding help to bring order to the historical narrative. It is first necessary to view Alsace and Lorraine as separate entities, each with its unique historical development. In this regard, it is particularly noteworthy that liberalism took deeper root in Alsace than in Lorraine. The gulf between conservative rural and liberal urban areas also shaped territorial politics. The emergence of a politically and economically dominant commercial-industrial bourgeoisie centered in the Alsatian cities of Strasbourg and Mulhouse is a case in point. When Bismarck united Alsace and Lorraine in a single administrative unit, the dominance of the Alsatian bourgeoisie virtually assured the predominance of Alsatian interests, second only to imperial interests, in the territorial administration. Finally, religious antagonism between Catholics, Protestants, and Jews influenced political and economic developments in Alsace and Lorraine, with the Catholic clergy emerging as a political force in the last years of the Second French Empire.

Lorraine (Lotharingia) was the name given first to a kingdom intermediate between the western and eastern kingdoms of the Carolingian empire, then to the two duchies into which Lotharingia was divided (Lower Lorraine and Upper Lorraine), and finally to a duchy based on the territory of Upper Lorraine alone. This latter region roughly included the Ardennes, the Moselle valley, and the upper Meuse valley. The duchy of Lorraine fell within the boundaries of the Holy Roman Empire, but beginning with the reigns of two French kings, Philip III (1270–85) and Philip IV (1285–1314), German control over Lorraine became progressively more tenuous. In 1297 the bishopric of Metz came under the control of French officials. By 1301 Lorraine had been virtually partitioned between France and the empire, with the duke of Lorraine now required to do service with sixty knights for the French king. In 1444 Charles VII of France entered Lorraine with an army and summoned the territory to accept his authority. At the same time, Burgundy, under Duke Charles the Bold (1467–77), was reaching its pinnacle of power, forcing the duke of Lorraine in 1473 to permit the Burgundians to occupy all of his strongholds. The Reformation, Wars of Religion, and the Thirty Years' War permitted France to gain a firm grasp on Lorraine. By the Treaty of Westphalia in 1648, the empire ceded to France the lands of the three Lorraine bishoprics of Metz, Toul, and Verdun, which French armies had occupied in

1552. After the War of the Grand Alliance, Lorraine was restored to its dukes by the peace of Rijswijk (1697); but with the betrothal of Duke Francis Stephen to the Hapsburg Maria Theresa, France demanded another change of dynasty in Lorraine. With the conclusion of the War of the Polish Succession, it was agreed that Francis Stephen would succeed to Tuscany and renounce Lorraine, which passed to the dispossessed Polish King Stanislaw Leszczynski, and then to his daughter Marie, the consort of Louis XV of France. Stanislaw took possession of Lorraine in 1737. On his death in 1766, Lorraine became a French possession, though treaties signed in 1735 and 1736 guaranteed a fair degree of autonomy in laws, privileges, customs, and tariffs until the French Revolution of 1789.

Alsace before the French Revolution developed along lines somewhat different from Lorraine. Bounded on the north by the Rhenish Palatinate, the east by the Rhine, the south by Switzerland, and the west by the Vosges mountains, Alsace was dominated by the Romans for 500 years after Caesar's conquest of Gaul. It was then occupied for a time by the Franks under Clovis. By the Treaty of Mersen (870) Alsace was united with the German territories of the Carolingian dynasty, and remained a territory of the Holy Roman Empire for the next 800 years. During the imperial period, the territory of Alsace was divided into a number of ecclesiastical and secular lordships and municipalities. Strasbourg, which expelled its prince-bishop in 1262, remained an imperial free city until Louis XIV annexed it in 1681. Ten other Alsatian towns formed a union (decapolis) in 1354, remaining under the protection of a governor appointed by the emperor.[1]

During the Reformation, Strasbourg became a center of Protestant activity, and the city turned Lutheran. The Treaty of Westphalia in 1648, under which the house of Hapsburg relinquished to the French crown its holdings in Alsace, jeopardized Protestant gains around Strasbourg. The process of incorporating the rest of Alsace into France occupied the remainder of Louis XIV's reign, for the Hapsburgs, the elector Palatine, the prince of Zweibrücken, the dukes of Lorraine and Württemberg, the margrave of Baden, the count of Veldenz, the bishops of Speyer and Basel, as well as countless other small princes all held fiefs in Alsace. Attempts to integrate the territory into France failed to blot out the Alsatian heritage, and in 1789 Strasbourg was somewhat more than half Catholic, bilingual, and culturally "mixed."

The French Revolution of 1789 tied Alsace and Lorraine closer to France. The revolutionary government replaced the former royal intendants with prefects, and established departments including Haut-Rhin and Bas-Rhin (Alsace) and Moselle, Meurthe, Meuse, and Vosges (Lorraine). Under a program to unify the national market by making customs points identical with political frontiers, the government abolished the status of "foreign lands in effect" for Alsace and Lorraine, under which they previously had traded freely with foreign countries. For Strasbourg, France's most important military, economic, and spiritual outpost during the revolutionary and Napoleonic period, the years 1789 to 1812 appeared in retrospect as a golden age. The Continental system propelled Strasbourg to a position of commercial preeminence which she never enjoyed again after Napoléon's fall.[2] Politically and religiously, however, Alsace responded to the revolution with disunity or even opposition, particularly with respect to the civil constitution of the clergy. During 1790, fear of German intentions produced greater unity in Alsace; but instead of creating all-out support for the central government in Paris, the new unity centered on the idea of provincial federalism expressed in a *Fédération de l'Est*.[3] As France went to war against Europe in 1792, the position of Alsace as a frontier war zone forced the local population into a more patriotic stance, and after 1795 the Alsatians demonstrated "robust loyalism." Because they viewed the Consulate as reactionary vis-à-vis the Directory, and welcomed the 1801 Concordat with the Vatican, the Alsatians supported Napoléon's empire.[4]

By 1815 Alsatians and Lorrainers had tired of the imperial regime and its never-ending wars. They wanted peace, but Lorrainers could hardly rejoice at the second Peace of Paris with its "mutilation of Lorraine," under which Prussia received Saarebrück, Saarlouis, Trèves, Aix-la-Chapelle, and Cologne.[5] The Bourbon Restoration threatened to wipe out many political and legal gains made during the revolution, as well as the economic stimulation brought by the empire. Lorraine seemed better prepared to accommodate the Restoration than was Alsace. Her relatively large agricultural units have evoked comparisons with Prussia's East Elbian region; her towns were poorer and her people more inclined to accept authoritarian government than those of Alsace.[6] Democratic, liberal, and republican sentiment predominated in Alsace's commercial and industrial centers, Strasbourg and Mulhouse. The Alsatian democratic spirit, however, refused to tolerate any form of extremism; Alsatian liberalism operated strictly within a framework of order and discipline.[7]

Although outright republicans constituted a rarity in Lorraine during the Restoration, the Bourbon regime commanded only lukewarm support. Particularly annoying to many Lorrainers was the government's obvious catering to the interests of the Roman Catholic clergy and the nobility. Both the government and the clergy intervened directly in the 1824, 1827, and 1830 parliamentary elections. Countering opposition to the government's imperialistic policy in the conquest of Algiers, the bishop of Nancy in 1830 labeled the king's opponents as enemies of God, glory, and the national interest of France.[8] Despite official pressure and outright election fraud, Lorraine sent a few members of the moderate opposition to the Chamber of Deputies in 1827. Although the ultraroyalist minister, Prince Jules de Polignac, purged most of the prefects in 1829, Lorraine elected three deputies in 1830 who adhered to either the moderate royalist or liberal opposition camp. On the eve of the July revolution, however, there was no true Orleanist party in Lorraine.[9]

Alsatian opposition to the Restoration monarchy was much more pronounced. In a region dominated by merchants, factory owners, and lawyers, government attacks on freedom of the press and freedom of association constituted a major issue. Protestant industrialists and anticlerical liberals in general feared a recrudescence of clericalism under the regime of Charles X. The greatest factor contributing to Alsatian political opposition was the economic demise occasioned by the collapse of the Napoleonic empire, and aggravated by the Bourbon regime's protectionist tariff policy. Mulhouse, whose textile, chemical, and machine industries experienced vigorous growth during the Napoleonic era, was occupied by Allied troops for four years after the second Peace of Paris, and suffered a severe financial and food crisis during the winter of 1816–17. Under the Old Regime, Alsace had enjoyed the benefits of being considered "effectively foreign," lying outside the French customs area; now, the protectionist policy of the Restoration governments interfered with the Mulhouse textile industry's operations in the international market. High tariffs also devastated Strasbourg's Rhine transit trade.[10]

Exactly where the opposition was leading Alsace remains unclear. In 1830 twenty-one of the twenty-nine Bas-Rhin deputies

and twenty-two of the thirty Haut-Rhin deputies belonged to the
"left." Haut-Rhin and Bas-Rhin were rated as among the "most
constitutional" in all France. But the success of the liberal opposition near the close of the Restoration era shared the stage with a
sharp revival of Bonapartism—Alsatians recalled the Napoleonic
regime as a time of military glory and economic prosperity.[11] None-
theless, the Alsatians welcomed the July monarchy with enthusiasm.
The Mulhousiens regarded Louis Philippe, who visited their city in
1831, as a king after their own heart.[12] In Lorraine, the July revolution unleashed the anticlerical pressures accumulated under
Charles X. A mob which invaded the seminary at Nancy committed
acts of vandalism, forcing the progovernment bishop of Nancy,
Charles Forbin-Janson, to flee the city. Another mob attacked and
temporarily closed the seminary at Metz on 6 October 1830.[13]

The "transports of joy" with which the July revolution was greeted
in Alsace and to a lesser extent Lorraine proved to be rather ephemeral. The early successes of the party of movement gave way to
electoral sweeps by the party of resistance after 1834. The wealthy
bourgeoisie dominated regional politics (under the July monarchy
there were never more than 7,000 voters wealthy enough to qualify
as electors in the four Lorraine departments of Meurthe, Meuse,
Moselle, and Vosges), accepted lucrative government posts, and
generally took care of their own interests. By 1846, thirteen of the
twenty-one Lorraine deputies also held positions as government
officials or civil servants.[14]

Results of elections based on such a limited *pays légal* (the entire
French electorate numbered only 247,972 in 1846) obscured the
growing sense of frustration which eventually produced the revolution of 1848. The Alsatian democrats had never been satisfied with
the accession of a "bourgeois prince." The dissolution of the Strasbourg National Guard, the political trials, laws against associations,
and rigorous police measures after 1834 stifled the political operations of the opposition; but the opposition was still there. Local
liberal and radical forces received an unexpected increment when
refugees from the unsuccessful Polish revolution of 1830–31 began
to stream into Strasbourg, Metz, Nancy, and Bar-le-Duc.[15]

In the long run, the "bourgeois monarchy" lost favor in Alsace
because it ultimately failed to advance the interests of the local commercial and industrial magnates. A first-rate transportation system
was the key to economic viability in a region which was at once close

to the heartland of Europe and distant from the locus of national power, Paris. Canal and railway development was essential to Alsatian interests. Although Strasbourg is generally considered as a Rhine port, the city does not lie directly on the great waterway, and has access to it only by means of the Ill River. To bring ships directly into Strasbourg during the July monarchy required the improvement (regularization) of Rhine navigation, and construction of an Ill-Rhine canal. Had the Strasbourg commercial interests been willing to construct port facilities outside the city limits, directly on the Rhine, the Ill-Rhine canal would not have been required. But the city fathers, fearful that a port directly on the Rhine would shift the commercial center out of Strasbourg and jeopardize the old-established interests in the city, held to their demand that all port facilities be constructed within the city. The Ill-Rhine canal finally opened in 1841, but the parliamentary debate on improving the Rhine navigation dragged on through the 1840s without any definite result. (The same scenario was destined to be repeated under the German regime.)[16] The Chamber of Deputies in 1838 approved a project for a Marne-Rhine canal which would have improved the connection between Alsace, Lorraine, and interior France. But funds adequate to build the canal were not appropriated under the July monarchy, due largely to the growing conflict between canal and railway interests.

Forward-looking industrialists such as Nicolas Koechlin of Mulhouse recognized the importance of railways for Alsatian industrial expansion. Largely responsible for the Mulhouse-Thann connection in 1839, Koechlin led a successful fight for a rail link between Strasbourg and Basel in 1841, though its completion was delayed by rural opposition, which feared the devastation of the countryside, and Strasbourg commercial interests, which echoed the arguments concerning port facilities in demanding that the railway station be located within the city itself.[17] The crucial Paris-Strasbourg line encountered stiffer opposition; it was debated throughout the 1830s, and the government in 1842 presented a plan to construct the line with state, local, and private collaboration, but it was not until 3 July 1844 that the Chamber finally sanctioned it. Responsibility for the long delay lies as much with regional interests as with the government and the Chamber. Eastern France found itself divided between one group seeking a railway through Nancy terminating at Strasbourg, and another group advocating a direct Paris-Mulhouse line.

The Strasbourg interests finally prevailed, as they also prevailed in an important banking controversy which developed during the 1840s. In 1842 the Bank of France decided to establish *comptoires d'escompte* in several eastern cities, believing that easier access to capital would encourage the region's economic development. The principle was sound, but its application was complicated by a dispute between Strasbourg and Mulhouse over the location of the Alsatian office. Strasbourg finally won the bank in 1846, but by that time the agricultural crisis which contributed to the 1848 revolution had already set in.[18]

Between 1830 and 1846 a combination of intraregional rivalries and sluggishness on the part of the government in recognizing and meeting the economic requirements of Alsace and Lorraine eroded support for Louis Philippe among the region's industrial and commercial aristocracy. When the agricultural and financial crises exploded in 1846, critics attacked the government for its alleged failure to protect the territory from economic disaster. In the context of declining economic fortunes, the Swiss civil war of 1847 made a profound impact in Alsace. Economic ties between the Alsatian textile magnates and Swiss bankers were very close, since over the years capital from Basel had helped finance Mulhouse industrial expansion. The success of the Swiss liberals in 1847 added fuel to the liberal cause throughout France, and particularly in Alsace.[19] Liberal demands for electoral reform culminated in a large banquet held in Strasbourg on 5 September 1847. More ominous in the long run than the political impact of the depression was the infusion of nationalism into Alsatian politics during the 1840s. Since 1840 threatening sounds had emanated from Germany, where there was growing interest in reuniting their Alsatian "German brothers" with the Fatherland. The possibility of becoming a war prize alarmed the Alsatians, but the government of Louis Philippe appeared unconcerned. It was not uncommon in Alsace to hear complaints about the "ministry of peace at any price."[20]

Louis Philippe's overthrow in February 1848 came as a surprise in Alsace and Lorraine. While support for the regime had steadily deteriorated since 1846, no one had expected a revolution. This may explain the relative calm which prevailed in Alsace and Lorraine in February. Economic dislocation in Mulhouse was now greater than it had been during the depression of 1846–47, but the infusion of credit from Basel and a sewage canal project which helped reduce unemployment saved the city from major trouble.[21] On 26 February the Strasbourg municipal council reconstituted itself as a *commission municipale*, added to its membership, stripped the prefect of his authority, and named a council of five to administer the department of Bas-Rhin. The government in Paris made no attempt to intervene, and the French minister of the interior confirmed this usurpation of power.[22] Metz accepted the republic without much fanfare. At Nancy, a few republicans gathered at the city hall to proclaim the republic and named a provisional commission to carry on official business. Although the commission held no mandate from the people, neither the mayor, the prefect, nor the local military commander made any move to interfere with its activities.[23]

Alsace did experience some violence during the February revolution, mostly in the form of anti-Semitic riots, which occurred in a number of towns during February, March, and April. The revolution released the traditional anti-Jewish sentiment of the region's peasantry, who burned and pillaged numerous Jewish properties. Authorities ultimately called out troops to put down the disorders. These disturbances may explain why the Alsatian Jews supported the 1848 republic only so long as they believed it could guarantee both order and liberty; eventually, they turned conservative, supported Louis Napoléon's coup, and generally endorsed official candidates in the Second French Empire.[24]

Republican zeal soon cooled in Lorraine, where the majority had neither expected nor desired a revolutionary regime. The elections for the Constituent Assembly, held on 23 April 1848, found all shades of republicanism from right to left represented; but for all the diversity, only one worker found his way onto an electoral list. Lorraine's deputies to the Constituent Assembly represented the bourgeoisie and peasantry, the very groups who were detached from the republic by the frightening experience of the June Days. Municipal elections in July 1848 and by-elections for the Constituent Assembly in the fall indicated a waning of interest in the republic's institutions. The voter turn-out was light, and the results were conservative. In the department of Moselle, Louis Napoléon Bonaparte won a seat in the Assembly in a 17 September by-election with only 17,800 votes, whereas it had required 69,000 votes to win a seat in Moselle in the April elections.[25] The presidential election of 10 December 1848 showed an overwhelming shift toward Louis Napoléon; while most of the Lorraine election committees and Lor-

raine deputies in the Constituent Assembly favored General Louis-
Eugène Cavaignac, the "butcher of Paris," Louis Napoléon won the
Lorraine departments of Meurthe, Moselle, Vosges, and Meuse by
margins as wide as six to one. The Bonaparte who won a seat in
Moselle with only 17,800 votes 17 September received 75,142 votes
for president in Moselle only three months later. Cavaignac's defeat
in Lorraine presaged the defeat of the republicans who had supported his candidacy. In the Legislative Assembly election of 13
May 1849, the conservative "party of order" swept Meuse and Moselle completely, and lost only one seat each in Meurthe and Vosges
to the republicans. Clerical influence in the elections produced the
desired result, as the Lorraine deputies generally supported the
Falloux Law of 15 March 1849, which restored clerical control over
elementary education. On 31 May 1851 only one Lorraine deputy
voted against the abolition of universal suffrage. Most of the Lorraine deputies voted against the Quaestors' Bill of 17 November
1851, thus helping to defeat a measure which might have prevented
Louis Napoléon's coup of 2 December.[26] Just how crucial the
Quaestors' Bill was has been pointed out by Karl Marx, who wrote
caustically that, "by debating the right to requisition troops, instead
of requisitioning them at once, it [the Legislative Assembly] be-
trayed its doubts about its own powers. By rejecting the Quaestors'
Bill, it made public confession of its impotence."[27] The deputies
appear to have gauged public opinion accurately, for the electorate
in both Alsace and Lorraine gave overwhelming support to the
Bonapartist solution in the plebiscites of 1851 and 1852.[28]

The bourgeois character of the revolution in Alsace was unmistakable. In the Haut-Rhin industrial district, only one worker appeared on the ballots for the Constituent Assembly—he lost.
Bourgeois to a man, the Alsatian deputies in the Assembly voted
unanimously to adopt the constitution, unanimously against the
proposition to submit the constitution to a popular referendum, and
unanimously for a resolution commending General Louis-Eugène
Cavaignac for his service to the nation during the June Days.[29] During the presidential campaign of December 1848, Alsatian industrial
and commercial interests refused to take Louis Napoléon's candidacy seriously; Cavaignac received the support of all but one Haut-
Rhin Assembly deputy, all of the Bas-Rhin deputies, and Bishop
Andraes Raess of Strasbourg. The public, nevertheless, voted over-
whelmingly for Napoléon.[30]

In legislative elections held under the Second Republic, Alsatians returned radical republicans; the trend toward conservatism in Lorraine was not duplicated in Alsace. Nevertheless, there was little opposition in Alsace to either of the Napoleonic coups in 1851 or 1852, which established the Second French Empire. The peasantry feared the Red spectre, and resented the republic's high taxation to finance urban welfare projects. Businessmen accepted Louis Napoléon's promises of peace and prosperity as easily as they had previously accepted General Cavaignac as the guarantor of law and order. The Mulhouse industrial-technocratic aristocracy heartily supported the Saint-Simonian aspects of the new emperor's program, and Strasbourg commercial interests dreamed of recapturing the commercial supremacy enjoyed by the city under the first Napoléon.[31]

Alsatian clerical reaction to the revolution, republic, and empire demonstrated remarkable flexibility. Before 1848 the Catholic clergy generally favored a Bourbon restoration; but in the revolutionary enthusiasm of 1848, Bishop Raess planted liberty trees. Raess supported Cavaignac for the presidency, but rallied to the empire, arguing that Louis Napoléon had saved France from terrible evils (*effroyables malheurs*).[32]

Only in 1863 did organized opposition to Napoléon's official candidates emerge in Alsace and Lorraine. In Lorraine, the government continued to squeeze out victories to the very end of the empire, though the margins of victory steadily diminished after 1863. But in Alsace, Catholic priests intervened to unseat the Bonapartist Baron Zorn von Bulach in 1863, and the first republican candidate since 1852, Maurice Engelhard, barely lost in Bas-Rhin.

In the closing years of the Second French Empire, Alsace and Lorraine once again were coming to life politically. Traumatic experiences have periodically disrupted or extinguished political life in Alsace and Lorraine. Abrupt transitions from royal absolutism to constitutional monarchy, from constitutional monarchy to republic, from republic to empire, and from empire back to republic, have temporarily stifled the normal play of political forces in Alsace and Lorraine as well as in France as a whole; but always the latent political, social, and religious forces have managed to regroup and rejoin the battle. Dormant forces were reawakening, particularly in Alsace, during the last years of the Second French Empire. Liberals, republicans, and Catholics vigorously joined the political fray, and for the first time in Alsace the proletariat openly challanged the political and economic supremacy of the industrial bourgeoisie. The disaster of the 1871 incorporation of Alsace-Lorraine into the autocratic, militaristic Bismarckian empire was accented by this revival: annexation represented not only an affront to national pride, but also catastrophically wiped out the hard-won gains made by liberals and Catholics in Alsace between 1863 and 1870.

But while temporarily engulfing these historic territorial forces, which soon emerged again in strength, war and annexation dealt a serious blow to the industrial bourgeoisie, whose political power was somewhat reduced by the tendency of the German administration to deal with the so-called notables, the large landowners and Catholic bishops. Newer socio-political forces, the Church and labor, ultimately received new vitality in the aftermath of the events of 1870–71. Local hostility toward the German regime, which was by no means universal, sprang more from these indigenous socio-political-economic considerations than from nationalistic anti-German sentiment.

2
LOCAL ATTITUDES AND GERMAN AIMS 1869-1871

As the Franco-Prussian conflict approached its climax in 1870, local dissatisfaction with Napoléon III assumed disquieting proportions. The old religious schism between Catholics and Protestants reappeared in Alsace, upsetting regional political tranquility. Political divisions along confessional lines ran much deeper than usual in Alsace's last regular French parliamentary election held in May 1869. Opposition parties did not confine their efforts to attacks on the government; liberal-monarchical and democratic-republican groups established popular journals to combat the clerical press while the Catholic clergy worked openly for the election of sympathetic candidates. Some Catholic leaders, skeptical of informal political activity, wished to organize a Catholic political party. Economic interests joined the fray along with the political and religious groups as the election in Mulhouse developed into a struggle between free-traders and protectionists.[1] The efforts of both Catholic and liberal forces opposed to the government proved quite successful without the benefit of formal political organization. Opposition candidates made a strong showing in Bas-Rhin and Haut-Rhin, though not in Lorraine. Léon Lefebvre and Emile Keller, both clerical opposition candidates, won at Colmar and Guebwiller-Thann, while Mulhouse elected Albert Tachard, candidate of the *Union Liberale et Démocratique*.

Napoléon III's efforts to win over the liberal opposition by granting parliamentary reforms achieved only marginal success in Alsace and Lorraine. Although the last plebiscite of 1870 vindicated the emperor and his program in the sense that he won a clear majority in France, his victory in Alsace and Lorraine fell short of government expectations. Local committees in Alsace campaigned against the plebiscite, with the *Courrier du Bas-Rhin* in Strasbourg providing free antigovernment publicity. While the Alsatians and Lorrainers sympathized with the Napoleonic parliamentary reforms, they could not accept the empire's aggressive foreign policy which threatened to precipitate a war in which they would find themselves in the front lines.[2] Despite official pressure to vote "yes," voter turnout in Alsace and Lorraine was relatively light, and the "no" vote showed a substantial increase over the last plebiscite in 1852. Whereas only 10,081 Lorraine voters cast negative ballots in 1852, there were 50,990 dissenters in 1870. The opposition vote in Bas-Rhin rose from 3,818 in 1852 to 20,551 in 1870; and in Haut-Rhin from 2,841 to 19,689. Another 51,291 registered voters in Alsace did not bother to go to the polls.[3]

Political unrest was not the only ominous sign for the French regime in the eastern regions. On the eve of the Franco-Prussian War a major upheaval in the labor movement threw the Alsatian industrial scene into chaos. The Alsatian industrial workers had come of age since their relative indifference during the 1848 revolution. In Haut-Rhin, the workers were pitted against a most formidable, close-knit oligarchy of inbred industrial families who had seized control of local politics after the revolution of 1789 had destroyed the local nobility. The textile industry was the life-blood of Haut-Rhin, and it was controlled by a closed society based on family alliances in both business and marriage. There were few "self-made men" in Alsace, and the few "upstarts" who did make the grade were generally to be found in commerce, the machine, or chemical industry rather than textiles. Nearly all of the textile families adhered to the Reformed religion, in an area where most people were either Catholics or Lutherans. Jews, who comprised 1.48 percent of the Haut-Rhin population in 1913, played an important role in Alsatian commerce, but the textile industry was virtually closed to them as it was to Catholics and Lutherans.[4]

True to their philosophy of political and economic liberalism, the Mulhouse industrialists rejected any government intervention in the industrial domain, particularly in questions of social reform. If any reforms were needed (which the industrialists doubted) they should come from the initiative of management, not the government. By 1870 labor had grown dissatisfied with its dependence on management's good will, which had brought the workers few gains. Alsatian workers began to organize their own power base, a difficult feat in view of the legal prohibition of strikes until 1864 and the bare toleration of labor unions after 1867. Many Alsatian textile workers were dispersed throughout the countryside and in the Vosges mountains, making organization difficult. Socialist doctrine penetrated France's eastern regions rather slowly, and the only significant strike during the pre-German era occurred in 1870–71, shortly after the founding of a section of the socialist International in Mulhouse.[5]

In June 1870 Colmar workers struck rather than accept a twenty percent wage reduction in the form of higher rents. Work soon stopped in Mulhouse, Guebwiller, Thann, Bischwiller, and Cernay as more than 15,000 men went on strike. Violent bands of strikers circulated from town to town, invading and closing down factories. Religion intruded into the dispute when Protestants accused the Catholic press of inciting the workers against the Protestant factory owners.[6]

Once the Franco-Prussian War began, disputants buried their controversy—at least for a time—beneath a wave of patriotism. Alsatians recognized the special significance of the war for them; everyone sensed that the destiny of Alsace was at stake.[7] Charles Boersch, editor of the *Courrier du Bas-Rhin*, proclaimed that the Alsatians would never consent to become Prussians.[8] When news that war was imminent reached Mulhouse 15 July, a compromise agreement quickly ended the strike. At Thann, Wesserling, Guebwiller, and Cernay, however, violence continued until 19 July, the day France declared war on Prussia. Only after political leaders passionately urged unity in the hour of crisis did those towns settle their strikes.[9]

Not even the call to arms could conceal the latent social, religious, and political antagonism in Alsace and Lorraine. Catholics alleged that treasonous Protestants welcomed the return of a Protestant power to sovereignty in Alsace.[10] Unrest reappeared in the industrial centers. While some workers supported Napoléon III, others threatened that if their conditions were not improved swiftly, they might prefer a Prussian government.[11] At Mulhouse the subprefect denied a petition from the bourgeoisie requesting rifles for defense against the onrushing Prussian forces. The internal threat posed by the workers, who had deserted the factories for the streets, concerned the subprefect far more than the external threat posed by Prussia. Confronted by violence from both within and without, Mulhouse and Colmar organized corps of volunteer constables to maintain internal law and order, but showed little enthusiasm for meeting Prussian aggression.[12]

Even where workers did not strike, it was practically impossible to keep the factories open. The war disrupted rail service, leaving factories starving for raw materials and choking with undistributed finished products. Most factories operated just three days a week, and some only during alternate weeks.[13] A silver shortage made it difficult to pay workers. Distress in the industrial centers menaced the established political order. In Strasbourg, workers forced the municipal council to reorganize with four additional working class members.[14] The advancing Prussians, though preoccupied with military operations, recognized the danger of social disorder. Later in August 1870, they permitted the resumption of coal exports from Germany to French territory occupied by Prussian troops. Without coal Alsatian factories could not operate, and the Prussians realized that forced layoffs would generate violence.

As Alsace and Lorraine slipped deeper into chaos, disaster struck Napoléon III. The Prussians captured him and the empire collapsed at Sedan while a new French republic was born in Paris. Infused with new hope, Alsatians, particularly those in the urban centers, warmly embraced the new republic. The mayor of Strasbourg, an imperial appointee, resigned, and the municipal council filled the vacancy with a staunch republican, Emile Küss, professor of medicine at the University of Strasbourg. All had high hopes for the republic; it would either prosecute the war more effectively, or it would conclude a prompt peace with the Prussians.

With all of its vitality, the new French Government of National Defense could not solve Alsace-Lorraine's social and economic problems. As the war closed, Alsatian factories were still idle, the workers still unemployed. Alsatian industrialists were principally concerned with getting the workers back to their jobs, reestablishing general prosperity, and avoiding labor violence. In August 1870 the textile magnate Frederick Hartmann suggested that industrialists request the French ministry of public works and commerce to restore rail service in Alsace.[15] The French government, however, was powerless to reinstate normal conditions in Alsace and Lorraine. French impotence, not disloyalty, led Alsatian industrialists in the spring of 1871 to send delegations to Berlin. Though most of them sympathized with the French cause, they realized that only German authorities could revive industrial activity and provide insurance against social revolution. Some of the Alsatian industrial leaders appreciated the advantages of a well-disciplined state such as Prussia, where a powerful and efficient army and bureaucracy guaranteed peace and order.

As French power declined, particularist sentiment grew stronger in Alsace and Lorraine. A relatively small but influential group hoped to establish the two regions as an independent state. The issue of religion, which inevitably found its way into nearly every political movement in Alsace and Lorraine, figured prominently in the autonomist program. Its early champions, Jacques Kablé, Auguste Schneegans, and Count Ferdinand von Eckbrecht Dürckheim-Montmartin, were all Protestants, and clearly reflected the anti-Catholic bias of the autonomist movement. Independence, Schneegans argued, would free the Alsatian Protestants from the oppressive Catholic government in Paris.[16] Kablé and Dürckheim proposed a "neutral" state which in fact would have been heavily dependent upon Germany.[17] It thus became difficult to distinguish between the desire for autonomy and outright sympathy for the German empire. Edmond About, an Alsatian who became editor of the *XIXme Siècle* in Paris after 1871, warned that Bismarck was not the most dangerous enemy after all. The real danger to Alsace and Lorraine came from within, from "the particularism adopted by some very intelligent men in the interest of their own private fortunes."[18] About attacked not only the autonomist movement but also those Alsatian businessmen who were seeking favorable tariffs from the Prussian government. Alsatians, particularly members of the League of Alsace, strongly supported his warning.

Resistors formed the League of Alsace the very day that Paris and Berlin announced the Frankfurt Treaty, under which France ceded what was now Alsace-Lorraine to Germany. A secret organization, it resisted Germanization and branded those who cooperated with the Germans as traitors. The society spread its propaganda through a periodical, *La Ligue d'Alsace*, which it printed in Basel and smuggled across the border into Alsace-Lorraine. German authorities never discovered the origins and membership of the League.

Although some believed that French republican leader Léon Gambetta was instrumental in establishing the organization, no evidence supports this contention. Gambetta is not mentioned in the firsthand account of the founding of the League by the Mulhouse industrialist Auguste Lalance.[19] Lalance himself probably originated the idea for the League, which was closely connected with the *Société Industrielle de Mulhouse*. Lalance was for some years president of this organization, and most League members were also members of the society. The overlapping membership suggests that the industrial society financed the League.

The League pledged to combat those who dealt with the "enemy." It accused industrialists such as Frederick Hartmann, who sought tariff concessions in Berlin for local industries, of protecting their private material interests and charged that the men who now extended suppliant hands toward Bismarck had only recently been the most dedicated supporters of the hated French empire.[20]

Hartmann defended himself by attacking the "unrealistic" thinking of the League. The League, he wrote, was living in a fantasy world of abstractions and chimeras. One had to view the situation as it really was; the people had to go on living, and French power was nonexistent in Alsace-Lorraine. Failure to cooperate with the Germans would only impede the revival of trade and commerce. The losses involved in protracted disruption of business would undoubtedly damage private interests, but Hartmann and other industrialists were even more anxious to prevent a social revolution. Only economic prosperity could stave off a major social crisis, and the beginnings of such a crisis were clearly visible in Alsace-Lorraine. Hartmann boasted of his attempts at both Berlin and Versailles to convince the German and French governments that after the annexation Alsace-Lorraine needed special economic arrangements.[21]

Confronted with the views of republicans, autonomists, and the League of Alsace, the historian is hard put to judge Alsatian public opinion in 1871. The historical record is largely confined to the writings of the leading industrialists, politicians, journalists, and religious leaders. There is, however, a statistical source from which one might judge public attitudes. The armistice agreement of 29 January 1871 permitted the French government to hold elections for a national assembly. This assembly would decide whether the war should continue, or on what terms France should seek peace. For the people of Alsace and Lorraine, the election was a plebiscite on annexation, although the Prussians had not anticipated a referendum when they agreed to permit elections in occupied territory.

The eighth of February 1871 was the day of decision for the French people. Despite some Prussian interference with the election conducted under the 1849 election law, it was as fair as any held under the regime of Napoléon III. Bismarck suggested that Prussian officials in Alsace and Lorraine impress the people with the consequences of failure to bring the war to an early conclusion.[22] The Prussians gave the mayors of Strasbourg and Colmar only three days to make the necessary arrangements for balloting, prohibited the posting of lists of candidates and party platforms, suppressed most of the independent press, and refused the bilingual *Courrier du Bas-Rhin* permission to publish names of the candidates. In a final attempt to discourage voting, placards bearing the signature of the Prussian governor general announced that the election had been postponed. The polls, however, opened as scheduled on 8 February. Only the Reichstag elections of 1874 and 1887 produced a larger turnout of voters under the German regime.[23]

Commentators focusing on the behavior of the Alsatian delegates to the Bordeaux National Assembly have mistakenly understood the 8 February election as a nearly unanimous victory for the war hawks and intransigent opponents of annexation. Particularly misleading was the victory of Léon Gambetta in all four departments later ceded to Germany; the popularity of this outspoken proponent of "war to the end" and opponent of annexation supposedly represented the views of most Alsatians and Lorrainers. Such interpretations imply a greater unity of opinion than actually existed. At least three different lists of candidates appeared in Bas-Rhin alone; the Strasbourg municipal council drew up one list, a dissident "democratic" group prepared the second, and the clericals proposed a third set of candidates. Constituting itself as an electoral committee, the Strasbourg municipal council drew up a slate of twelve candidates to represent the entire department of Bas-Rhin. The council's action touched off vigorous protests from those who felt the Strasbourg municipal council did not reflect popular opinion in Bas-Rhin. The council had been elected under the French imperial system, in which government-supported "official" candidates commanded an unfair advantage. During the war, the imperial prefect had further increased government influence in the council by appointing new members without bothering with the formality of elections. Had the

Strasbourg municipal council been democratically elected, it would
still have been presumptuous for it to claim competence to represent
the entire department of Bas-Rhin.

Mayor Küss rejected all complaints against the legality of the
council's action, and refused to add Léon Gambetta and Jules Favre
to the list. Although Gambetta and Favre were not Alsatians, many
Alsatians wished to vote for them to demonstrate their loyalty to
France. The Strasbourg municipal council, however, did not wish
the election to degenerate into an emotional plebiscite. The elected
representatives of Bas-Rhin and Haut-Rhin might play an important
role as negotiators with both the German and French governments.
While prominent figures such as Gambetta and Favre might have
great propaganda value, native Alsatians were more likely to protect
regional interests.[24]

Obtaining no satisfaction from the mayor and council, a dissident
group numbering two hundred persons nominated its own list of
"democratic" candidates. Seeking merely to complement the council
list by adding Gambetta and Favre rather than oppose the council
candidates, the democrats retained six council nominees, including
Mayor Küss himself. Catholic interests, directed by the bishop of
Strasbourg, selected a third slate of candidates. Emile Küss, Jacques
Kablé, and Charles Boersch, all Protestants, were included on the
clerical list to make it palatable to the Protestants.[25]

Since the election lists duplicated many names, no single group
could claim a clear-cut victory. No candidate won a seat unless he
appeared on at least two of the competing lists. Persons running
solely on the clerical ticket invariably suffered defeat.[26] The election
results provided something for everyone. War or peace, the basic
issue in the election, remained somewhat ambiguous after the votes
in Alsace and Lorraine had been counted. In the nation as a whole,
Adolph Thiers, who emerged as a moderate willing to negotiate
with Bismarck, was elected in twenty-six departments, while Léon
Gambetta, representing the cry "war to the end," won in ten. But in
Haut-Rhin, Bas-Rhin, Meurthe, and Moselle, departments to be
ceded to Germany, Thiers won no seats while Gambetta was elected
in all four (he chose to represent Bas-Rhin). Emile Keller, who as
a French parliamentary deputy had voted against the war in August
1870, now supported Gambetta's program of resistance as he won a
National Assembly seat in Bas-Rhin. Keller's attitude indicates the
unique position of Alsace and Lorraine at this time of crisis; he was

one of the very few deputies of the right in the Assembly (clerical Legitimist) who backed Gambetta on the war issue. The election of Gambetta and Keller, however, did not tell the entire story. Although Gambetta won his seat in Bas-Rhin with 56,271 votes, Jules Favre, who favored peace on honorable terms, won a seat in the same department with 54,514 votes. Haut-Rhin returned two staunch anti-German delegates, Auguste Scheurer-Kestner and Alfred Koechlin, but also voted for the autonomist Louis Chauffour and for Frederick Hartmann, the first Alsatian labeled a traitor by the League of Alsace.[27] Bas-Rhin voters endorsed two other prominent autonomists, August Schneegans and Jacques Kablé.

Despite cleavages of opinion, delegates from Alsace and Lorraine did indeed submit two protests to the Assembly, holding null and void any act which gave the territory to the Germans. The first of the protests marked the beginning of an alliance between the Catholics and "protesters" in the two territories. Drawn up by Gambetta, it was read to the Assembly by Emile Keller, a clerical from Haut-Rhin.[28] Bowing to Prussian military superiority, the Assembly ratified the Frankfurt Treaty. Expressing their disdain for a parliament which had handed their homelands to the Germans, the Alsace and Lorraine delegates withdrew from the French National Assembly. Even in this overt act of defiance, one could detect a divergence in outlook between Alsace and Lorraine. Of the forty members from Meurthe, Moselle, Bas-Rhin, and Haut-Rhin who resigned, nine—seven from Meurthe and two from Moselle—continued to sit as representatives of the newly formed department of Meurthe-et-Moselle.[29]

The vigor of these protests obscured the lack of unity among the delegates as they converged on Bordeaux. Autonomists such as Hartmann and Schneegans had wished to obtain concessions from the Germans, rather than alienate them with inflammatory speeches.[30] Lacking sufficient public support and vigorous leadership, the autonomists lost out at the National Assembly. The death of Emile Küss in his Bordeaux hotel room silenced at a critical moment the most influential autonomist advocate. Sparked by the fiery Gambetta, the protesters carried the day. Schneegans later criticized Gambetta's radical influence, complaining that his policy of intransigence led only to sensational acts which jeopardized the true interests of Alsace and Lorraine. Schneegans conceded that walking out of the National Assembly vividly set their grievance before the high court of world opinion; but it left Alsace-Lorraine unrepresented in later tariff negotiations between France and Germany.[31]

Had Schneegans the gift of prophecy he might have criticized Gambetta's radical policy even further, for the departure of the Alsace and Lorraine representatives served neither the interests of Alsace-Lorraine nor those of the Third French Republic. The president of the Assembly ruled that the deputies from Alsace and Lorraine could sit in the French parliament after 1871. Their presence in support of the republican ideal might have changed the history of the Third Republic. Adolph Thiers, the chief executive toppled by a sixteen-vote margin in 1873, might have survived, an alliance might have been formed between the moderate Thiers and the more radical Gambetta, and the republic might have been spared the years of sterility between 1873 and 1877.[32]

Germany unfortunately accepted the Bordeaux protests as an accurate index of Alsatian opinion. Initially, the German administration believed the Alsatians harbored no ill-will for Germany. Maximilian du Prel, a German imperial official in Alsace-Lorraine during the 1870s, reported many Alsatians welcoming the change of regime as an opportunity to sweep away hated prefects and mayors and tyrannical municipal councils.[33] Another German official, Wilhelm Fischer, described the Alsatians as rejoicing in their new freedom from the army of police spies that maintained the Napoleonic military dictatorship.[34] With the Bordeaux protests, the German administration received its first hint that these "long-lost German brothers" would renounce a new set of bonds fashioned in Berlin.

The Bordeaux protests, however, were not an accurate measure of hostile public opinion in Alsace-Lorraine. Germany did not inherit an irreconcilably hostile population in 1871, nor was the prospect of integrating this territory into the German empire completely hopeless from the outset. A significant group of industrial and political leaders in Alsace-Lorraine championed the ideal of an autonomist state. Failing to achieve this, they would enter the German community on the basis of equality with the other German states.

Yet, the majority of Alsace-Lorrainers preferred to remain with France, but not necessarily because they were anti-German in a nationalistic sense. Opposition to the German regime was based on two factors: a nationalistic preference for France, and a liberal political predisposition inherited from the closing years of the Second French Empire. The second factor was at least as important as the first. With its strong militaristic tendencies, the French imperial regime had aroused strong opposition in Alsace and Lorraine. The French republic proclaimed after Napoléon III's debacle at Sedan had gained wide acceptance in Alsace and Lorraine. Many Alsace-Lorrainers who felt no hostility toward the Germans nevertheless balked at being citizens in a German empire. So recently emancipated from Napoleonic dictatorship, they had no desire to become citizens of another imperial regime which found its legitimacy in military violence.

In Berlin, where annexation was already a foregone conclusion, the feelings of the Alsace-Lorrainers made little impression. Pressure for the annexation of Alsace and part of Lorraine had been an important factor in German politics since the 1840s. As revolution swept Germany in 1848, the future chancellor Bismarck counseled taking Alsace from France as a means of promoting German unity. The Austrian Kaiser Franz Joseph, seeking aid in Berlin during the Italian war of 1859, indicated he would support German attempts to regain Alsace and Lorraine.[35] King Wilhelm of Württemberg and the Tübingen historian Julius Weizsäcker also supported annexation.[36] Although some broad popular demand for annexation existed by 1870, public clamor for annexation was rather weak during the early weeks of the war, until Bismarck himself began to encourage the press to stir up the issue. German presses cast forth hundreds of annexationist pamphlets, while university professors argued that Alsace was a German land by virtue of its historical and "racial" background. Although Bismarck scoffed at such arguments as "professors' ideas," he recognized their utility in stirring up nationalistic fervor.[37] Bismarck made equally good use of the religious implications of the annexation. No supporter of Catholic aspirations, Bismarck nevertheless responded to the south German Catholics' favorable attitude toward annexation of Alsace-Lorraine, which might properly be considered one of many concessions Bismarck made to win south German support for German unification. By adding a territory whose population was eighty percent Catholic, Bismarck helped allay fears that south German Catholics could expect little sympathy from a unified Germany dominated by Protestant Prussia.

It mattered little whether Germany had an historical right to

Alsace-Lorraine, or whether south German Catholics favored annexation: military advantage demanded German control over the
territory. The nationalist historian Heinrich von Treitschke admitted
that the annexationist argument based on the "return of our German
brothers" was nothing but a ruse. If the Alsatians had been Jap-
anese, remarked Treitschke, Germany would have annexed them
anyway, in order to capitalize on the military value of Metz and
Strasbourg.[38]

The striking Prussian victory over the French in 1870 created
ideal conditions for the consummation of German annexationist
aims. With the weight of German public opinion behind him, Bismarck could take advantage of a favorable international situation
if he acted quickly.[39] There would not be another Congress of Vienna, with its coalition of allies trying to reestablish a European
balance of power. Because Prussia had fought and won alone in
1870, Bismarck could dictate his terms to a prostrate French nation. Such an opportunity to take Alsace-Lorraine might never occur
again.

In 1878 Bismarck claimed in retrospect that at the beginning of
the Franco-Prussian War, Prussia sought no territorial gains at
French expense.[40] By the middle of September 1870, however, Bismarck had committed Germany to the annexation of Alsace and
some portion of Lorraine. Bismarck unfolded his annexation plan
in early August, after the first major Prussian victories at Wörth and
Wissembourg. On August 14 he informed Prince Friedrich Charles
of Prussia that he planned to take Alsace and the "German" portion
of Lorraine. Bismarck notified Tsar Alexander II the following day
that Prussia intended to hold Alsace. In mid-September, Bismarck
circulated a message to the neutral powers, announcing his intention
to retain Metz and Strasbourg as guarantees against French aggression.[41] In a memorandum to Bismarck from his army command
post in France, dated 14 August 1870, Crown Prince Friedrich
Wilhelm (later King Friedrich III) echoed the Prussian chancellor's
sentiments, but with some reservation. In his *Kurze Denkschrift für
den Fall eines Friedens*, the crown prince agreed that France must
be deprived of some territory so as to make her incapable of disturbing the peace in the future; but this might be done without necessarily enlarging Germany or Prussia. The prince recognized that the
return of Alsace had become a popular demand which would be
difficult to resist, but failed to explain how the return of this territory

might be accomplished without enlarging either Germany or Prussia.[42]

Prussia evidenced her determination to hold Alsace-Lorraine by promptly establishing administrative organs in the occupied region. On 14 August 1870, King Wilhelm named Bismarck's uncle, General Lieutenant Friedrich Count Bismarck-Bohlen, as governor general in Alsace. Bismarck-Bohlen administered the territory under instructions prepared jointly by the Prussian ministry of war and Bismarck. On 26 August, King Wilhelm appointed the Catholic administrative director of Düsseldorf, Friedrich Christian Hubert von Kühlwetter, as civil commissar in Alsace. Kühlwetter's duties as general director of the territorial administration ranged from collection of taxes to cooperation with the army in matters of supply.[43] Concurrent with Kühlwetter's appointment, the king extended Bismarck-Bohlen's area of authority to include not only Alsace, but also five *arrondissements* in Lorraine: Metz, Diedenhofen, Saargemund, Saarburg, and Chateau-Salins, designating the entire area as the General Government of Alsace and German Lorraine.

During the occupation period Prussian authorities actually exceeded the limits of international law. Only with the ratification of the Preliminary Peace on 2 March 1871 did Prussia inherit the right to exercise sovereign power over occupied French territory. International law permitted an occupying power to exercise authority only for the purpose of maintaining security and order, but Bismarck-Bohlen regulated education and religion as well. Some experts supported Prussia's loose interpretation of international law. After a lengthy discussion of legal niceties, Edgar Löning, a University of Strasbourg law professor, concluded that "necessity" defined the rights of an occupying power. Since war was still considered a permissible and sometimes necessary activity, any act necessary to achieve the ends of war must be considered legitimate.[44]

Once Bismarck resolved to retain control over French territory, he had only to decide how much territory to annex. Two incompatible objectives governed Bismarck's decision; he sought to combine maximum insurance against French aggression with minimum annexation of the French-speaking population of Lorraine. Bismarck never questioned the necessity of acquiring the Strasbourg fortress; he took seriously the warning made to him by the grand duke of Baden during the Crimean War that south Germany would always be vulnerable to attack so long as Alsace remained in French hands. In this sense, Bismarck regarded the annexation of Alsace as a prerequisite for the expansion of the new German Reich southward beyond the Main.

But why annex Lorraine and the city of Metz? Bismarck, in fact, did not wish to take Metz, and included that city in his original demands only for bargaining purposes.[45] King Wilhelm of Prussia wrote Queen Augusta on more than one occasion that the neutral powers, notably Russia, were "making noises about the integrity of France."[46] Because Bismarck hoped to effect a quick settlement before any of the neutral powers could raise objections, he was not prepared to negotiate at length over Metz. Bismarck appreciated the military value of Metz, but he had no desire to re-create in Alsace-Lorraine the problems which Prussia already faced in governing her hostile Polish provinces.[47]

Enlisting the aid of the grand duke of Baden and Crown Prince Friedrich, Bismarck attempted to influence King Wilhelm against taking Metz, but he was obliged to annex the city against his better judgment. General Helmuth von Moltke's opinion that the fortress of Metz equalled in value a German army of 120,000 men was decisive. Moltke wanted a *Diktatfrieden*—he would have dealt France such a blow as to cripple her for a hundred years. General Gustav von Alvensleben, a die-hard reactionary and close advisor to the king, wanted to take France right up to the Marne. Bismarck acquiesced on Metz without admitting that Moltke was correct. The chancellor's relations with Prussia's generals had deteriorated in the course of the wars of unification; constant disputes over strategy and tactics had spawned mutual recriminations. Bismarck could renounce Metz only at the cost of a total breach with the military. Because Bismarck chose to conciliate the generals, military necessity as understood by Moltke determined the extent of the annexation. The peace of 1871 was not the *Versöhnungsfrieden* of 1866; this time, Bismarck did give in to Moltke on Metz. But without the moderating influence of Bismarck, the Prussian generals would have taken even more in 1871.[48]

If strategic military factors prevailed in determining the extent of annexation in Alsace and Lorraine, one must hasten to add that in the modern world, real military power rests on a strong industrial base. It is therefore ironic that the German chancellor who supposedly recognized the dominant role of "blood and iron" in deciding political questions gave practically no consideration to the factor of iron ore resources in determining the Franco-German boundary in 1871. Everyone knows that by 1914, Lorraine (both French and German) had become one of the world's great suppliers of iron ore; and nearly everyone has assumed that France retained much of the iron ore region in 1871 only because of a German oversight or mistake. Robert Parisot, whose somewhat dated history of Lorraine remains the best work on the subject, typifies the generally-held view that, "if, at the time, they had known of the iron ore wealth of the Briey basin, the Germans would not have failed to demand that territory."[49] The Germans did, in fact, know about the Briey deposits. Prior to the Preliminary Peace of 1 March 1871, Wilhelm Hauchecorne, director of the Mining Academy in Berlin, prepared a report on "The Exploitation of Mines, Factories, and Saltworks in the Parts of France Formerly German." It is not clear who authorized Hauchecorne's report, but it may have been prepared at the request of the Prussian minister of commerce, industry, and public works. Although the report seems to have been buried in the office of the military governor of Lorraine at Nancy and never reached higher authorities, the value of the French iron deposits was a matter of public record available to any German official who bothered to consult official French production statistics. After the conclusion of the Preliminary Peace, Hauchecorne was appointed to the official boundary commission, and made repeated attempts to secure more of the iron-bearing deposits for Germany. Bismarck, who was engaged in negotiations with the French over the exact limits of the Belfort area to be left to France, could have demanded a larger share of the iron ore area in return for making concessions to the French in the Belfort region. Instead, as Richard Hartshorne has shown, the Germans appeared more interested in military cemeteries than iron ore, and took little or no advantage of the bargaining over the final Frankfurt Treaty to secure additional mineral resources. In the end, Germany took less than half of the Lorraine deposits then being worked, and somewhat over half of the blast furnaces of the northern field (excluding the Nancy region) and the most important iron fabricating plants.[50]

Although the Germans wasted little time in annexing Alsace-Lorraine, they vacillated in choosing a means of incorporating the region into Germany. They had several alternatives: they could give it to one of the south German states as a reward for participation in the war; they could add it to Prussia; or they could establish it as a

neutral buffer state. Bavaria was the south German state most anxious to gain by the annexation, but Grand Duke Friedrich of Baden
as well as Treitschke and the National Liberals viewed Bavaria's
designs for expansion with grave misgivings. The enhancement of
Bavarian power would simply create a Bavarian-Prussian dualism
similar to the old Austro-Prussian rivalry. Since the other south
German states were too small to handle Alsace-Lorraine, Duke
Friedrich and the National Liberals favored the cession of Alsace-
Lorraine to Prussia.[51]

The south German liberals, who had long opposed German unification under a Prussian military dictatorship, rejected any plan that
would award the recently annexed territory to Prussia. Disappointed
with the results of Prussian annexation of Hanover, Hesse-Cassel,
and Nassau in 1866, they discounted National Liberal assurances
that liberal forces from Alsace-Lorraine would soften Prussia's hard
militaristic posture. The south German liberals realized that in a
contest between Alsatian liberalism and Prussian authoritarianism,
the Alsatians must lose. They considered Kühlwetter's appointment
as civil commissar the first step toward creation of a police state in
Alsace-Lorraine. In their disillusionment, they gravitated toward
Bismarck's plan to create an imperial territory (*Reichsland*) over
which they might exercise some influence.[52]

The idea of establishing an imperial territory belonging to all of
the German states emerged gradually from the shadows of Bismarck's consciousness. He first considered the possibility of creating
a neutral buffer state between France and Germany, but rejected
this as an ideal which could not be realized. No buffer state could
be neutral in the long run. Eventually, he reasoned, it must lean
toward one of the great powers; and considering its liberal tradition,
Alsace-Lorraine would probably establish closer ties with France.[53]
The creation of a Reichsland seemed to Bismarck the best solution
to several problems. He did not wish to raise Bavaria to great-power
status in Germany, and he recoiled from stirring up dynastic rivalries
by incorporating the annexed territory into Prussia. Bismarck now
began to recognize the value of Alsace-Lorraine in his plan to create
a German empire. If he succeeded in convincing the German princes
of the necessity of incorporating Alsace-Lorraine into Germany as
an imperial territory, the princes would then be forced to create an
empire.[54] The beauty of the Reichsland idea was that both liberals
and conservatives could accept it. The liberal unitarists had long be-

lieved that German unification must await the destruction of German particularism. They hoped the organization of Alsace-Lorraine as an imperial territory might set a precedent for the eventual transformation of all German states into imperial provinces.[55] The conservatives supported the Reichsland solution for different reasons. Fearing the creation of a highly centralized state, they considered the establishment of Alsace-Lorraine as an imperial territory a step toward decentralization.[56]

If the plan to set up Alsace-Lorraine as an imperial territory contained certain advantages, it also had serious shortcomings. The Reichsland was a unique political configuration which did not fit into the administrative structure of the rest of the empire. Particularly during the years 1871–79, the search for a way to accommodate Alsace-Lorraine in the imperial structure led to constant experimentation with the territorial government and frequent changes of personnel. This continuing fluctuation confused and disordered the implementation of German Reichsland policy.

Confusion in the administrative system merely reflected a basic contradiction in Germany's attitude toward the territory. Hoping to win the sympathy of the people of Alsace-Lorraine, Bismarck nevertheless regarded the region as Germany's first line of defense. Many German officials felt that the military security of the empire could be achieved only by depriving the Alsace-Lorrainers of the basic rights enjoyed by other German citizens. In denying these rights, the Germans blasted their own hopes for conciliation. Although Alsace-Lorraine stood out as a shining symbol of German military supremacy, the task of defining an organization and policy for the region was one which Bismarck never mastered.

3

CIVIL-MILITARY CONFLICTS AND PUBLIC ADMINISTRATION IN ALSACE-LORRAINE 1871-1918

When the governor, Prince Chlodwig Hohenlohe-Schillingsfürst, remarked in 1886 that the best policy is a good administration, he unwittingly explained much of Germany's difficulty in governing the Reichsland.[1] Cumbersome administrative machinery frustrated attempts to govern wisely and effectively. The complex division of authority and responsibility between Strasbourg and Berlin provided nearly every ranking German bureaucrat an opportunity to meddle in the affairs of Alsace-Lorraine. Between 1871 and 1918, frequent changes in administrative structure and personnel caused shifts and inconsistencies in German policy. The root problem was a continuing struggle for supremacy between civil and military authorities; but some major changes in Reichsland administration reflected shifts in Bismarck's imperial political and economic policies. The year 1879, during which Bismarck ended the *Kulturkampf*, shifted from free trade to protection, and broke with the National Liberals, also witnessed a radical reconstruction of Alsace-Lorraine's administrative structure.

The imperial law of 9 June 1871 established basic regulations for the government of Alsace-Lorraine. As an agent of the Federal Council (*Bundesrat*), the emperor exercised sovereign power in the Reichsland. Pending introduction of the imperial constitution in Alsace-Lorraine on 1 January 1873, the emperor, with Federal

Council approval, made all laws for the Reichsland. After that date, the ordinary procedure for imperial legislation, involving action by the Federal Council, Reichstag, and emperor, applied to Alsace-Lorraine. Selection of a date for introducing the imperial constitution exposed a basic disagreement between the government and the Reichstag. The dispute was more than a squabble over timing; for the liberals, progressives, and Catholics, it was a matter of preserving Alsace-Lorraine from dictatorship by the emperor, since the Reichstag played no role in the territorial government until the introduction of the imperial constitution. The government suggested 1 January 1874, but Franz Duncker, a Progressive, amended the date forward to 1 January 1872. Reichstag committee hearings eventually produced a compromise agreement on 1 January 1873. Convinced that nothing short of a territorial government in Strasbourg could prevent dictatorship from Berlin, a group of deputies led by August Reichensperger (Center) rejected the compromise.[2] Bismarck, always mindful of the requirements of military security, declared emphatically that all important decisions would be made in Berlin, not Strasbourg.[3]

The highest authority for Alsace-Lorraine was the Office of the Reich Chancellery (*Reichskanzleramt*) in Berlin. Although Chancellor Bismarck held ultimate responsibility for Reichsland affairs, Rudolf von Delbrück, president of the Reich Chancellery and Germany's leading free trade advocate, also influenced territorial policy. Responding to Bismarck's request in August 1871, Wilhelm I created a special Section III in the Reich Chancellery to deal exclusively with Reichsland affairs. He appointed Karl Herzog, an official in the Prussian ministry of commerce, director of the new bureau. Creation of Section III only complicated Alsace-Lorraine's administration, for no less than seven departments in Berlin now shared responsibility in the Reichsland: Section III of the Reich Chancellery; the central section responsible for commerce; Section I for postal matters; Section II for the telegraph; the *Reichsjustizamt* (until 1877 Section IV of the Reich Chancellery); the Prussian war ministry; and the Prussian foreign office.

The bureaucracy in Strasbourg implemented policies formulated in Berlin. Frequent changes in the territorial administration reinforced the confusion caused by fragmentation of authority in Berlin. When friction developed between Bismarck-Bohlen, Kühlwetter, and Bismarck, the military-civil general government of the occupa-

tion period broke down. Bismarck, not yet prepared to begin his
Kulturkampf against German Catholicism, objected to Bismarck-
Bohlen's separation of local teachers' seminaries on a confessional
basis. He demanded his uncle's resignation, and recalled Kühlwetter
to Berlin in August 1871, thus preparing the ground for a completely new high authority in the Reichsland.[4] The emperor named
Eduard von Möller, an outstanding Prussian bureaucrat, to the
newly-created post of high president (*Oberpräsident*) for Alsace-
Lorraine. Möller had entered government service in 1838 as state
commissioner for the Cologne-Minden railway. As Möller quickly
proved his ability, the Prussian king widened his commissariat to
include all railways in the western provinces. During the crisis of
1848, Möller had been named district president of the Rhine provinces, where he had forged close bonds of friendship with Prince
Wilhelm of Prussia, the future Prussian king and German emperor.
Möller's reputation as an experienced troubleshooter won him appointment as high president in electoral Hesse after the Prussian
annexations of 1866. Weighing his success in integrating Hesse
into Prussia, the government hoped he might repeat the feat in
Alsace-Lorraine.

   Bismarck, who did not share the emperor's admiration for Möller,
succeeded in limiting the high president's powers. Under the law of
30 December 1871, Bismarck alone determined the authority delegated to the high president.[5] While Bismarck wanted a strong administration in Strasbourg, he nevertheless wished to retain ultimate
control of all power. Having established in principle the high president's dependence on the chancellor, Bismarck proceeded to assign
him sweeping authority. Paragraph ten of the law of 30 December
1871, the so-called dictatorship paragraph, invested the high president with wide emergency powers which in other constitutions are
generally reserved to military authorities after the proclamation of
a state of siege. The dictatorship paragraph provided the framers
of the Weimar Constitution of 1919 with a precedent for Article
Forty-eight.

   The high presidency was a Prussian institution grafted to a replica
of the old French administrative structure. Alsace-Lorraine under
the Germans comprised three districts (*Bezirke*) of Upper Alsace,
Lower Alsace, and Lorraine, each administered by a district president. Below the district level, twenty-two counties (*Kreise*) headed
by county directors handled local matters. Elected district and county

councils dealt with regional economic affairs, but were not permitted to deal with "political" questions. Holding powers of the former French prefects, the district president's chief function was to formulate police regulations. Police commissioners in Strasbourg, Metz, and Mulhouse reported directly to the district president. The county directors, replacing the French subprefects, supervised communal administration, prepared communal budgets, and appointed mayors in rural towns.

Popular opinion found no institutional outlet in the Reichsland. Prompt introduction of the imperial constitution would have enabled the people to speak through their Reichstag deputies, but the government convinced the Reichstag to delay introduction until 1874, one year later than originally scheduled. Government spokesmen claimed agitation caused by the approaching citizenship option deadline ruled out the holding of Reichstag elections in Alsace-Lorraine until 1874.[6] Möller, an anti-Catholic, backed the government with the warning that elections in 1873 would produce a solid delegation of ultramontanes.[7] Möller also feared increased control from Berlin with the introduction of the imperial constitution; Herzog, supported by Bismarck, threatened to centralize Reichsland administration under Section III of the Reich Chancellery.[8]

Implementation of the imperial constitution brought Alsace-Lorraine fifteen seats in the Reichstag, but no representation in the Federal Council. Because the Reichstag now made laws for Alsace-Lorraine, debates on territorial issues gave the Centrists and Progressives new opportunities to attack the government. To avoid the embarrassment of public debate in the Reichstag, Bismarck proposed the creation of a territorial assembly in Strasbourg. Seeing a chance for greater independence from Berlin, Möller originally supported Bismarck's plan. After the territorial clerical-protester victory in the 1874 Reichstag election, however, Möller reversed his position, convinced that an opposition coalition would control a territorial parliament.[9] Deciding to gamble, Bismarck late in 1874 secured permission from the emperor to establish a territorial committee (*Landesausschuss*). As an advisory body of thirty-four, selected by the three district councils from among their own membership, the territorial committee had no real power. The government was not required to consult it, nor was it bound to respect the opinion of the committee when it did consult it. The territorial committee did not represent a significant step toward self-government. It approved

bills which the Reichstag would have passed in any case, but could
not prevent the passage of bills it opposed.[10] Bismarck had snared
himself in a self-defeating contradiction. Limitation on the competence of the territorial committee meant that the Reichstag still
legislated for the Reichsland, leaving unfulfilled the chancellor's
desire to remove the Alsace-Lorraine debate from the imperial parliament. Totally emasculated, the territorial committee commanded
little respect in Alsace-Lorraine. Most of the delegates were autonomists, willing to cooperate with the Germans; protesters generally
refused to participate in any of the organs of local government. It
was to their Reichstag deputies rather than the territorial committee
delegates that the people of Alsace-Lorraine turned for leadership.

Moves to expand the powers of the territorial committee began
in 1876, with a visit to Berlin by the autonomist leader Auguste
Schneegans. Suspecting that Möller wished to use the committee as
a lever to increase his own power, officials in the imperial capital
gave Schneegans a cool reception. Herzog refused to consider any
changes in the Reichsland until the 1877 Reichstag election enabled
the government to judge public opinion.[11] Bismarck voiced fears that
a territorial parliament dominated by anti-German clericals would
incite another Franco-German conflict.[12]

When in 1877 the autonomists unexpectedly won five of the six
Reichstag seats for Lower Alsace, Bismarck decided that government support for Schneegans and his followers might be a worthwhile investment. He upgraded the territorial committee from an
advisory committee to a parliament, with the significant reservations
that the emperor initiated all legislation and the Federal Council
granted ultimate sanction. Although the Reichstag now played no
role in territorial legislation, it could resume its function as law-
maker for the Reichsland should the territorial committee become
refractory.

Final responsibility for German policy in Alsace-Lorraine still
rested with the chancellor. Already overburdened with the awesome
charge of general imperial affairs, Bismarck wished to transfer full
accountability for Reichsland affairs to some other official. The
tension between Möller and Berlin authorities had convinced Bismarck that the high president could not fill such a position of responsibility. Möller, however, still held the emperor's confidence.[13]
Unable to dismiss the high president completely, Bismarck determined to move him to Berlin where he could at least hold him in

check. With this end in mind, Bismarck offered Möller directorship of a separate ministry for Alsace-Lorraine headquartered in Berlin. Arguing that the Reichsland could not be governed effectively from Berlin, Möller declined.[14] Bismarck's setback was only temporary, for Delbrück's resignation from the presidency of the Reich Chancellery in 1875 under pressure from the protectionists opened the way for a complete reorganization of the Reichsland administration. Section III was removed from the Reich Chancellery and placed directly under Bismarck's supervision; Karl Herzog stayed on as the department's senior administrator, but now reported directly to the chancellor.[15] This was only a temporary arrangement; blueprints for the reorganization of the entire imperial administration already lay on Bismarck's drawing board.

By December 1877 the reorganization plans were complete. The scheme called for conversion of Reich Chancellery divisions into separate departments, each headed by a secretary of state. The new structure included a department designated the *Reichskanzleramt für Elsass-Lothringen*, with Herzog as secretary of state. Neither Möller nor Bismarck was satisfied with this latest attempt to find a proper administration for the Reichsland. Hoping to capitalize on his personal relationship with Wilhelm I, Möller suggested that Alsace-Lorraine either be converted into a "Grand Duchy of Alsace-Lorraine," or joined to Germany through a personal union under the emperor. Both Bismarck and Herzog rejected the idea of a personal union, believing experience had shown that such a system could work only in conjunction with a true parliamentary system. Bismarck held more enthusiasm for sending the crown prince to govern the Reichsland, but the emperor feared the prince and his family would become "foreigners" in Strasbourg.[16] The autonomist leader Julius Klein objected to the crown prince plan, predicting that Alsace-Lorraine would become a *Dauphiné* governed by a child supervised by private tutors.[17] When the prince temporarily assumed imperial command in 1878 after the Hödel-Nobiling attempts on the emperor's life, the possibility of sending him to the Reichsland was no longer seriously considered.[18]

When the autonomists lost one of their five seats in the 1878 Reichstag election, Bismarck decided to shore up the party by making more concessions to territorial self-government. At the same time, he could relieve himself of responsibility for Reichsland affairs. In February 1879 Bismarck invited the autonomist leader

Schneegans to discuss plans for a definitive constitution for Alsace-Lorraine. Intimating to Schneegans that Möller's days were numbered, Bismarck said he was considering naming a governor (*Statthalter*) for the Reichsland. The governor would be supported by a full ministry, two sections of which, suggested Bismarck, could be headed by Alsatians. Asked to advise on filling the posts, Schneegans offered the name of his autonomist colleague, Julius Klein.[19] As the interview closed, Schneegans asked if Bismarck would object to the introduction of a Reichstag resolution embodying the chancellor's views. Bismarck readily concurred, since such a resolution would create the impression that the initiative for change came from the Alsace-Lorrainers themselves.

Supporting Schneegans' resolution, Bismarck told the Reichstag he was overburdened, and wanted a fully responsible official to direct the Reichsland administration. It was time to end the chronic weakness of the territorial government.[20] Bismarck gained a great deal by appearing to meet the demand for self-administration in Strasbourg. He removed Möller from office, lightened his own administrative load, and strengthened the hand of the Alsatian autonomist party. The chancellor stood to lose nothing, for he could withdraw the concessions if at any time they endangered national security. Imperial authorities in Berlin still held decisive military and civil powers.[21]

The so-called constitution of 1879 satisfied neither Bismarck's desire for a final solution, nor the popular demand for real self-government. The governor occupied an ambiguous position. As a "responsible" minister, he exercised powers formerly held by the imperial chancellor and the high president, but he also acted as a nonresponsible sovereign when exercising powers delegated by the emperor in the name of the Federal Council. The governor's ambivalent status was more important theoretically than practically, since most administrative matters were handled by the new ministry directed by the secretary of state. The ministry contained four sections, each headed by an undersecretary of state, dealing with the interior, religion, education, justice, finance, industry, agriculture, and public works. As the fulcrum of power, the secretary of state reviewed all decisions made by the undersecretaries, and possessed authority to transfer or dismiss all ministry officials.

Under normal conditions, full legislative responsibility rested with the territorial committee and the Federal Council; the territorial committee gained the right of initiative, and the emperor lost the right to block bills passed by both the committee and the Federal Council. Although increased in size from thirty-four to fifty-eight members, the territorial committee was still chosen by an indirect balloting system. Bismarck opposed retention of the indirect system; he had suggested direct suffrage for district and county councils, as well as the territorial committee, but Schneegans and Klein, anticipating the weakness of their autonomist party in direct, popular elections, persuaded Bismarck to settle for indirect voting.[22]

Local politicians who had hoped the 1879 constitution would raise Alsace-Lorraine to full *Bundesstaat* status felt they had been shortchanged. As a true federal state, Alsace-Lorraine would have received votes in the Federal Council. The emperor, who was also king of Prussia, would have instructed the Alsace-Lorraine Federal Council delegates, in effect giving Prussia two or three more votes. Bismarck's imperial constitution had achieved a very delicate balance among the particularist German states; giving Prussia more votes in this manner would in effect change the balance of the federal union. Although Bismarck admitted the desirability of seating Alsace-Lorraine in the Federal Council in a purely advisory capacity, he rejected any plan which might revive the particularist sentiment so skillfully overcome in 1871.[23]

In any administration, the quality of the leadership is no less important than the organization of the bureaucracy it directs. Both the kaiser and the territorial committee wished to appoint Möller as first governor of Alsace-Lorraine, but Bismarck was determined to remove Möller from Strasbourg.[24] The call to the governorship instead went to General Fieldmarshal Edwin von Manteuffel. Manteuffel played a very important role in Prussian court politics; he alone of Friedrich Wilhelm IV's *camarilla* remained a trusted adviser to Wilhelm I. Had Bismarck failed to end Prussia's constitutional crisis of the 1860s, Manteuffel himself would have settled matters with parliament. He steadfastly advised his king to refuse any limitation on royal prerogatives, thereby preventing any compromise between crown and parliament.[25] It was perhaps inevitable that in the course of the wars of unification, a deep personal rivalry developed between Bismarck the master politician and Manteuffel the conquering general. Manteuffel shared the feeling of many military officers that Bismarck had received more than his share of the credit for establishing Germany as a great power; the army, after all, had brought home the victories of 1864, 1866, and 1870–71.

While compiling an outstanding military record in the wars of unification, Manteuffel also distinguished himself as a diplomat and as commander of Prussian occupation troops in France after the war of 1870. The son of a Saxon state official, Manteuffel was born in Dresden, 24 February 1809. Entering military service in 1827, he soon gained the trust of the Prussian King Friedrich Wilhelm IV. In 1848 and 1849 Manteuffel performed diplomatic missions in Sweden and Denmark, after which he completed another round of assignments in Moscow, Warsaw, Vienna, and Hanover. By 1857 his reputation had earned him the post of chief of the Prussian war ministry's personnel section.

Following the Danish war in 1865, King Wilhelm named Manteuffel governor (*Statthalter*) of Schleswig; but he soon relinquished that post to return to active command during the 1866 Austrian campaign. The outbreak of the Franco-Prussian War in 1870 found Manteuffel serving as aide-de-camp to the Prussian king. After holding several field commands during the war, he was named head of the army of occupation in France, serving in that capacity until the last Prussian troops withdrew from France in September 1873. His experience as chief of the occupation forces foreshadowed problems he later encountered as governor of Alsace-Lorraine, particularly in defining the relationship between military and civilian authority.

Manteuffel was a truly political general. As commander of the occupation army he interpreted his wide powers in the widest possible manner. He considered himself not simply a general, but also a statesman and diplomat. When Manteuffel challenged Bismarck's control of foreign policy by concluding an agreement with French Finance Minister August Thomas Pouyer-Quertier in August 1871, Bismarck sent Count Harry von Arnim as special plenipotentiary to Paris to restore normal diplomatic channels. As for the occupation itself under Manteuffel, it was strict but not unduly repressive.[26] His military and political detractors in Berlin accused Manteuffel of being a Francophile, and the chief French historian of the occupation maintained the general was "seduced by the charmer Thiers."[27] Manteuffel's own chief of staff, Major General Albrecht von Stosch, objected to Manteuffel's conciliatory stance, as did Bismarck himself in Berlin.

Despite his differences with Manteuffel, Bismarck supported the fieldmarshal's nomination to the governorship of Alsace-Lorraine in 1879. Manteuffel's appointment rested on the supposed advantages of his high military rank. Frequent clashes between civilian and military authorities had marred Möller's administration as high president. A conspiracy between General Julius von Hartmann, division commander in Strasbourg, and Ernst von Ernsthausen, district president of Lower Alsace, sought to remove Möller from office in 1875. Hartmann obtained an audience with the emperor, only to find that Wilhelm still supported his long-time friend. At Möller's suggestion, the general was pensioned, and Ernsthausen was transferred from Strasbourg to Colmar.[28]

The kaiser fully expected that the appointment of a governor holding the highest military rank in the territory would eliminate conflicts both within the military establishment and between civil and military authorities. Should territorial political movements threaten imperial security, the governor could rely on complete support from his military subordinates.[29] The kaiser, however, had miscalculated. Manteuffel set out to pursue in the Reichsland the same conciliatory policy which had alarmed military and bureaucratic circles during his command of occupation forces in France. He soon lost control over his own bureaucracy, alienated the officers of the XV Army Corps garrisoned in Strasbourg, and rekindled Bismarck's suspicions in Berlin. The unity of high military rank and civilian authority in a single person proved to be a liability rather than an asset. Manteuffel's responsibilities were simply more than one man could handle. As the governor (*Statthalter*) he exercised certain delegated sovereign rights of the empire; but he was also chief of the territorial administration, and commanding general of the XV Army Corps. The attempt to exercise all of these functions led to jurisdictional disputes and personal jealousies.[30]

Manteuffel's difficulty with subordinate military officers was the most unexpected development during his governorship. Having chafed under the strong bureaucratic regime of Möller, the territorial military commanders now hoped for more responsibility and a freer hand. Manteuffel, true to his previous performances, placed his political responsibilities as governor far above his obligations as military commander. His duties as commander of the XV Army Corps he left to his chief of staff; he signed orders without actually exercising command. On the few occasions when he did take personal charge of military affairs, his presence was unwelcome. Subordinate officers complained that the governor neglected the army, an unpardonable sin in imperial Germany. The governor received reports from his civil cabinet daily, but met with his military command only once each week. General Ernst von der Burg, the military governor of Strasbourg who had served as a military and political adviser to the crown prince, opposed Manteuffel's conciliatory policy while retaining his close personal friendship with the governor. Reluctantly, Manteuffel gave up formal command of the XV Army Corps, which was turned over to General Wilhelm von Heuduck. Comparing Manteuffel's regime with that of his successor Hohenlohe-Schillingsfürst, Manteuffel's adjutant in Strasbourg, Count Bogdan Hutten-Czapski, concluded many years later that, "it soon became apparent that a civilian governor was much more suitable for this difficult office than a military commander."[31] Czapski has exaggerated a basic kernel of truth, for as stormy as Manteuffel's regime was, it was rather placid compared to that of Hohenlohe-Schillingsfürst.

Manteuffel's control over his civilian bureaucracy remained even more tenuous than his grip on the military command. In personnel matters, the governor possessed theoretical but not practical authority. Bismarck used the Reichsland as a dumping ground for bureaucrats who had outlived their usefulness in Berlin, and as a testing ground for new programs and new men. Manteuffel's cabinet had to accommodate the chancellor's predilection as well as the governor's. The year 1879 saw Bismarck's renunciation of economic liberalism in an effort to find new revenue for the Reich government. The shift in economic policy produced widespread personnel adjustments in both the Reich and the Reichsland. Rudolf von Delbrück's resignation from the Reich Chancellery presidency in 1876 had already deprived the government of a vigorous advocate of free trade. When the chancellor himself abandoned economic liberalism in 1879, Möller, a free-trader, became a sacrificial offering in honor of the new protectionist program.[32] Manteuffel's first secretary of state, Karl Herzog, a free-trader, lost his post in July 1880 when he tried to block a Prussian liquor tax bill. Schleswig High President Karl von Boetticher, Manteuffel's choice as Herzog's successor, declined the transfer to imperial service and loss of his Prussian pension rights.[33] Bismarck finally appointed Karl von Hofmann, the Prussian minister of trade and Delbrück's successor at the Reich

Chancellery. An economic liberal, Hofmann was of no further use to Bismarck in Berlin. Manteuffel accepted Hofmann on the condition that Delbrück's brother-in-law be relieved of his post as Alsace-Lorraine undersecretary for the interior.[34] At the same time, Bismarck named a protectionist, Georg von Mayr, as undersecretary for finance. Having shifted from free trade to protection, Bismarck set out to purge economic liberals from imperial administration. When their services were no longer desired in Berlin, the liberals might be exiled to the Reichsland; but even in Strasbourg, the government tolerated only a limited number of economic liberals.[35]

In the tumult of incessant personnel transfers, not even Manteuffel's position was safe. Increasing tensions between the governor and the chancellor finally led the kaiser to send Count Czapski to Strasbourg as Manteuffel's adjutant in the hope that he could moderate the conflict.[36] The powerful Count Alfred von Waldersee, dissatisfied with the governor's lenient administration, joined Bismarck in voicing objections to Manteuffel.[37] Talk of replacing Manteuffel abounded in 1883–84, with Waldersee being mentioned as a possible successor. Nothing but the kaiser's unwillingness to dismiss his trusted adviser saved Manteuffel. When Manteuffel proscribed a planned torchlight procession in Strasbourg honoring Bismarck's seventieth birthday late in March 1885, his closest aides feared the governor's career was finished. Manteuffel's death in June 1885 fortunately brought an honorable end to a lifetime of distinguished service to the monarchy. It also set the stage for the most devastating release of pent-up military opposition under Manteuffel's successor, Prince Chlodwig zu Hohenlohe-Schillingsfürst.[38]

Hohenlohe, a Bavarian liberal Catholic, was sixty-six years old when called to Alsace-Lorraine. Although he was to move on to the imperial chancellorship in 1894, he had already achieved a distinguished position in politics and diplomacy by 1885. He received the news of his appointment as governor of Alsace-Lorraine while serving as German ambassador in Paris, and his reaction resembled that of a twenty-year-old receiving his army induction notice. "When one has been Ambassador in Paris for eleven years," wrote Hohenlohe, "one only goes to Strasbourg as a matter of patriotic duty."[39] Hohenlohe had good reason to accept his appointment reluctantly. He correctly judged that his lack of military rank would create difficulties in a territory where military security was of prime importance. But there were certain advantages as well. The position

offered interesting work, relative independence, and the highest
salary in the imperial service, 200,000 marks.[40]

Bismarck's reasons for appointing Hohenlohe help to explain the
governor's subsequent difficulty. Holstein's judgment that "he was
picked because they wanted a nonentity" is at best misleading.[41]
After the Manteuffel experience, Bismarck felt that the next governor
ought to be an experienced administrator and diplomat. The kaiser
wanted General Count Otto Stolberg-Wernigerode, who had served
as vice president of the Prussian State Ministry from 1878 to 1881.
Bismarck convinced Wilhelm of the wisdom of separating the functions of governor and commanding general in the Reichsland. Filling
the governorship, however, was only one part of Bismarck's overall
plan for overhauling the foreign ministry. Exactly what Bismarck
had in mind remains unclear; the complexity of Bismarck's own
thought-process, combined with the petty jealousy of the dozens of
bureaucrats and diplomats competing for the chancellor's favor,
render a definitive interpretation impossible. According to Helmuth
Rogge, Bismarck felt it was time for a change of ambassador in
Paris; Hohenlohe had held the post eleven years. In the chancellor's
view, London was becoming more important than Paris, and the
English capital deserved no less than the best of Germany's diplomats. Bismarck could accomplish everything he desired by sending
Hohenlohe to Strasbourg, shifting Count Georg Herbert zu Münster
from London to Paris, and sending to London the state secretary
of the foreign ministry, Count Paul von Hatzfeldt-Wildenburg.[42]
Other accounts mention all the factors discussed by Rogge, but so
transform the priorities as to throw an entirely different light on
the matter. Hohenlohe's son, Prince Alexander zu Hohenlohe-
Schillingsfürst, contended that his father's assignment to Strasbourg
formed part of Bismarck's scheme to appoint his own son Herbert
to the post of state secretary for foreign affairs.[43] Correspondence
between Holstein and Hatzfeldt supports Alexander's contention,
although Hatzfeldt was not exactly a disinterested observer. Hatzfeldt, in fact, felt that if he were forced to surrender his post at the
foreign office to Bismarck's son, he should be compensated with
nothing less than the governorship of Alsace-Lorraine.[44] Hatzfeldt
indeed went to London, Münster transferred to Paris, Hohenlohe
assumed the governorship in Strasbourg, and Count Herbert von
Bismarck became state secretary for foreign affairs.

Hohenlohe's difficulties with the military began 5 November 1885, the day he arrived in Strasbourg to assume the governorship. As the governor's party approached the governor's palace, Hohenlohe's son Prince Alexander and one of his aides noticed that the two sentry-boxes outside the palace were not manned. Manteuffel, as a field-marshal, had had sentries, as well as two military adjutants. If Hohenlohe were not accorded the same privileges, the prestige of his office would decline. For Manteuffel, obtaining sentries and adjutants was a simple matter; but how did a civilian go about securing such favors? Inquiries to the commander of the XV Army Corps, General Wilhelm von Heuduck, produced no results. Hohenlohe sought help from the chancellor himself, who, through his son Herbert, passed on the governor's request to the kaiser. The German emperor made the final decision on assigning two sentries to the governor of Alsace-Lorraine! On 14 November 1885, Hohenlohe recorded in his *Journal*: "Today I received my two sentries, which will contribute to the quieting of the civilians, who were already beginning to be annoyed because their Governor was so badly treated."[45] Not only had the kaiser ordered sentries for Hohenlohe, but he had also commanded the officers at Strasbourg, including Heuduck himself, to turn out for installation ceremonies for the sentries.[46] The assignment of adjutants to the governor, however, involved more complex negotiations. Hohenlohe wished to have Manteuffel's adjutants stay on; they would be assigned to the "Governor" rather than to the "Fieldmarshal." The matter created quite a stir among the Prussian generals, who regarded the governor's attempt to obtain adjutants as an infringement on their privileges. In a letter to Army Quartermaster General Count Alfred von Waldersee, General Baron Walter von Loë argued against military adjutants for Hohenlohe. Loë conceded that the governor might be entitled to adjutants if he functioned as *alter ego* to the kaiser; but this was not the case, because Hohenlohe's immediate superior, he claimed, was another civilian official, the Reich chancellor.[47] When the case first came before the military cabinet, Hohenlohe's request was refused. Thirteen months after taking office, Hohenlohe finally received permission for one of the two adjutants he had sought.[48]

Considering the outcome of the sentry and adjutant affairs, one might conclude that Hohenlohe was more than holding his own against the generals. His son, Prince Alexander, claimed that once the sentry affair had been settled, the governor's relations with General Heuduck were good. The imperial cabinet order granting the sentries, Alexander maintained, had established once and for all the preponderant position of the governor over the military commanders.[49] Alexander grossly overestimated the significance of the sentry affair. The granting of sentries and an adjutant brought no permanent solution to either the general problem of civil-military relations in the Reichsland or the specific problem of Hohenlohe's relations to the generals with whom he had to deal. In January 1886 Lieutenant Colonel Max von Bock, chief of staff of the XV Army Corps, complained to Waldersee of the lack of definition between civil and military authority, and advised that the difficulty be ironed out before the French took the confusion as a sign of disunity in the German empire.[50] Hohenlohe noted in his diary on 13 August 1886 that army officers in Alsace-Lorraine, concerned with what they considered the governor's laxity in dealing with French reserve officers and other foreigners in the Reichsland, were pressuring Heuduck to try to bring the cases before military courts.[51]

Hohenlohe continued his efforts to regulate his relations with the military during 1886–87. The difficulty over the sentries and adjutants convinced the governor that his only recourse was to obtain a high military commission for himself. He discussed this possibility with a number of generals, who advised him that the simplest method of obtaining a commission was to have the kaiser designate him commander of the territorial *Landwehr* battalions. The kaiser himself appeared sympathetic toward Hohenlohe's plight; the obstacle was the military cabinet, upon whose advice the kaiser made the ultimate decision. Hohenlohe's brother, Prince Victor Hohenlohe-Schillingsfürst, duke of Ratibor, personally interceded with the military cabinet—with no result. Nothing could be done against the determined opposition of the chief of the military cabinet, General Emil von Albedyll, believed by Hohenlohe to desire the governorship for himself.[52]

During the war scare of 1886–87, fanned by militant Boulangism in France and the arrest of the French border guard Schnaebele in Alsace-Lorraine, Hohenlohe's uneasiness continued to grow. In February 1887 the Ministry of Alsace-Lorraine and the Prussian General Staff held conversations concerning the impact of the possible declaration of a state of siege in the event of mobilization. Hohenlohe wrote to Bismarck that the conversations had, "induced me to consider the question what may be the position of the Imperial Governor in such an event." Noting that according to the

Prussian law of 4 June 1851, the executive power passed to the military commander upon the declaration of a state of siege, Hohenlohe concluded that he would "be condemned to inactivity in a moment of danger, which would be an extremely painful position to myself." To insure himself a role in the event of war, Hohenlohe suggested to Bismarck that the governor might assume the functions of governor-general of Alsace-Lorraine; if that were not feasible, the governor indicated a preference for duty at "headquarters."[53] Bismarck responded with a devastatingly brutal reply. In the event of the proclamation of a state of siege, the governor's position would be "generally analogous to that of most of the German Federal princes who have transferred their military supremacy to the King of Prussia; in other words, there would be no change in the situation." Nor would a military title help Hohenlohe; Bismarck was a general, but he would not therefore inherit any military powers in a state of siege. Modification of Hohenlohe's title to governor-general would be equally useless, as would a transfer to army headquarters. The right to cooperate in the management of a state of siege, Bismarck concluded, belongs only to the military authorities on active service at the point in question. Obviously exasperated by Hohenlohe's continuous attempts to secure military privileges, Bismarck scorned the governor's plea for support against the military cabinet. "His Majesty," wrote the chancellor, "probably would not care to consider these and other points of difficulty before the beginning of the mobilization."[54]

Hohenlohe had reached the end of the road in his efforts to achieve a degree of security within the military hierarchy; after the *Septennat* Reichstag election of 21 February 1887, the generals mounted a withering offensive against the governor. Not a single progovernment candidate succeeded in the Reichsland. While Bismarck was winning the election in Germany, Hohenlohe was losing control in the militarily sensitive Reichsland. The ultranationalist press joined the generals in demanding radical measures against the recalcitrant traitors; among the possibilities mentioned were the partitioning of Alsace-Lorraine among Baden, Bavaria, and Prussia, the abolition of the governorship and transferral of the territorial administration to Berlin, abolition of the territorial committee, revocation of the right to representation in the Reichstag, and the removal of all officials responsible for the apparent failure to Germanize the territory. Hohenlohe's own ministers joined the cry from

Berlin, proposing to suspend the territorial committee or to demand the resignation of the mayor of Mulhouse.[55] Hohenlohe's fear of the declaration of a state of siege now assumed a measure of reality. The generals, led by Julius von Verdy du Vernois, the military governor of Strasbourg, and Waldersee in Berlin, regarded the state of siege as the simplest way to remove Hohenlohe from the territorial administration.[56] At least some of the generals really meant business. This would not simply be a formal declaration of a state of siege; it would be war with France. Cavalry General Baron Walter von Loë told Waldersee shortly after the election that pro-French sentiment would never be erased in Alsace-Lorraine until Germany crushed France in another decisive war. Lacking this demonstration of the futility of French agitation, it mattered little whether the kaiser appointed a Manteuffel, a Hohenlohe, or anyone else to govern the Reichsland.[57]

The military's challenge to Hohenlohe constituted an implicit threat to the chancellor himself. Serious talk of war, the declaration of a state of siege in Alsace-Lorraine, and the dismantling of the territorial government constituted a direct attack on Bismarck's control over both domestic and foreign policy. For Bismarck, the Hohenlohe crisis had developed at the worst possible moment. Kaiser Wilhelm I, whose support Bismarck had managed to retain during the darkest moments of his career, showed the strains of his ninety-one years and died 9 March 1888 without settling the Alsace-Lorraine issue. The new emperor, Friedrich III, was a dying man, and Bismarck would have difficulty manipulating the future Wilhelm II. When Bismarck resisted the most drastic measures demanded by the military, he did so to protect his own position; but to conciliate the military party, Bismarck had to prove he could be as tough as any general by ordering some repressive measures for Alsace-Lorraine.

Hohenlohe wished to save his own skin, and sensing that his political career might be drawing to a premature close, the governor went to Berlin to try to salvage his honor. Hohenlohe did convince Bismarck that he (Hohenlohe) should not be made the scapegoat for the election fiasco in the Reichsland. But the military party demanded satisfaction; someone had to be held responsible for the vote in Alsace-Lorraine. The unanimous choice for this sacrifice was Karl von Hofmann, Hohenlohe's secretary of state. Hofmann was convenient. As a holdover from the Manteuffel administration, he could be accused of pursuing the fieldmarshal's discredited policy of conciliation. Everyone Hohenlohe consulted, including Bismarck, Holstein, and the chief of the civil cabinet, Baron Karl von Wilmowski, advised the governor to dismiss Hofmann. Hohenlohe resisted, for his conscience told him that Hofmann was not responsible for the debacle. But when the governor saw the list of repressive measures Bismarck intended to introduce in the Reichsland, Hohenlohe admitted that Hofmann was not the man to implement such a program, and asked for his resignation.[58]

Technically, there appears to be no reason why Hohenlohe, as the direct representative of the kaiser and Federal Council in Alsace-Lorraine, should not have been held "responsible" for the failure of the government's policies there. The lines of responsibility were defined by the 1879 *Statthalter* law, which held the secretary of state responsible for actions taken by the governor under sovereign powers delegated to him by the kaiser. But we are dealing here with a question of political rather than legal responsibility. The "war scare" tactic employed so successfully in the rest of Germany during the *Septennat* campaign backfired in Alsace-Lorraine. The Alsace-Lorrainers wanted peace, because their homeland would be the battleground in any future war. Giving the generals a more powerful army would only encourage the more foolhardy among them to attack France. Hohenlohe himself employed the war-scare tactic in a speech—which was widely reported in the press[59]—to the territorial committee on 9 February 1887. Did Hohenlohe misjudge the political temperament in Alsace-Lorraine? The governor informed Bismarck on 11 February that, "the apprehensions of war, which exert a favorable influence upon the elections in Germany, have a contrary effect here."[60] Ultranationalists and militarists who discounted Hohenlohe's opinion might have placed more credence in the report of Lieutenant Colonel Max von Bock, chief of staff of the XV Army Corps, who predicted to Waldersee the day before the election a severe government defeat in a territory where no one wanted war.[61] Who, then, advised Hohenlohe to intervene in the election with his war-scare speech? Helmuth Rogge believes it was Hofmann.[62] But in a letter to his brother, Prince Ratibor, Hohenlohe depicted the uproar over Hofmann as exaggerated and unjust. The governor had intervened in the 1887 election against his better judgment under pressure from German ultranationalists.[63] Nevertheless, Hohenlohe felt he had no alternative but to follow everyone's advice and dismiss the secretary of state.[64]

The ultras had overthrown Hofmann, but they lacked the power to name his successor. Hohenlohe recommended one of his undersecretaries, Max von Puttkamer, as Hofmann's replacement. The chancellor was at first inclined to agree, then decided Puttkamer was "too liberal and not sufficiently energetic." In a move which must have disappointed the militants, Bismarck finally decided that a secretary of state was superfluous, and left the post vacant until 1889, when he did permit Hohenlohe to appoint Puttkamer.[65] Hofmann's dismissal triggered a complete overhaul of Hohenlohe's cabinet. Puttkamer took over the department of justice, Konrad von Studt left his post as head of the administration in Königsberg to become undersecretary for the interior, and Otto Back, the Strasbourg commissar, replaced Georg von Mayr as undersecretary for finance. When Back requested permission to rejoin the Strasbourg government after only a few months in the ministry (he had been elected mayor), Hohenlohe appointed Max von Schraut, an *Oberregierungsrat* in the imperial treasury department.[66] Exactly how much freedom Hohenlohe had in making these appointments remains unclear. On the secretary of state, Bismarck clearly retained final decision. Hohenlohe reported that, "for the Interior I may choose whom I will."[67]

Considering the intensity of the campaign mounted against him, Hohenlohe obtained impressive concessions during his consultations in Berlin in March 1887. He successfully withstood attacks from the semiofficial *Strassburger Post*, which prematurely announced 30 March that the governorship had been abolished, and from generals such as Verdy du Vernois, who observed to Otto Back that there was a vacant ambassadorial post in Rome to which Hohenlohe might be appointed.[68] In the ministerial council, Robert von Puttkamer, Prussian minister of the interior, and Heinrich von Friedberg, Prussian minister of justice, supported Hohenlohe, but Karl Heinrich von Bötticher, secretary of state in the imperial department of the interior, and Franz Johann von Rottenburg, chief of the Reich Chancellery, favored dismissing Hohenlohe, abolishing the *Statthalter* post, and transferring the administration to Berlin. Bismarck refused to split his cabinet with an open confrontation, and played a waiting game until the kaiser himself settled the issue. In the 28

March ministerial conference, Bismarck listened to arguments from both sides, and finally commissioned Bötticher to draw up a draft bill abolishing the governorship.[69]

Bismarck was playing a double game, throwing a sop to conservatives like Bötticher while telling Hohenlohe that he would not permit the Reichsland territorial administration to be dismantled.[70] Removing the administration to Berlin would have run counter to the chancellor's objective in establishing the governorship in 1879; he wished to relieve himself of the burden of directly supervising the government of Alsace-Lorraine. Hohenlohe correctly recognized that his future ultimately depended on the kaiser's decision. The governor obtained two audiences with Wilhelm; on 20 March the emperor assured Hohenlohe that he had no intention of restructuring the entire territorial administration "merely because the elections have turned out badly." But when Bismarck gave Bötticher permission to draw up the draft legislation abolishing the governorship, Hohenlohe returned to the palace on 1 April with the outline of a plan projecting the major personnel changes described above, but retaining the administrative structure intact. The kaiser approved Hohenlohe's program, signed it in quadruplicate, and Hohenlohe returned to Strasbourg with his honor and integrity more or less unimpaired.[71]

Before Hohenlohe left Berlin, Bismarck informed him that sweeping personnel changes in Strasbourg would not be sufficient to satisfy the demands of the military radicals. The governor would have to implement a "hard line" policy against pro-French elements in the Reichsland. Hohenlohe's friends had already urged him during the autumn of 1886 to conciliate his military critics with "a few acts of rigor," but the governor believed repression would only complicate the task of governing Alsace-Lorraine.[72] Now Bismarck presented Hohenlohe with a list of eight measures required to insure the security of the Reichsland, including the dissolution of certain associations, restrictions on residency for French officers and Frenchmen in general, expulsion of all agitators whether foreigners or natives, introduction of a political police, abolition of municipal council election of mayors, redistribution of election districts, suppression of all dangerous newspapers and exclusion of French newspapers, and the imposition of a passport system for all French citizens visiting the Reichsland. Hohenlohe objected to many of these measures, particularly the passport system, but returned to

Strasbourg considering himself fortunate to have preserved his own position.[73]

Hohenlohe's troubles were not yet ended. In July 1887 he noted a report from his undersecretary for the interior, Studt, that in Berlin they were still discussing a possible "simplification" of the Alsace-Lorraine administration. The most likely plan would have merged Section I (interior, religion, and education) with Section II (justice), and shifted Section IV (industry, agriculture, and public works) to Section III (finance). The ministry would then consist of a secretary of state managing Sections I and II, and one undersecretary managing Sections III and IV. Studt believed the acceptance of such a plan would strengthen Hohenlohe's standing in Berlin, but Hohenlohe saw only the possibility of more problems. The plan placed too great a burden of work and responsibility on the secretary of state; and if something went wrong, the governor would receive the blame. Hohenlohe's greatest concern, however, was the possibility that his critics in Berlin hoped to scrap the entire administration by slowly chipping it away.[74]

Conservative efforts to "reform" the territorial administration failed, but the implementation of repressive measures agreed upon by Bismarck and Hohenlohe in Berlin proceeded smoothly during 1887 and the first months of 1888. Leading opposition politicians such as Jules Antoine and Jacques Kablé were forced to relinquish their Reichstag seats and leave the Reichsland, factory owners suspected of harboring French sympathies were expelled, and gymnastic and musical societies suspected of serving as front organizations for pro-French activists were ordered disbanded. On the matter of imposing passport requirements on French visitors in Alsace-Lorraine, however, Hohenlohe procrastinated. In May 1888 Bismarck finally ordered the governor to introduce a system of compulsory passports against the French. Fearing the storm of protest such a measure would raise in both the Reichsland and in France, Hohenlohe balked. The injustice of the passport regulation was the least of Hohenlohe's concerns; he was much more concerned with the impact of the measure on his own position as governor. He wrote in his diary that, "It seems that Berlin desires to introduce these irritating measures with the object of reducing the inhabitants of Alsace-Lorraine to despair and driving them to revolt, when it will be possible to say that civil government is useless and that martial law must be proclaimed. The power will then pass to the general-in-command, the governor will be obliged to retire . . . and will be an object of ridicule for his failure."[75] The governor resolved to resist, even at the risk of a total break with Bismarck. "If I yield now," he wrote, "I cannot avert the final catastrophe of a military government, and shall be unable to resign with honor."[76] To the chief of the civil cabinet, Wilmowski, Hohenlohe wrote that the introduction of the passport system would probably lead to war with France, and the governor had "no desire to draw on myself in the eyes of the world the odium of having by my administration prepared the way for war."[77]

Others shared Hohenlohe's fear of a military solution to the Alsace-Lorraine problem. Holstein advised Hohenlohe that the civil government in the Reichsland faced a grave crisis; the generals were pressing for the declaration of a state of siege. As a concession to the military, Paul Kayser, an embassy official in the foreign office, had proposed that the civilian government relinquish to the army control over espionage cases, and allow such cases to be tried in military courts. Holstein thought Kayser's proposal was "the only conceivable means of avoiding an immediate abolition of the civil government." Hohenlohe, however, thought it inadvisable to give in to the military, since in any event the governor would be held responsible for what happened in the Reichsland.[78] Implementation of the passport system constituted an alternative to military dictatorship, and Hohenlohe seemed determined to resist that course, too.

Bismarck viewed the passport system as an aspect of imperial foreign policy; in view of the possibility of war, the government must secure the borderland. Robert von Puttkamer, the Prussian minister of the interior, expressed the Bismarckian approach when he told Hohenlohe in May 1887 that the decision on implementing the passport system depended on the outcome of the latest French cabinet crisis; if Boulanger was included in the new government, then the passport measure would be introduced, but if Boulanger was excluded from the cabinet, the passport system would be unnecessary. When Maurice Rouvier, a proponent of reconciliation with Germany, formed a government without Boulanger, Bismarck delayed introduction of the passport regulation.[79] Boulanger made a new move in 1888 by standing in as many parliamentary by-elections as possible, his so-called plebiscitary campaign to win popular support. The war threat was still very real, and the passport system could not be delayed indefinitely. The Schnaebele incident, and the widespread belief that the French operated a vast espionage system in Alsace-Lorraine contributed to the deterioration of Franco-German relations.[80] In January 1887 well before the unfortunate *Septennat* election, Bismarck had informed Hohenlohe that the passport system was needed to "emphasize the existing separation and alienation" between France and Germany.[81] Crown Prince Wilhelm (future Wilhelm II) "considered the compulsory passport measure necessary, and shared the view of the military that the French ought to be treated roughly."[82] In the final analysis, though, the merit of the passport system itself was not the critical factor. Bismarck regarded the passport question as part of his foreign policy program, not as a domestic affair; and in the field of foreign policy, no one could challenge the chancellor.

Hohenlohe's difference with the chancellor was fundamental. Whereas Bismarck assumed the possibility of war, and regarded the passport system as part of the preparation for an almost inevitable conflict, Hohenlohe refused to concede the inevitability of war, and maintained that the passport regulation would simply add one more unnecessary burden to Franco-German relations.[83] Hohenlohe still held out hope that Alsace-Lorraine could be integrated successfully into the German empire, but measures such as passports would not help. The disruption of communication across the border, warned Hohenlohe, would most adversely affect those who were most friendly to the German cause, the small farmers and workers, the "little people" of Alsace-Lorraine. The educated, wealthy middle class, mostly anti-German, would always find ways of maintaining their ties with France. If Bismarck was concerned with halting all economic intercourse between the Reichsland and France, the tariff barriers had already accomplished this and passports were unnecessary. Bismarck coldly replied that Alsace-Lorraine was annexed to insure the military security of the Reich, and not out of concern for the inhabitants of the territory.[84]

Disregarding Hohenlohe's objections, the Prussian ministry approved the passport measure 13 May 1888. Bismarck was prepared to replace Hohenlohe with General Leo von Caprivi as governor general if Hohenlohe refused to implement the order. That would be the military dictatorship Hohenlohe so desperately wished to prevent. The governor's choice was limited; he could resign or give in. After consulting with his friend the grand duke of Baden, who "did not consider the occasion a suitable one for resigning," Hohenlohe informed Wilmowski and Bismarck that, "I must withdraw my opposition to a measure the responsibility for which will not be mine."[85]

Controversial though it was, the passport system was instituted even though no one had proved it was either necessary or workable. Hohenlohe's brother, Prince Ratibor, thought it was a senseless measure which would only stir up trouble.[86] On the surface, the regulation appeared quite stringent and effective. Designed to erect a barrier between France and Alsace-Lorraine, the passport system served much the same purpose as the Berlin wall of the 1960s. Certain categories of persons could not enter Alsace-Lorraine under any circumstances. Qualified foreigners desiring to enter the Reichsland from France had to secure a passport from the German ambassador in Paris, and the red tape and delay was designed to discourage applicants. If granted, the passports expired after eight weeks; visitors were required to report to the local police whenever they remained at one locale over twenty-four hours. French military personnel, whether active or reserve, and students in French military academies required special authorization in addition to the passport.

Before the passport measure became law on 22 May 1888, the French laws of 2 October 1795, 19 October 1797, and 30 April 1817 regulated the entry of foreigners into Alsace-Lorraine. Originally designed for use against Germans, these laws were turned against the French after 1871. The government never introduced Germany's own law on passports (12 October 1867) into Alsace-Lorraine. The new 1888 measure was much stricter than the 1867 German law, but it had one major loophole. It applied only to visitors entering the Reichsland across the Franco-German border. Anyone, including Frenchmen, could still gain easy access to Alsace-Lorraine by entering from Germany, Switzerland, or Luxemburg. The ineffectiveness of the measure may explain why the French did not retaliate with stringent measures of their own until they finally imposed similar restrictions on German military personnel in October 1912.[87]

Hohenlohe tenaciously pursued his struggle against the passport system. When he raised the matter in a conversation with Bismarck in December 1889, the chancellor expressed his satisfaction with the passports and rejected any relaxation.[88] Wilhelm II's accession to the throne upon the death of Friedrich III on 15 June 1888 brought Hohenlohe no relief. As crown prince, Wilhelm had already expressed enthusiasm for the passport measure, and despite their conflict after he assumed the imperial title, the emperor and chancellor remained united on this particular issue. Hohenlohe's audience with Wilhelm on 21 January 1889 failed to move the young emperor. "When I spoke about the repressive measures," wrote Hohenlohe, "he wrapped himself in silence and refused to express an opinion. I saw that he stood entirely under the influence of the Imperial Chancellor, and did not trust himself to express an opinion different from his."[89]

Bismarck's magic failed to control the willful Kaiser Wilhelm II for long, and the Iron Chancellor submitted his resignation 18 March 1890. Bismarck had "resigned" during many crises in the past, but this time the kaiser accepted the chancellor's retirement. Bismarck's successor, General Leo von Caprivi, offered Hohenlohe greater hope for a relaxation of the passport restrictions. In a casual dinner conversation with the new chancellor only four days after Bismarck's resignation, Hohenlohe asked Caprivi about the possibility of a "more sensible" administration of the passport measure, and repeal of the ban on issuing hunting licenses to French citizens. Caprivi sympathized, but advised waiting a few months to avoid giving the impression that the new administration intended to turn everything upside-down. "On the whole," recalled Hohenlohe, "we got on very well, and I rejoiced that he had been appointed Imperial Chancellor."[90]

Caprivi was flexible, but would the kaiser bend on the passport issue? On his annual visit to the Reichsland during April 1890, the emperor had made vague remarks promising to meet the needs and wishes of the people so long as this was compatible with the security requirements of the empire. Interpreting the kaiser's remarks in the most liberal sense, the territorial committee passed a resolution requesting the total suspension of the passport regulations. In response, Caprivi assured the Alsace-Lorrainers that although the government could not immediately repeal the measure, it would continue to administer it in the most enlightened manner.[91] So stood the matter when the kaiser's mother Victoria and sister Margaret visited Paris on 18–27 February 1891. From a purely legal standpoint, the German royal family had as much right to visit the French capital as anyone else; but their sidetrips to St. Cloud and Versailles revived memories of the Prussian conquest of 1870–71 and enraged French public opinion. Responding to Parisian demonstrations against the royal visitors, Wilhelm II issued orders for the rigorous enforcement of the passport regulations in Alsace-Lorraine.[92] Reaction to the tightening of the passport regulations was instantaneous. The German ambassador in Paris, Count Münster, warned that actions taken in anger seldom produced good political results. Münster opined that some of the restrictions constituted violations of the Frankfurt Treaty; and on the practical level, the passports were causing economic hardship in some of the south German states as well as Alsace-Lorraine. The passports merely provided French agitators with more ammunition. "If the Alsatian administration, despite the extensive police powers at its disposal, is incapable of holding in check pro-French agitation or of winning over the Alsatians by a policy of rigorous justice without enforcing compulsory passports," wrote Münster, "then it is worthless."[93] The territorial committee sent a delegation to Berlin to seek the repeal of the passports. The kaiser received them 14 March, expressed his gratitude that they had come to him for redress (their action demonstrated that the people of Alsace-Lorraine finally recognized the sovereignty of the German Empire), and told them that unfortunately the situation on the western border permitted no relaxation of the passport regulations at that time. Hohenlohe noted that while "the deputation was not entirely satisfied with the official answer . . . they are under the impression that instructions will soon be sent from Berlin ordering milder treatment. This I do not believe. Of the two spirits predominant in the leading circles in Berlin, the military has the upper hand."[94] The governor had reason to doubt the good will of Berlin's governing clique. Foreign Secretary Baron Adolf Marschall von Bieberstein had told one of the territorial committee's delegates that no one in Berlin cared whether the people of Alsace-Lorraine were satisfied or not. Prussian Finance Minister Johannes Miquel had recently expressed to Hohenlohe the opinion current among the military that the Alsatians would become good Germans only after another successful war with France.[95]

As the situation began to cool, Caprivi indicated to Hohenlohe that the compulsory passes could be relaxed. The governor was wary; would not a softening of enforcement stir new attacks from the generals? Caprivi, perhaps counting on his military rank as well as his authority as chancellor, assured the governor that the matter was of no concern to the military, and that he would order them not to interfere.[96] Apparently neither Hohenlohe nor Caprivi could exercise effective control over the enforcement of passport regulations, as Caprivi admitted in a message to Hohenlohe in July that "it seems to me that the denial of passports has become more rigorous since I last discussed the matter with you."[97] While he warned that dropping the passport system would be interpreted as a sign of weakness, the chancellor sought to avoid any tightening of the restrictions which might give the impression of official chicanery. Caprivi favored a milder application of the pass system, but for all of the wrong reasons. The influence of the military point of view was beginning to work its effects upon the chancellor. If it should come to war with France, said Caprivi, we would need a *causus belli*. As unpopular as the passport system was in all of Europe and England, it did not, in Caprivi's opinion, furnish such a just cause for war; therefore, it must be administered so as not to cause any international difficulties.[98] Far from taking a stand against war, Caprivi simply argued that Germany ought to find an issue offering more plausible justification for an attack on France.

At Caprivi's request, Hohenlohe, accompanied by his under-secretary of state for the interior, Ernst Mathias von Köller, Karl Wilhelm Mandel (an official in the interior department), and Heinrich Hosëus (curator of the Strasbourg university and close advisor to Hohenlohe) traveled to Berlin in September 1891 for discussions concerning relaxation of the pass system. Several days of talks, in which representatives of the foreign office participated, resulted in a revision of the original passport measure, which the kaiser approved 21 September 1891. Henceforth, passports would be required only of active French military personnel, retired officers, students in foreign military schools, and emigrants from Alsace-Lorraine wishing to return for visits. "At last," remarked Hohenlohe, "this unpleasant business has been settled."[99]

Hohenlohe's last years as governor, prior to being called to the imperial chancellorship in 1894, were relatively peaceful. The vacancy left in Strasbourg by Hohenlohe's elevation provided another opportunity for the military to try to lay hold of the governorship. Count Botho zu Eulenburg, Prussian minister-president from 1892 to 1894, and Count (later Prince) Guido von Henckel-Donnersmarck, whose industrial interests in Silesia and the Rhineland made him the second richest man in Prussia (Krupp was first), considered themselves top contenders for the governor's post; but Fieldmarshal Count Waldersee and General Verdy du Vernois also figured as candidates. Waldersee has claimed that Hohenlohe recommended Eulenburg as his successor, but Hohenlohe's son Alexander maintained that Hohenlohe accepted the chancellorship only on the condition that Eulenburg did not get the governorship. The kaiser eventually suggested Prince Hermann zu Hohenlohe-Langenburg, Prince Chlodwig's cousin and a distant relative of the kaiser by marriage. A native of Württemberg, Hohenlohe-Langenburg was a professional soldier, attaining the rank of general, though without distinction. As a Free Conservative Reichstag deputy, he had served as Reichstag vice president in 1877–78. He had also served as president of both the Württemberg House of Lords and the *Kolonialverein*. Though he had some public experience, Hohenlohe-Langenburg had never been responsible for policy formulation or administration in a government agency. Unimpressed as he was with his cousin's qualifications, Hohenlohe-Schillingsfürst supported his nomination, simply because he abhorred the alternative of Waldersee or Verdy du Vernois.[100]

Once again, the military party had been thwarted in its attempts to gain control over the administration of the Reichsland. Hohenlohe-Langenburg's thirteen-year tenure, longest of any governor, meant a long wait for another chance. Langenburg, however, was not a particularly strong governor, and left most affairs to his secretary of state. The kaiser, meanwhile, continued to surround himself with more and more military officers while receiving his civil cabinet hardly more often than once each year. The military advisors gradually coalesced into what Holstein called an organized secondary government, a sort of shadow cabinet. The kaiser assigned aides-de-camp to various departments; one of these was a colonel assigned to keep track of affairs in Alsace-Lorraine.[101]

Perhaps because the struggle for power shifted to Berlin after 1894, there were no major civil-military conflicts in the Reichsland until the disastrous Zabern affair in 1913.[102] Because the Zabern affair illustrates the general constitutional crisis faced by Germany on the eve of World War I, it will be dealt with in the concluding chapter. It is already clear that civil-military conflicts contributed greatly to the instability of the territorial administration, and prevented the implementation of coherent, continuous programs of conciliation. Although the 1879 organizational scheme remained intact until 1911, Bismarck at least was not committed to maintaining it.[103] What Bismarck, Caprivi, and Hohenlohe were committed to was a defense of the civilian authority of both chancellor and governor against the generals' demands for military dictatorship in both the Reichsland and the Reich. Until 1913 the generals were unable to unseat a governor of Alsace-Lorraine, but they were able to force the civilian administration to take strong measures simply to prove to the kaiser that a Bismarck, a Hohenlohe, or a Caprivi could be as tough as any general.[104] With the Zabern affair, the military party at last achieved a predominant position in the Reichsland, and set the empire on a course which ended with the military dictatorship of Hindenburg and Ludendorff during World War I.

4
PROGRAMS FOR THE REICHSLAND: CONCILIATION OR COERCION?

To govern Alsace-Lorraine as a conquered hostile territory, or to integrate the province into the German Reich; this was the eternal dilemma facing the Germans. "National security" and "Germanization" formed the essence of German policy in Alsace and Lorraine throughout the forty-eight-year regime. Prince Chlodwig zu Hohenlohe-Schillingsfürst, the second governor of Alsace-Lorraine, concisely outlined the principles of German policy in a speech at Buchsweiler in 1887. "We have duly united Alsace and Lorraine with the German Empire . . . because the experience of centuries forced us to secure our western frontier. As soon as the European situation is threatening, or appears threatening, the question confronts us whether this frontier is really secure. This lays obligations on the Government of the country, which it must fulfill. I do not mean to regard this zeal for the safety of the country as the only business of the Government. Our problem is greater; it embraces a wide field of fruitful activity in intellectual and material matters. The Government will endeavor to solve problems and looks for the confidence and co-operation of the people."[1]

The basic conflict between the demands of military security and Germanization produced a good deal of the inconsistency and vacillation in official policy. But the very concept of Germanization itself proved difficult to implement. Germanization, stated in other terms, meant a program to integrate the population of the annexed territory into the mainstream of the German Reich. This turned out to be no simple task, even for the highly-touted Prussian bureaucrats. Some Germans explained the "failure" of Germanization by pointing an accusing finger at "French agitators," while liberal Germans admitted that the imperial administration had shown little skill or good will in dealing with the Alsace-Lorrainers.[2] Both of these explanations are valid. There was hostility toward the new regime after 1871, but much of this hostility could have been mitigated had the Germans treated the territorial population fairly and as the equals of other German citizens.

Misconceptions about German Reichsland policy persist to this day; what is needed is a clear exposition of German policy, and an explanation as to why the Germans felt it necessary to pursue programs which stirred up local opposition. Citizenship option policy provides a suitable starting point, since of all Reichsland regulations it was the most controversial and confused.

Alsace-Lorrainers wishing to retain French citizenship could do so under the citizenship option provisions of the Frankfurt Treaty. The option clauses, however, lacked clarity and precision, and the German interpretation of the option agreement caused great anguish, distress, and confusion. The Preliminary Peace of 26 February 1871 assured inhabitants of the annexed lands the right of emigration, and security of person and property. The option agreement itself, article two of the Frankfurt Treaty, provided that

> French citizens, born in the ceded territories, actually domiciled in the territory, who expect to preserve French citizenship, may do so, up to October 1, 1872, by means of a preliminary declaration made to the competent authority, and by means of transferring their domicile to France and fixing it there, without this right being subject to alteration by laws of military service, in which case they will retain French citizenship.[3]

The additional convention of 10 December 1871 established option procedures for native-born Alsace-Lorrainers residing outside the ceded territory at the signing of the peace treaty.

Three issues clouded the option clauses: who was entitled to or required to opt in order to preserve French citizenship? Need one move physically from Alsace-Lorraine to French territory, or could one opt validly by establishing a purely legal residence in France while continuing actual residence in Alsace-Lorraine? Could minors secure French citizenship while their parents or guardians became

German citizens? Reviving the "gap" theory of the Prussian constitutional crisis of the 1860s, German authorities argued that the treaty failed to clarify certain points and completely neglected others. In view of the treaty deficiencies, some German official would have to clarify matters.[4] During the ten months following treaty ratification, no clarification was forthcoming. Diplomatic notes exchanged on the option problem indicated only that the French and German governments sharply disagreed on an interpretation. In a unilateral directive of 7 March 1872, High President Möller finally cleared the air by ruling that annexation affected the citizenship of three classes of people: natives of Alsace-Lorraine who were domiciled in the territory 2 March 1871; non-natives who happened to be domiciled in the territory 2 March 1871; and natives of Alsace-Lorraine who were not domiciled there 2 March 1871. If they wished to preserve French citizenship, members of all three groups were required to move physically to French territory by the option deadline of 1 October 1872.[5]

Möller's decree included one category of persons not mentioned in the treaty—non-natives who happened to be living in Alsace-Lorraine at the time of annexation. While German legal scholars recognized the treaty did not cover this group, they nevertheless felt it necessary to provide for them. The nature of the arrangement, however, was hotly disputed. Some experts argued that in the absence of specific mention of option rights for non-natives in the treaty, their only legal choice was to become German citizens.[6] Others contended that non-natives automatically became French citizens living in a foreign country, subject to German police regulations concerning foreigners on German territory.[7] German authorities rejected the latter interpretation, which would have created a large dissident French population within the German empire. As in so many other Reichsland matters, the Germans evidenced an ambivalent attitude toward option and emigration. Refusing to believe that many of their "brothers" really wished to leave the Reichsland, many Germans regarded option declarations as mere gestures by people fearful of appearing less patriotic to France than their neighbors. But those who viewed the optants as "malcontents" found satisfaction in the growing number of emigrants.[8]

As the 2 October 1872 option deadline approached, option declarations rose sharply. Following Möller's ruling that valid options entailed physical departure from Alsace-Lorraine, emigration also

increased radically. Fearing that mass emigration would tarnish
Germany's public image, Möller tried to stem the flow by making it
more difficult for minors to leave Alsace-Lorraine. To avoid German military service, scores of minors opted and emigrated, leaving
their parents behind to protect family financial interests. They intended to return to their homes in Alsace-Lorraine after passing the
German military draft age. Möller's decree of 16 March 1872 prohibited independent options by nonemancipated minors; if a minor
wished to opt for French citizenship, his parents or guardian had to
make the same choice.[9]

While the Germans tried to break the option and emigration
movement, the League of Alsace urged every patriotic Frenchman
to file an option declaration. The League, however, tried to discourage emigration, proclaiming the duty of all Alsace-Lorrainers
to stay and resist the Germanization program.[10] The *Société de
Protection des Alsaciens et des Lorrains Demeures Français* did
encourage young men to emigrate, noting that German authorities
had granted several youths special emigration permits.[11]

Estimates of actual emigration during the first year of German
rule lack sound statistical support. Of the 159,791 option declarations submitted prior to the 2 October 1872 deadline, the Germans
considered only 50,148 valid; the others failed to transfer their real
domicile to France.[12] Option figures do not reflect actual emigration
rates, since many left the territory without making option declarations or securing emigration permits. Official emigration figures for
the period between the signing of the Frankfurt Treaty and the
option deadline apparently do not exist. Long-range population
statistics, however, indicate that annexation merely accelerated a
process of mass emigration which had already begun before 1871.[13]

Option and emigration rates varied considerably among the three
Reichsland districts. Upper Alsace, the League of Alsace stronghold,
produced 91,962 declared optants, twenty percent of the district's
population. Option declarations totaled 39,190 (seven percent) in
Lower Alsace, and only 28,639 (six percent) in Lorraine. The emigration picture, however, was exactly the reverse. Seventy-five percent of Lorraine's declared optants actually emigrated, twenty-nine
percent left Lower Alsace, and only eighteen percent of declared
optants emigrated legally from Upper Alsace. Valid options were
most numerous in regions accessible to France, where one could
move to French territory and continue to maintain personal and

economic ties with the Reichsland. Economic factors weighed heavily in the decision to emigrate. The assumption that property owners most likely to suffer financial loss were least likely to emigrate is supported by an occupational analysis of Strasbourg optants. Of 3,239 Strasbourg citizens making valid options, 2,087 were listed as being of "no particular trade." The list also included 451 artisans, 151 day laborers, 141 merchants and shopkeepers, 70 military pensioners, 53 civil pensioners, 23 teachers, 22 notaries and solicitors, 20 artists and chemists, 19 lower state officials, 17 doctors, 14 judicial officers, 3 druggists, 2 Jesuit priests, and 1 factory owner.[14]

No one knows exactly how many people left Alsace-Lorraine during the German regime. Estimates based on official sources place emigration between 1871 and 1910 at approximately 460,000. It is reasonable to estimate that in the early years of the regime alone, from 1871 to 1886, about 156,000 left the territory, indicating that the emigration movement was more than a mere ephemeral gut reaction to the German takeover. In December 1871, 64,112 Frenchmen born in other departments resided in Alsace-Lorraine; only 30,223 remained in 1880.[15] As the émigrés moved out, Germans moved in to replace them. At the moment of annexation in 1871, 78,687 Germans resided in French Alsace and Lorraine; in 1880 there were 123,538 non-native Germans residing in Alsace-Lorraine, and by 1910 the figure had risen to 295,436. In 1875 there were twenty-six non-native Germans per 1,000 population in Alsace-Lorraine; twenty years later there were 101 per 1,000, and by 1910, 123 of every thousand were non-native Germans. The concentration of Germans in the cities far exceeded the average. Metz in 1910 counted 410 non-native Germans per thousand, and Strasbourg claimed 293 per thousand.[16]

Well into the Manteuffel era of the 1880s, the "option problem" continued to excite popular emotion in the Reichsland. Although German bureaucratic obtuseness generally receives the blame for the problem, French diplomats negotiating the Frankfurt Treaty demonstrated great laxity in failing to demand greater precision in the treaty itself. Since the Frankfurt Treaty option clauses closely reproduced article six of the treaty of 24 March 1860, ceding Nice and Savoy from Sardinia to France, the French assumed practical application would also be identical. In the earlier case, France had not required the native population to emigrate in order to preserve Sardinian citizenship. The German government tacitly accepted the

Sardinian precedent, until Möller's decree of 7 March 1872 produced a radical change of course.[17]

The 7 March decree automatically conferred German citizenship on those optants who failed to emigrate by 1 October 1872. Möller soon obscured the clarity of this pronouncement when he ruled that declared optants who had not emigrated could not vote in the 1873 district and county council elections unless they formally retracted the option declaration.[18] The 7 March edict conferred German citizenship on all who had made invalid options; subsequent orders implied that persons failing to retract their option declarations were not German citizens. If they were Germans, they were clearly second-class citizens, deprived of the right to vote. Möller, however, never claimed that declared optants who failed to emigrate were considered French citizens. Through contradictory and confusing directives, the Germans created a group of 100,000 persons who had no assurance of citizenship in any state. Voting restrictions on declared optants remained in force until 1877; meanwhile, 100,000 Alsace-Lorrainers withheld their support from the German regime.

With the passing of the option deadline, an unexpected problem confronted German officials; persons who had made valid options for French citizenship later sought to return to Alsace-Lorraine and become naturalized German citizens. Believing the return of optants would reduce Alsatian ties with France, Möller raised no objections. Bismarck, however, argued that optants who had forfeited their rights as German citizens could not regain them through naturalization.[19] Möller's view prevailed, and in 1880 Secretary of State Herzog reported to the territorial committee the naturalization of 1,036 optants in 1878, and 611 in 1879. Of 5,000 applications from optants desiring naturalization between 1872 and 1880, all but a few hundred had been granted.[20]

German option policy was contradictory, confusing, arbitrary, and discriminatory. Civil authorities were not entirely to blame for the deficiencies in option regulations, for the option problem was really a military issue. Option and emigration drained potential manpower from the German army; between 1871 and 1880, the twenty-to-forty age group in the Reichsland declined from 102,178 to 86,506.[21] Civilian authorities at first pursued a liberal option policy, but when the military pressed for immediate introduction of German military conscription, the administration had to insure that draft-age men did not escape duty through loose option regulations.

Young men leaving Alsace-Lorraine to avoid German military service were neither pacifists nor cowards. Since the 1789 revolution, Alsace and Lorraine had given France some of her most outstanding generals and fighting men. Bismarck recognized that annexation would sever France from the source of her best soldiers.[22] While refusing German service, Reichsland emigrants willingly joined the French military forces. An average of 500 Alsace-Lorrainers enlisted in the French Foreign Legion each year between 1870 and 1914. From 1882 through 1908, about forty-five percent of all Legion troops were emigrants from Alsace-Lorraine; most members of regular French units stationed in Algeria were former Alsace-Lorrainers.[23]

Although the Germans considered Alsace-Lorrainers to be politically unreliable, many high officials pressed for early introduction of compulsory military service as the surest method of Germanizing the Reichsland. Bismarck, who believed political opposition to compulsory service would impede Germanization, was overruled by Moltke and the emperor, and compulsory military conscription became the law in Alsace-Lorraine 1 October 1872.[24] If they were unreliable for combat purposes, the Alsace-Lorrainers could be used as garrison troops in the eastern provinces; in any event, men drafted into the German army could not bear arms for France.[25]

German draft calls and recruiting drives met with little success in Alsace-Lorraine. Draft evasion most commonly occurred in the urban centers and regions bordering France. Historically, the urban bourgeoisie had avoided military service by hiring substitutes or paying a tax; members of the Alsatian middle class who had served in the army of the Second French Empire were rare. But while the cities failed to meet their draft quotas after 1872, the rural districts often provided a surplus of volunteers.[26]

Optants returning to Alsace-Lorraine became prime targets for German recruiters bent on filling draft quotas. Territorial committee delegates charged that optants reentering the Reichsland as naturalized German citizens were conscripted, imprisoned, or fined as much as 3,000 marks. Secretary of State Herzog, however, professed official leniency in exempting naturalized optants from military service under justifiable circumstances. He minimized the seriousness of the situation by observing that in 1878, only 63 of 1,036 naturalized optants sought military exemption; in 1879, only 42 of 611 applied, and just three requested exemption during the first quarter of 1880.[27]

Neither conciliation nor coercion succeeded in stemming mass draft evasion. To conciliate families of wealth and education, Bismarck and Prussian war minister Count Albrecht von Roon devised a plan permitting short, one-year enlistments for men meeting certain educational standards, and willing to pay for their own food, clothing, and equipment. Less educated men able to provide for their own upkeep could volunteer for three or four year tours of duty, serving in the unit of their choice. Men choosing this option generally elected to serve in the Berlin Guard Corps, opened to Reichsland volunteers by special order of the war ministry.[28] When these conciliatory measures failed, the government held trials and sentenced *in absentia* draft-age men who emigrated without permission. Legal action against absentees, of course, did not fill draft quotas, and in 1878 the government finally offered amnesty to all absentees offering to fulfill their military obligations.[29] Despite the amnesty, the 1879 draft call met with the usual resistance. Only after twenty years of German rule did the draft evasion problem show signs of abating. The 1879 evasion rate of approximately twenty-five percent had dropped to eight percent by 1904. The conviction rate for draft evasion declined steadily from 2,405 in 1890 to 1,217 in 1900 and only 539 in 1910.[30]

Table 1.   Military Conscription[a]

Year	Called	Failed to Appear	Inducted
1872	32,073	20,509	2,402
1873	34,789	20,925	2,097
1874	36,490	20,756	3,507
1875	32,178	14,535	3,695
1876	33,880	13,999	4,225
1877	36,723	13,920	4,576
1878	40,800	9,580	. . .
1879	40,850	10,101	. . .

a. Source: Kaiserliches Oberpräsidium, *Mittheilungen aus der Verwaltung von Elsass-Lothringen während der Jahre 1871–1879* (Strasbourg, 1879), pp. 81, 89.

Given the annual draft evasion rate during the first half of the German regime, the introduction of compulsory military service contributed little toward the primary goal of national security. France, in effect, continued to recruit soldiers in Alsace-Lorraine, as youths by the hundreds evaded German conscription and enlisted in the French army. Security requirements had to be met by some other means, and because Alsace-Lorraine was a strategic frontier region, the German military garrison in the Reichsland was unusually large. Two and one-half army corps maintained headquarters in Alsace-Lorraine: the XV at Strasbourg, the XVI at Metz, and one division of the XXII in Saarbourg. By 1910 the German military contingent in the Reichsland had swelled to 82,276, including 6,628 native Alsace-Lorrainers. A 1912 estimate placed 90,000 German troops, about one-sixth of the whole German army, in Alsace-Lorraine. Strasbourg's 1910 population of 178,891 included 15,455 men attached to the military, while in Metz the military accounted for 13,978 of the 79,318 residents. The military comprised 4.47 percent of the territorial population, considerably higher than 1.1 percent common in other parts of the empire.

In 1912 the entire German army included about 14,000 Alsace-Lorrainers, nearly 7,000 of whom were stationed in the Reichsland. These figures seem to indicate a growth of confidence in the reliability of the territorial recruits since 1892, when only 1,110 were stationed in Alsace-Lorraine. Alsace, with a figure of 66.7 percent, stood first among all German states in the ratio of draft-eligible men who were found fit for service. Lorraine, with 58.9 percent, ranked fourth, surpassed only by East and West Prussia.[31] Although the draft calls met strong resistance, many youths volunteered their services. Thirty-six percent of all Alsace-Lorraine recruits entered the service as volunteers, whereas the volunteer rate for the rest of Germany was only twenty-four percent. Once in the army, however, the rate of advancement for Alsace-Lorrainers was slow. Of the 14,000 Alsace-Lorrainers in the German army in 1912, only 1,215 had reached noncommissioned officer rank. Overall, noncommissioned officers comprised 18.8 percent of the German army, but only 7.8 percent of the recruits from the Reichsland ever achieved that rank.[32]

Despite the heavy concentration of troops, Alsace-Lorraine did not immediately become an impregnable military fortress after 1871. With the exceptions of Forbach and Faulquemont, the Germans garrisoned no towns which had not previously supported troops under the French regime. Even more surprising in view of Moltke's insistence on its strategic value, nothing was done to strengthen the fortifications at Metz until 1886. Military policy in the Reichsland seems to have been dictated by high-level strategy. The General Staff possessed complete confidence in the maneuverability of the German armies. The strategy was to permit the French to penetrate Lorraine, and then counterattack somewhere between Metz and the Vosges Mountains. With such a plan, there was no need to convert the Reichsland into a Maginot-type fortified barrier.[33]

Boulangism in France and the Schnaebele incident along the border forced a reevaluation of the military situation after 1886. Metz received three additional infantry regiments, raising the total there to seven. More regiments were added in other towns, in some instances where none had been garrisoned before. After 1898 there was another round of troop reinforcements in the Reichsland. In 1899 the Germans began major improvements in the Metz fortifications, and strengthened the defenses on the hills surrounding Thionville. Although the Metz fortifications remained incomplete when war broke out in 1914, the fortress was still considered to offer one of the most impregnable defenses in the world.[34]

Compulsory military service worked badly as a vehicle of Germanization, but it was only one weapon in the government's arsenal. Efforts to revive the German language in Alsace-Lorraine occupied a whole army of bureaucrats, and aroused strong opposition in the territory. Alphonse Daudet's *La dernière classe* portrays the Germans as ruthlessly suppressing the French tongue so dear to the hearts of the people. Numerous linguistic experts have already impaled themselves upon the complexities of the linguistic composition of Alsace and Lorraine; there will be no attempt here to produce a completely fresh account. The political boundary of the annexed region followed the linguistic boundary more closely than is generally believed. With the notable exception of Metz and the larger part of the Château-Salins region, which were without question French-speaking areas, most Alsatians and many of the inhabitants of annexed Lorraine spoke either German or a Germanic provincial dialect.[35] Sharp delimitation of a linguistic boundary in Alsace and Lorraine is impossible. French-speaking enclaves crop up in German-speaking regions, and linguistic districts seem to merge with each other or break with each other for no apparent reason, there being no natural geographical barriers to promote linguistic distinctions. Between the conquest of Alsace and Lorraine by Louis XIV and the Prussian victory of 1870–71, the linguistic boundary, vague as it was, changed very little. Many nineteenth-century German studies indicated a larger German-speaking area than actually existed, but German exaggeration should not obscure the fact that in nearly two centuries of French rule, the French language had made only minimal gains in Alsace and Lorraine. No one recognized this uncomfortable fact better than Napoléon III, who during the 1860s launched a vigorous campaign to impose the French language on the territory. The emperor's efforts met strong resistance from the Catholic clergy and the press in both Alsace and the bilingual parts of Lorraine.

Table 2.   The Linguistic Composition of Alsace-Lorraine, 1879[a]

	Communes	Percentage of District Population
LORRAINE		
French-speaking	341	30.37
German-speaking	370	53.25
Mixed	41	16.38
LOWER ALSACE		
French-speaking	27	4.09
German-speaking	531	95.52
Mixed	2	0.39
UPPER ALSACE		
French-speaking	17	3.71
German-speaking	324	78.71
Mixed	43	17.58
ALSACE-LORRAINE		
French-speaking	385	12.12
German-speaking	1,225	77.39
Mixed	86	10.49

a. Source: Maximilian du Prel, *Die deutsche Verwaltung in Elsass-Lothringen, 1870–1879* (Strasbourg, 1879), pp. 100–2. "Mixed" represents a 50–50 mixture of French and German. Other studies, Richard Böckh, *Der deutschen Volkszahl und Sprachgebiet in der Europäsichen Staaten* (Berlin, 1869), and Henri Kiepert, "Der Sprachgrenze in Elsass-Lothringen," *Zeitschrift der Gesellschaft für Erdkunde zu Berlin* 9 (1874): 307–20, use different criteria, but arrive at substantially the same results.

When the Germans introduced their language program in Alsace-Lorraine after 1871, they were simply implementing Napoléon III's program in reverse. The German program and local reaction to it raise some interesting questions. If most Alsatians and many annexed Lorrainers already spoke German or a Germanic dialect, why was a forced program of Germanization needed in the first place? If a Germanization program was required in the French-speaking parts of annexed Lorraine, why did the people who already spoke German object to it? Answers to such questions can never be definitive; but the questions themselves suggest the complexity of the linguistic issue. The language conflict was not simply a national issue separating pro-French from pro-Germans. It was as much a political issue as a national issue; this became apparent as soon as the Catholic clergy reversed its previous opposition to Napoléon III's program and protested against Germany's suppression of the French language after 1871. What we are dealing with here is not a choosing of sides in favor of either France or Germany, but rather a particularist provincial revolt against the imposition of any uniform language by any central government.[36]

German authorities never issued a blanket order suppressing the use of French in the Reichsland. Recognizing the futility of trying to teach German to French-speaking adults, they concentrated on the younger school-age generation. The first language directive of 14 April 1871, prohibited the teaching of French in lower elementary grades; this regulation took effect in middle and upper elementary grades in October 1872. In regions where commercial relations required fluency in French, exceptions to the rules permitted French instruction up to four hours weekly in upper elementary grades.[37] A decree issued on 4 January 1874 required elementary schools to use German in all classes; but, as usual, there were significant special cases. Classes composed solely of French-speaking students were conducted in French. In classes containing a mixture of French- and German-speaking pupils, the high president selected the language to be used. Schools in French and "mixed" districts could offer instruction in the use of French from three to six hours per week, a rather reasonable allowance compared to the five hour requirement for German language courses. In 1881 classes were still conducted in French in 435 communes having a total population of 303,000.

Secondary school language regulations were somewhat more restrictive than elementary level standards. If all students in a class used French as their mother tongue, teachers were permitted to use French; otherwise, French was spoken only in French courses. In the *Gymnasia*, French courses met four to six hours per week, while German courses met only three hours. An 1878 regulation redressed the balance, providing for three hours of instruction in both French and German. A new ruling in 1883 reduced French instruction to two hours weekly. As late as 1888, teachers conducted mathematics and science classes in French; pupils learned French and German equivalents for all technical terms. German-speaking examiners administered science examinations, but students could respond in either French or German. Officials accepted French or German to satisfy the composition requirement, reducing stylistic and grammatical requirements for students born in French-speaking regions electing German for the composition examination.[38]

Language regulations in teacher-training institutions (normal schools) remained rather flexible until 1888. When the Germans reopened the normal school in Metz as a Catholic teachers' seminary in October 1871, the language of instruction was French. Other normal schools in French or mixed districts continued to use French until otherwise instructed by the high president. Three-year normal schools operated on two tracks for first and second year students, one track for French-speaking students, the other for those who spoke German. They were united only in the third year of training. Teaching examinations were conducted in German, but exceptions permitted teachers educated in French or mixed areas to take the examinations in French. Not until 4 January 1888, in the repression following the disastrous *Septennat* election of 1887, did the *Oberschulrat* order German to be used in all teacher training institutions for women.[39]

By 1890 the Germans recognized that in the linguistic question, Alsace and Lorraine had to be treated as separate entities. Lorraine still held the bulk of the French-speaking population in the regions of Metz and Château-Salins; but even in these areas drastic changes had occurred since 1871. The previously well-defined linguistic boundaries had become blurred through a combination of intense German immigration, and a diminishing ratio of French-speaking children caused by an excess of the death rate over the birth rate in the French-speaking areas.[40] Recognizing the population shifts since 1871, the government introduced a special linguistic plan for Lorraine schools in 1890. The new scheme increased the number of hours of French by two hours in the lower elementary grades (one and two), but totally eradicated French instruction in the upper elementary grades (five through eight).[41] The 1890 Lorraine plan was only the first in a series of attempts by the government to "fine tune" the language regulations. In 1892 a new arrangement divided Lorraine's elementary schools into three categories, based on the proportion of French-speaking students, each of which taught French and German under a different formula. Under this scheme, schools enrolling less than twenty-five percent children of German-speaking parents remained under the 1890 plan; mixed schools enrolling between twenty-five and seventy-five percent children of French-speaking parents were reduced from eight hours of French per week to five in grades one and two; and schools whose enrollment of French-speaking students was less than twenty-five percent followed the normal teaching plan for German schools, which did not include French. The 1892 plan lasted only until 1897, when Group I schools were permitted two additional hours of French in grades one and two, one hour less in grades three and four, and two hours in grades five through eight, in which no French instruction had been permitted under previous plans. German instruction was reduced by one hour in all elementary grades.

This continual juggling of language requirements only served to disrupt educational planning in Lorraine, without satisfying the intensifying demands in the territorial committee for French instruction in all elementary schools. Local agitation for the extension of French instruction in elementary schools dated back to the early 1870s, when the League of Alsace first took up the issue. The first territorial committee action on the language question came in 1875, when Baron Hugo Zorn von Bulach (elder) introduced a resolution (unanimously adopted) requesting permission to teach French in elementary schools to the same degree that German had been permitted under the French regime.[42] In view of Napoléon III's campaign to extirpate German, this was not a particularly intelligent motion. Language regulations prior to 1871 were no less confusing than they were after the annexation. An 1855 regulation established French as the language of instruction in elementary schools. An 1859 order limited German lessons to thirty-five minutes per day, and they were to be taught in French! An 1860 regulation technically provided for German instruction up to five hours per week in the upper grades of primary schools, but since the "hours" were only forty-five minutes in length, the actual time for German was only 225 minutes. In 1869 the prefect of Bas-Rhin set a maximum of five hours per week for German, and banned German instruction in the first grade.[43]

The 1875 territorial committee resolution had no effect on official policy. The Strasbourg chamber of commerce followed it up with a demand for French instruction in all elementary grades, and the territorial committee adopted a resolution in the 1881–82 session asking the government to permit each commune to make its own decision in the matter of French instruction. Between 1885 and 1900, a period of political repression in Alsace-Lorraine, the linguistic question remained dormant; but after 1900 the territorial committee renewed its campaign. In 1909 the territorial assembly approved a resolution demanding instruction in French two half-days per week, and another vague request for "more instruction in French than before." A special eighteen-member territorial committee commission appointed in 1909 recommended making French instruction compulsory for at least four hours per week in upper grades of elementary schools, and advised the government to drop restrictions on teachers who desired to teach French privately outside normal school hours.[44] The government in turn advised the territorial committee to reject the commission report. Presentation of the government's case fell to one of the few Alsatians holding a responsible post in the Reichsland, the Secretary of State Hugo Zorn von Bulach (younger). The territorial committee considered von Bulach as little less than a traitor, and with only two abstentions unanimously adopted the commission report. Chancellor Theobald von Bethmann Hollweg, who subsequently promoted the 1911 constitution for Alsace-Lorraine, told the Reichstag in 1909 that passage of the territorial committee's language resolution had damaged the government's efforts to liberalize the constitution. When the 1911 constitution was approved, it granted authority to regulate the language question to the governor rather than to the new *Landtag*.[45]

Pressure from the territorial committee did induce the government to promote one more plan for Lorraine in 1910. The new scheme reduced the number of Lorraine communes permitted to teach French under special dispensation from the governor; but it also reduced the number of communes classified as purely German and enlarged the category regarded as "mixed." Schools transferred from the "pure German" category to the "mixed" group could now teach

French in all grades, and schools in mixed districts could now add French in grades five through eight, which had not been permitted under the 1892–97 plans. Schools with French-speaking enrollment between fifty and seventy-five percent could now teach French seven hours per week in grades one and two, whereas the previous limit had been five hours.[46]

All areas of public life felt the impact of language regulations. Official documents appeared in German, debates in the district and county councils and the territorial committee were conducted in German, and court cases were argued in German unless witnesses, parties to the suit, or testifying experts knew no German. The statistical bureau in Berlin supplied new German names for all railway stations, new German inscriptions appeared on all state and public buildings, Strasbourg streets received German designations, and street signs in Metz displayed German translations beneath the traditional French names.

Government language regulations penetrated the spiritual realm as well as public areas of life. Displaying its usual inconsistency and vacillation, the government permitted sermons in French every Sunday in Mulhouse, but only three times each month in Colmar. When authorities reduced the Colmar quota of sermons in French to two per month, the Protestant Directory and Consistory complained and secured a reversal of the decision in 1891. During World War I, when German military commanders either restricted or suspended preaching in French for the duration of the war, Protestant pastors in areas of Lorraine which had experienced heavy German immigration seemed quite pleased. But when the government indicated the ban on sermons in French would be retained after the war, Friedrich Curtius resigned from the presidency of the Protestant Directory in Alsace-Lorraine after his attempts to change the government's decision failed.[47]

Given the usual stereotype of the zealous Prussian bureaucrat, one cannot escape the conclusion that the German administration propagated the national language in Alsace-Lorraine with great reserve. Exceptions to the regulations provided for the needs of French-speaking localities, and the use of German expanded gradually over a long transition period. The ultranationalist Germans failed to convince some of the highest territorial officials that the use of French constituted a danger to German national security. During discussions concerning a plan to require the use of German in the district councils, Governor Chlodwig zu Hohenlohe-Schillingsfürst commented that Germany would not be endangered "if a few old gentlemen who speak no German or speak it badly prefer to conduct the business of their councils in French."[48] An 1883 government survey indicated that fourteen-year-old Lorraine students who had been attending German schools for eight years still knew no German. Compulsory education, combined with the emigration of many teachers loyal to the French regime, placed a heavy burden on the inefficient educational system inherited by the Germans in 1871. Schools in French-speaking regions seldom found enough teachers fluent in German. Even when teachers competent in German were available, the cost of retiring the French-speaking teachers on pensions was prohibitive.[49] Germanization, insofar as it referred to the extension of the German linguistic boundary in Alsace and Lorraine, had made little progress by 1919; and changes in the language pattern which had occurred resulted more from emigration and immigration than from the success of government language regulations.[50]

Linguistic regulation of the elementary schools was only part of the over-all government program to place education in Alsace-Lorraine under state control, in conformity with the Prussian system. Aside from the army, the schools were considered the best vehicle for implementing the Germanization program. Because the policy of extending state control over the educational system represented a direct threat to clerical control of the schools, the anticlerical aspects of the government's educational program will be dealt with in greater detail in the following chapter on church-state relations. The breadth of the state's concern in educational matters was all-encompassing; the government regulated not only public elementary and secondary schools, but also set standards for technical schools, teachers' colleges, and even seminaries training priests.

The crown jewel in the educational establishment was the *Kaiser Wilhelm Universität* in Strasbourg. First established in 1621, the university at Strasbourg was tolerated by the Catholic Bourbon regimes even though its faculty was predominantly Lutheran. The revolutionary government, however, was not so tolerant, and abolished the university in 1793 on the grounds that the Lutheran faculty provided a German base on French soil. Until 1872 what had once been a university was nothing more than a Lutheran academy training Lutheran ministers.[51]

When the Germans assumed control of Strasbourg and created the Reichsland, it occurred to a number of the more imaginative nationalists that the new imperial territory might be the ideal place to establish a truly national German university. Such a university would serve both as a lasting monument to the achievements of the German regime in Alsace-Lorraine, and as a constant reminder to the local population that they were now Germans. The process of Germanization begun in the elementary schools could be completed in a German university.

The new university opened its doors 1 May 1872. In accordance with the principle of Germanization, it was expected that the bulk of the student body at this "German" university would be composed of Alsatians and Lorrainers. But Alsace-Lorraine was predominantly Catholic, and the university as originally constituted had no Catholic theological faculty. Few local students were willing to attend a university which was both German and Protestant. The founding of a Catholic theological faculty in 1903 (about which more will be said in the following chapter) encouraged more local students to attend, but as late as 1910 half the student body was still recruited from Germany; moreover, perhaps as many as fifty percent of the "local" students were actually sons of German immigrants.[52]

Failing to recruit an indigenous student body, the university played only a minor role in assimilating the territorial population into the German Reich. Furthermore, the faculty, though predominantly German, proved difficult to control. Friedrich Althoff, a one-time professor and administrator at Strasbourg, moved to Berlin where he attempted to direct the university's affairs from his post in the Prussian ministry of education. During his governorship, Hohenlohe-Schillingsfürst attempted to appoint a *Ministerialrat* named Richter as provisional curator of the university in 1887, but the faculty strenuously objected that Richter was simply one of Althoff's puppets. The governor backed down, and instead appointed Heinrich Hosëus, who held the curator's post until 1895.[53]

Disenchantment with the university as an instrument of Germanization expressed itself in a dwindling university budget. Because universities in other German states feared the "national" university in Strasbourg might drain off their best students, the federal government had supported the institution in miserly fashion from the beginning. Most of the cost of the physical plant, which eventually came to a value of fifteen million marks, was borne by the people of Alsace-Lorraine, and the federal government paid only half of the annual operating cost of approximately one million marks. The federal government paid for only one building, the so-called *Palais* completed in 1884 at a cost of 3,800,000 marks. The Federal Council approved its 400,000 mark share of the 1876 university budget "contrary to the opinion of the middle states." At that time, the Strasbourg university budget exceeded that of any south German university; in north Germany, Bonn and Göttingen boasted budgets nearly equal to Strasbourg's, but only Leipzig and Berlin carried budgets exceeding that of Strasbourg, by twenty percent and fifty percent respectively. The ensuing years witnessed a drastic relative decline in the Strasbourg university's budgetary position. By 1916 Munich's budget was larger, and the other south German universities were close behind. In north Germany, only Marburg and Greifswald trailed Strasbourg by a small margin; Kiel and Königsberg had forged ahead, and Leipzig's budget was now four times greater than Strasbourg's.[54]

Intellectual development of the Strasbourg university, as significant as it was, inevitably succumbed to political reality. The reality was that the university was simply one more pawn in several different wars: the Franco-German conflict, the Protestant-Catholic antagonism, civil-military disagreements, liberal-conservative differences, and the petty jealousies of the various German states at one time or another had some bearing on the affairs of the university. Conflicts between German and local professors divided the university community, the struggle to establish a Catholic theological faculty further split the university along confessional lines, and government-appointed administrators often found themselves engaged in battle with the faculty. The impact of these political and religious controversies on the intellectual life of the university cannot be underestimated. Controversial subjects simply could not be offered. There was, for example, no course on the history of Alsace and Lorraine, which in that time and place was a controversial subject, until Georg Wolfram introduced it into the curriculum in 1911.[55]

If programs such as universal military conscription, language regulations, and educational projects failed to transform the Alsace-Lorrainers into "good Germans," then the government was prepared to take other steps to insure the security of the Reich. It was a cardinal principle that no Alsace-Lorrainer should hold a responsible position in the territorial administration. Because only Prussian bureaucrats could be trusted with the task of Germanization, the discriminatory staffing policy extended to all non-Prussian Germans; the first non-Prussian appointed to the territorial ministry was Georg von Mayr, a Bavarian Catholic named to head the department of finance in 1879. For an Alsatian or Lorrainer, loyal service to the German regime provided no guarantee of promotion to high office. Jean Schlumberger, the Strasbourg industrialist who served for many years as president of the territorial committee, demonstrated such devotion to the empire that the kaiser rewarded him with several decorations. When Governor Manteuffel died in 1885, Schlumberger gave the fieldmarshall's daughter Isabella a villa at Müllheim in Baden and contributed to her support.[56] Yet, when Schlumberger's name was mentioned for appointment as district president in Colmar in 1886, the new governor, Hohenlohe-Schillingsfürst, opposed the nomination as a sign of "great weakness, and a superfluous, dangerous concession to the Alsatians."[57] In the wave of repression triggered by the defeat of government-sponsored candidates in the 1887 *Septennat* election, military critics in Berlin forced Hohenlohe to fire Karl Ledderhose, the undersecretary of state who had originally recommended Schlumberger for the district presidency.

Only one Alsatian headed the territorial government under the German regime; Rudolf Schwander was named governor 27 October 1918. His appointment, of course, was meaningless, since the German empire was about to expire. Another Alsatian, Emil Petri, entered the ministry as undersecretary of state for religion and justice in 1898. There were some who doubted that Petri, a Protestant, could sympathetically direct the religious affairs of a predominantly Catholic territory. The most successful Alsatian was Baron Hugo Zorn von Bulach (younger), who received the post of undersecretary of state for agriculture in 1895, and in 1908 advanced to the top administrative post, secretary of state for Alsace-Lorraine. The baron's father had served as chamberlain to Napoléon III. Residing in the family castle *Osthausen* on the Rhine plain near Strasbourg, Baron von Bulach was one of the few surviving members of the nobility in Alsace in 1871. The elder Bulach, a leader in the "autonomist" movement after 1871, actively cooperated with the Germans and arranged promising careers for both of his sons. The youngest of them, Baron Franz Anton Phillip von Bulach, entered the German diplomatic corps and worked for a few years in the foreign office. His real ambition, however, was to enter the priest-hood. He eventually carved out a brilliant career, rising to become coadjutor to the bishop of Strasbourg in 1901, a post he resigned in 1918 as the French occupied the city. As coadjutor, Franz von Bulach maintained his intellectual independence, which is more than one can say for his older brother Hugo, the secretary of state.[58]

While Franz von Bulach was making his way in the Church hier-archy, his older brother Hugo Zorn von Bulach was making his name in Alsatian politics. He served in the district council of Lower Alsace, the territorial committee, and the Reichstag. Bulach gener-ally accompanied the kaiser on his annual visits to the Reichsland. When the government took over the old Alsatian castle at Hohkö-nigsberg and restored it as a royal hunting lodge, the kaiser named Bulach *Schlosshauptmann*, similar to the post his father had held under Napoléon III. Friendship with the emperor paid its first major political dividend in 1895, when Bulach received the post of under-secretary of state for agriculture under Governor Prince Hermann zu Hohenlohe-Langenburg. Bulach's appointment stirred consider-able uneasiness; though no one questioned the theoretical com-petence of an Alsatian to administer the agriculture department, it was seriously doubted that Bulach could command the respect of his subordinates, all of whom were Germans.[59] Bulach survived and in 1908 won the appointment as secretary of state, a position sub-ordinate only to the governorship. The price for success was higher than most Alsatians and Lorrainers were willing to pay. Bulach had to defend every objectionable government program in the territorial committee and after 1911 in the *Landtag*. He opposed attempts by the territorial committee to extend French instruction in public schools in 1909, he cautioned the territorial committee against de-manding real autonomy during the 1911 constitutional debate, and he defended the government proposal to introduce special repressive laws against the press and civic organizations in 1913. As one critic aptly described the situation, Bulach had proved himself to be a good Prussian.[60]

Sometimes, particularly in the sphere of municipal government, Alsace-Lorrainers did not prove to be good Prussians; in these cases, the Germans applied the appropriate remedy. They appointed new mayors, or replaced recalcitrant mayors and municipal councils with specially appointed commissars. Attempting to minimize the impression of German tyranny, Heinrich Pauli, a Reichsland district president just prior to World War I, claimed that commissars governed only about one hundred Lorraine communes and "hardly any" in Alsace.[61] Quantitative analysis, however, tells only part of the story, for the key cities of Strasbourg, Metz, and Colmar had been placed under commissars by 1877.

Strasbourg's mayor, the banker Ernst Lauth, was deposed because he refused payment for new German street signs and denied use of municipal funds for construction of a German theater. In addition to being uncooperative, Lauth allegedly told the Strasbourg district president Ernst von Ernsthausen that he hoped for an early return of French power. Ernsthausen reported the conversation to High President Möller, who removed Lauth from office 12 April 1873, and appointed as commissar Otto Back, the imperial police director in Strasbourg. Considering Back's appointment illegal, the municipal council refused to meet under his direction. Möller responded by suspending the council for one year, giving Back the powers formerly exercised by both mayor and council. When the suspension expired, Berlin authorities told Möller to try for a settlement with the council. Ernsthausen opposed this tactic, arguing that the pro-French council would never come to terms with the government. Möller, however, proposed the Alsatian autonomist Julius Klein as commissar, the council accepted the proposal, but Klein declined to serve. His patience exhausted, Möller finally ordered permanent dissolution of the Strasbourg municipal council.[62]

Lacking a municipal council, Strasbourg lost its representation in the territorial committee, since it was the council which elected the city's delegate to the territorial assembly. Governor Manteuffel considered reviving the council in 1879, but he eventually decided that government by commissar involved fewer political risks. The cities were being held as political hostages; Ernsthausen had made this clear in 1877 when he dismissed the Colmar mayor during the Reichstag election campaign as a warning against the election of candidates unfriendly to the government.[63] In defense of the government, it might be noted that the mayors functioned ambiguously as both organs of state power responsible to the government, and as representatives of the people responsible to the popular will. The use of commissars, which resolved the troublesome dualism, impressed the government as an attractive alternative.[64]

If Germanization programs supplemented by political coercion failed to provide for the real or imagined security requirements of the

German regime, the territorial government could select weapons from a vast arsenal of French and German repressive legislation. The Germans probably could have managed quite well with nothing more than the authoritarian legislation of the two Napoleonic regimes, which under international law remained valid in Alsace-Lorraine unless specifically repealed by German legislation.[65] The Germans, however, were taking no chances when they inserted paragraph ten into the organic law of 30 December 1871. Known as the "dictatorship paragraph," it empowered the high president and later the governor to take any measure considered necessary to preserve public safety and order. Although the imperial constitution required the emperor to declare a state of siege before local officials in other parts of the empire could invoke exceptional powers, no such limitation applied in the Reichsland. Nor did the dictatorship paragraph provide for parliamentary repeal of executive decrees.

While the potential threat of the dictatorship paragraph caused considerable popular animosity, officials seldom applied the regulation because there were numerous ordinary laws which accomplished the same ends. Möller did use the paragraph to muzzle the Catholic press and expel Catholic "agitators" such as Ignace Rapp, vicar general to the Strasbourg bishop.[66] Manteuffel also used it to suppress anti-German newspapers following government reverses in the 1881 Reichstag election. Nevertheless, Möller found the law a nuisance; it caused much popular bad feeling, and added nothing to administrative effectiveness.[67]

Prince Alexander zu Hohenlohe-Schillingsfürst, son of the governor, Prince Chlodwig zu Hohenlohe-Schillingsfürst, and a one-time district president in Alsace-Lorraine, admitted the dictatorship paragraph was seldom used and caused the people to feel like second-class citizens, but opposed its repeal because he feared such action would simply encourage pro-French agitators. Prince Alexander also admitted to being influenced by Alsatian industrialists and landowners who regarded the dictatorship paragraph as insurance against workers' uprisings.[68]

Opposition to the dictatorship paragraph grew steadily. The Reichstag passed a bill repealing the exceptional law on 27 February 1895, but the Federal Council rejected it. Meanwhile, the disparity between the provisions of the dictatorship paragraph and the rest of the legal code in the Reichsland continued to grow as imperial legislation was made applicable to Alsace-Lorraine during the

1890s. The Reichsland came under the imperial municipal code in 1892; the imperial press law, which guaranteed the right to publish French-language newspapers, in 1898; the new imperial penal, civil, and commercial codes in 1900; and the imperial law on associations in 1905.[69] How could the government continue to justify the exceptional law of the dictatorship paragraph while simultaneously attempting to normalize the situation in the Reichsland through the introduction of the German legal code? The government finally conceded, and from the heights of the Hohkönigsberg the kaiser announced the repeal of the dictatorship paragraph, effective 18 June 1902.[70]

Combined with the new Alsace-Lorraine constitution of 1911, the repeal of the dictatorship paragraph appeared to signify the end of second-class status for the Reichsland. Freed from the threat of a police state, the Alsace-Lorrainers began to act like free men, a result which the Germans had apparently not anticipated. The period of exhilaration passed quickly. When expressions of freedom increasingly took the form of a revival of French culture and language, the government concluded that its policy of "weakness" had been a mistake.[71] In 1913 the government sought new exceptional laws permitting the suppression of French-language newspapers and the banning of any organization considered to pose a threat to public order or demonstrating anti-German tendencies. The *Landtag* rejected the bills, but the battle lines between the people and the government were clearly drawn.[72]

Had any progress toward "Germanization" been achieved since 1871? The government's 1913 demand for new exceptional laws, followed by the Zabern affair, convinced many that the answer was a resounding "no." One might compare the situation in Alsace-Lorraine with the problem of Germanization faced by the Prussians in the Polish provinces. It is probably no coincidence that the man chosen to assume the governorship of Alsace-Lorraine after the disastrous Zabern affair—the Prussian minister of the interior, Hans von Dallwitz—counted several responsible posts in the Polish provinces among his years of administrative experience. Dallwitz considered the government's Germanization policy as a failure in both Alsace-Lorraine and the Polish provinces. But he made an important distinction between the two cases; the Polish program had failed because it was too aggressively anti-Polish, whereas the Reichsland policy had failed because it was too weak and tolerant.[73]

Systematic attempts to Germanize the Polish provinces began in 1885 with a large-scale expulsion of Polish Jews, Russians, and Austrians. The expulsions served as the prelude to the 1886 colonization (*Ansiedlung*) program, under which the Prussian government appropriated one hundred million marks to purchase from Poles land that would then be turned over to German peasants. The Prussian *Landtag* voted an additional 100 million marks in 1898, and 250 million more in 1902. The government inaugurated the same program in Schleswig in 1912 with a grant of one hundred million marks. The colonization program formed part of a total Germanization package introduced in 1886–87 consisting of school regulations, language ordinances, and controls on the Catholic clergy. The program did not work. Polish peasants refused to sell land to the Germans, and Catholic priests resisted what they rightly considered a renewal of the *Kulturkampf*. In a mood of exasperation, the Prussian *Landtag* enacted legislation in 1908 permitting the expropriation of land from unwilling Polish peasants.[74]

Dallwitz unfortunately was not the only Prussian bureaucrat to conclude that the policy which had produced completely counterproductive results in the Polish provinces might provide the final solution to the Alsace-Lorraine problem. The first administrative correspondence concerning a colonization project dates from 10 August 1887 when the district president at Metz, attempting to explain the antigovernment vote in the 1887 *Septennat* election, pointed to the large number of French proprietors of small holdings in Lorraine. Similar reports were summed up in a 28 December 1888 statement signed by Governor Hohenlohe-Schillingsfürst and sent to the chancellor. According to this report, French citizens or Alsace-Lorrainers whose sons had emigrated owned 67.7 percent of all Lorraine properties over fifty hectares, 54.4 percent of such properties in Lower Alsace, and 35.2 percent in Upper Alsace. Citing the political risks stemming from this situation, the report recommended that the government purchase land and promote German colonization as it did in the Polish provinces. Similar official reports originated in Metz in 1890 and 1900, and in Strasbourg in 1906.[75]

Unimpressed by the results of the Polish colonization program (but still unwilling to admit its failure), authorities in Berlin ignored the pleas from the Reichsland until the critical war years after 1914. In a secret conference held at Bingen on 15 and 16 June 1917, high

German civilian and military authorities adopted the "Polish" plan
for Alsace-Lorraine. Legislation passed by the Reichstag on 14
December 1917 authorized the founding of the Westmark Land
Corporation, capitalized at 7,500,000 marks. Backers of the corporation included real estate companies in Königsberg, Stettin, Bres-
lau, and Halle, iron and steel companies from the Ruhr, Sarr, and
Lorraine, including the Krupp interests, and private investors such
as Prince Henkel von Donnersmark and his son. Supposedly this
was a private corporation with no official connections, but Westmark's contract with the imperial chancellery, signed on 17 January
1918, touched off vigorous protests in the Reichstag. The corporation represented a last desperate attempt to Germanize the Reichsland; it made only a few purchases of land, all of which were declared
null and void by the conquering French.[76]

In simple terms, the Germanization of Alsace-Lorraine had failed.
But "Germanization" is not a simple concept. If by Germanization
one means that the people must become the pliant stooges for Prus-
sian bureaucrats and Prussian generals, then one can argue that the
Bavarians were never Germanized, either. German policy in the
Reichsland was far too complex to be summed up in a single word.
Because German policy centered on real or imagined military security requirements, it was generally repressive and unpopular.
When the government extended its view beyond military questions
and tried to win popular support, it offered occasional concessions.
German Reichsland policy emerged as a strange mélange of coercion
and conciliation, forceful action and vacillation. Policy fluctuation
paralleled the irregular development of administrative structure and
personnel previously described. The total result satisfied neither
the government nor the people.

5
PERMANENT *KULTURKAMPF* IN ALSACE-LORRAINE 1871-1918

To transform the population of Alsace-Lorraine into a loyal German citizenry, the new regime above all else had to win over the Catholics. For a Protestant power to have successfully integrated a predominantly Catholic territory would have been difficult in any case. In Bismarck's mind, "Germanization" included the destruction of Roman Catholic political and "cultural" opposition, whether it be in Prussia, the Reich, or Alsace-Lorraine. In the empire, the *Kulturkampf* impaired Bismarck's ability to maintain a parliamentary majority in the Reichstag; in the Reichsland, the *Kulturkampf* added to the inherent difficulties of administering the territory and destroyed any possibility of rapid assimilation of the "German brothers" so recently reunited with the fatherland.[1]

Memories of the Prussian assault on Catholic Austria in 1866 were still fresh. Catholic priests in Alsace-Lorraine, wrote Christian Hallier, equated Germany with Prussia, and Prussia with Protestantism.[2] The priest Carl Marbach, writing to the bishop of Strasbourg in March 1871, claimed the Prussians were universally hated in Alsace-Lorraine.[3] The bishop of Angers, Charles-Emile Freppel, warned King Wilhelm of Prussia that Alsace would never belong to a Prussian monarch.[4] Given the apparent hatred for the Prussian, Protestant regime, the initial moderate response of most of the Catholic hierarchy in the Reichsland is rather surprising. For some years prior to the annexation, however, leading Alsatian Catholics had maintained close ties with German Catholicism. Andreas Raess and his successor as bishop of Strasbourg, Peter Paul Stumpf, along with the canon of Hagenau, Joseph Guerber, followed the Mainz circle of German Catholicism. Decrying state control over the Church, the Mainz circle hoped to enlist popular support for its efforts to free the Church from foreign power, state power, and the forces of feudalism.[5]

Shortly after the annexation, Joseph Guerber, who later became a leader of the Catholic-protester group, counseled the Alsatian Catholics against clinging to dreams of an early French restoration "with narrow-minded obstinacy." A Father Griser of Lixheim in Lorraine philosophically concluded that since Alsace-Lorraine had been detached from France by a "definitive" treaty, the people might as well try to make the best of the situation.[6] The Reichstag session of 1874 uncovered a division in the Catholic attitude toward the German regime. The fifteen deputies from the Reichsland, including the clerical delegates, protested against the annexation of their homeland. But Bishop Raess immediately mounted the speakers' platform and assured the Reichstag that the Catholic priests of Alsace-Lorraine recognized the validity of the Frankfurt Treaty. Most of his subordinate priests repudiated Raess by declaring that the bishop was speaking only for himself.

The nonpolitical attitude exemplified by Paul Dupont des Loges, bishop of Metz, was fairly typical of the clerical reaction to the new order. The *Norddeutsche Allgemeine Zeitung* claimed that Dupont had greeted the German emperor as the "restorer of authority in the territory," but Dupont's vigorous denial of that charge seems justified.[7] Although the bishop was elected to the Reichstag in 1874, he counseled his priests to devote themselves to their religious duties and avoid any "compromising" political activity.[8] The spirit of political noninvolvement prevailed in an address presented to the emperor in November 1871 by 797 members of the Alsatian clergy, in which they recognized the principle, "Give to God what appertains to God; give to the kaiser what appertains to the kaiser."[9]

While trying to avoid political controversy, Dupont des Loges sent his vicar general to the negotiations in Brussels, hoping to secure protection for local Catholic interests in the Frankfurt Treaty. Dupont's biographer, Father Félix Klein, believed the bishop's efforts were successful, and that the Alsace-Lorraine Catholics could expect to receive just and tolerant treatment at the hands of the Germans. The *Kulturkampf* rudely shattered such expectations.

The Germans equated ecclesiastical opposition with political opposition; in Prussia, the answer to Catholic opposition was the *Kulturkampf*. Lujo Brentano correctly observed that, "to have brought the *Kulturkampf* into a Catholic territory which they desired to win over would have been madness."[10] Despite claims that high officials in Strasbourg and Berlin never promoted anticlerical policies in the Reichsland, the government clearly did succumb to the madness described by Brentano.[11] Authorities applied Prussian and imperial anti-Catholic laws in Alsace-Lorraine, and drafted special anticlerical legislation to meet the specific requirements of the Reichsland. Bismarck himself charged the ultramontanes in Alsace-Lorraine with trying to undermine government authority, and referred to the German Catholic leader Ludwig Windthorst as the "disturber of the peace in Germany, and the underminer of trust in the newly-acquired provinces."[12] Fearing clerical control of the territorial assembly, Bismarck opposed extension of the powers of the territorial committee.

Bismarck's difficulties with the Alsace-Lorraine Catholics began with the signing of the Frankfurt Treaty. Two questions in particular demanded prompt attention; revising boundaries of the Catholic dioceses to conform to the new political boundary between France and Germany, and determining the status in Alsace-Lorraine of the French Concordat of 1801. Article Six of the Frankfurt Treaty provided for negotiation of new diocese boundaries "without delay," but a solution equally acceptable to Germany, France, and the Holy See came only in 1874.[13] In the interim, by the additional act of 11 December 1871, existing diocese boundaries remained in effect until revisions were agreed upon. Under this awkward arrangement, French bishops retained jurisdiction over territory which was now part of the German empire, while the bishop of Metz, now German, continued to administer the part of his diocese which remained in France. Settlement of the diocese boundaries was more important than is generally realized. Count Karl von Tauffkirchen, the Bavarian ambassador to Austria, advised Bismarck that regulation of the boundary question was the key to settlement of all church-state problems in Alsace-Lorraine.[14] Both Tauffkirchen and High President Möller urged Bismarck to end the boundary dispute with a provisional *modus vivendi* with the Holy See. Without an agreement, warned Möller, French bishops could continue to spread anti-German propaganda in Alsace-Lorraine.[15] Bismarck, however, re-

fused to make any overtures to the pope until the Holy See had
"changed its present attitude toward the political position of our
supporters in Germany."[16] The chancellor refused to relax pressure
on the Church long enough to settle a problem that greatly complicated the task of governing the Reichsland. The struggle to preserve
German culture took precedence over the rational administration of
Alsace-Lorraine.

When in 1874 some thirty Alsace-Lorraine priests received prison
sentences for disseminating an allegedly anti-German pastoral letter
from the bishop of Nancy, the German government finally recognized
the desirability of regulating the dioscese boundaries.[17] Since Bismarck had no direct diplomatic connections with the Vatican, he
had to initiate negotiations through Count Harry von Arnim, the
German ambassador in Paris. To get talks started, Bismarck proposed a meeting of a special Franco-German boundary commission
at either Strasbourg or Nancy. Duke Louis Charles Decazes, the
French foreign minister, indicated French preparedness to negotiate,
but warned that Vatican approval would be needed for any binding
agreement. Decazes told Bismarck he was instructing the French
ambassador in Rome to begin talks with the Holy See, and that
he was asking the French minister of religion to obtain the agreement of the bishops whose dioceses would be affected by a
settlement.[18]

The commission proposed by Bismarck met in Paris on 22 May
1874, drafted a set of proposals, and sent them to Rome for papal
approval. In consistorial decrees of 10 July and 14 July, the pope
approved the separations and incorporations necessary to achieve
conformity between the diocese boundaries of Nancy, St. Dié,
Besancon, Metz, and Strasbourg, and the political frontiers established by the Frankfurt Treaty. Strasbourg and Metz were removed
from the ecclesiastical province of Besancon, declared exempt from
all archepiscopal or metropolitan jurisdiction, and placed under the
direct control of the pope. By placing Strasbourg and Metz directly
under the Holy See, the Church prevented these dioceses from
coming under the jurisdiction of a German archbishop. According
to the *Augsburger Allgemeine Zeitung*, this was "not an uncommon
case in the hierarchical constitution of the Catholic Church."[19]

While settlement of the diocese boundary problem removed a
major source of church-state conflict, the status of the French Concordat of 1801 in the Reichsland remained in doubt. Unable to

resolve differences of interpretation of certain articles of the Concordat, Berlin and the Vatican never reached agreement on this issue. The crux of the problem was Article Seventeen of the Concordat, which provided that non-Catholic rulers of France lost the right to name priests and bishops. The privilege of making appointments, however, could be renegotiated with the Vatican by a non-Catholic ruler. Emperor Wilhelm I was neither a Catholic nor a Frenchman. Was he required or entitled to renegotiate only the appointment rights mentioned in article seventeen, or did the annexation invalidate the entire Concordat in Alsace-Lorraine?

Local Catholic leaders rejected a legalistic approach to the status of the Concordat; for them, it was a matter of whether the Concordat afforded sufficient protection to Catholic interests. On that point, the Catholic hierarchy disagreed and vacillated. Father Griser in Lorraine viewed the Concordat as protection for Church liberties, especially if the Germans would drop the Organic Articles added by Napoléon I without papal consent. Optimistic about prospects for Catholicism under the German regime, Griser believed Prussia allowed its Catholic subjects more liberties than any other German state. He assumed that the Prussian king and German emperor would be no less tolerant of the Catholics in Alsace-Lorraine.[20]

Bishop Raess of Strasbourg, on the other hand, took the position that the annexation invalidated the Concordat. Influenced by the Mainz circle of German Catholicism, Raess saw the annexation as an opportunity to break state control over the Church. While Bismarck-Bohlen served as governor general of the occupied territory, Raess appointed priests to vacancies without securing state approval, and notified the governor general that he regarded the Concordat as null and void in Alsace-Lorraine. To protect himself, Raess asked the Vatican for an official opinion on the Concordat's validity. Before the papal reply arrived, however, Bismarck-Bohlen rejected Raess' opinion with the announcement that priests named without government sanction would be neither recognized nor paid by the state.[21] Civil commissar Kühlwetter informed Catholic authorities that the Concordat and Organic Articles remained in force. The German foreign office admitted that renegotiation of royal rights in the naming of priests and bishops might be required, but denied that the rest of the Concordat had been affected by the annexation. In any event, the terms of the original Concordat were to remain in effect until a new agreement had been reached.[22]

Replying to Raess' query on the status of the Concordat, the pope sent a message through the papal secretary of state, Cardinal Giacomo Antonelli, indicating that the Concordat no longer applied in Alsace-Lorraine, and instructing Raess to discontinue application for state approval of ecclesiastical appointments. At the proper time, wrote Antonelli, the Church would conclude a new agreement with the German government.[23] Berlin authorities interpreted Antonelli's letter to Raess as a unilateral abrogation of the Concordat. While it was willing to accept the Vatican's apparent rejection of the Concordat, the government pointed out that political authorities were now free to regulate religion in the Reichsland in any manner they pleased. The possibility of more stringent government control in the absence of the Concordat had not occurred to Antonelli, and he quickly reversed himself in subsequent communications with Raess. He now recognized the need for a special agreement regulating religious affairs in the Reichsland; until such an accord could be reached, the original Concordat, including royal prerogatives in the naming of priests and bishops, would remain in force.[24]

On the government side, High President Möller saw no need to negotiate a new agreement with the Vatican. Under international law, if the Concordat and Organic Articles were regarded as ordinary French legislation, they remained in effect unless specifically replaced by German regulations. So long as Möller felt the Concordat permitted sufficient state regulation of the Church, Bismarck accepted Möller's interpretation. But Bismarck demanded that the Church make up its own mind. Religious authorities could not claim the Concordat was valid when it served the Church's advantage, and not valid when it was detrimental to the Church's interests. If the Vatican adopted such an ambivalent policy, then the government would draft its own legislation concerning religious affairs in the Reichsland.[25]

Given the lack of any better agreement, both Church and state gave the Concordat *de facto* recognition. Germany's diplomatic break with the Vatican in 1872 precluded the possibility of negotiating a new accord. The Church viewed the Concordat as protection against arbitrary religious laws in the Reichsland, while the government felt the Concordat assured adequate secular control over the Church. But the Concordat was not an effective means of protecting Catholic interests in Alsace-Lorraine. Although the Prussian May Laws of 1873 were never introduced in the Reichsland, the government found other ways of repressing the Catholics. The imperial law of 25 June 1872, which expelled the Jesuits and "related orders" from Germany, was extended to Alsace-Lorraine. High President Möller exceeded the zeal of the Bundesrat by classifying the Marian Congregation and other teaching orders of nuns as "related orders," thus earmarking them for expulsion.[26] Other anti-Catholic measures followed the expulsion of the Jesuits. The government applied the *Kanzelparagraph* in the Reichsland, imprisoning two priests for allegedly disturbing the peace with inflammatory sermons. Divorce, abolished by the French law of 8 May 1816, became legal again in Alsace-Lorraine under the German law of 27 November 1873. The high president siezed the bishops' pastoral letters if they contained any anti-German references. Salaries of Catholic priests did not measure up to the level paid to Protestant pastors. The government also tried to force the Church to sell its French government bonds and purchase German bonds. When Dupont des Loges refused to comply with the order, the government retaliated by refusing legal recognition for any new Catholic-endowed institutions.[27]

Church-state relations were thus already strained in 1880 when, for the first time under the German regime, there arose the question of nominating a bishop in Alsace-Lorraine. The case involved the appointment of a coadjutor, with the right of succession, to Dupont des Loges, bishop of Metz. In 1874, Dupont had urged the Vatican to dictate procedures for the naming of bishops, as the price for a settlement of the diocese boundary problem. The Vatican, however, had passed up that opportunity to bargain with the German government on the appointment of bishops, and when Dupont decided it was time to appoint a coadjutor, there was some doubt as to the proper procedure. The state was just as uncertain in this matter as the Church. Governor Manteuffel, who was on friendly terms with the bishop of Metz, finally asked Dupont to explain the proper course for naming a bishop. To protect himself, the governor suggested that Dupont provide an answer which, "in recognizing the rights of the state, cannot compromise me with my Emperor." Dupont replied that the pope named coadjutors at the request of the bishop desiring this favor; but the Holy See never made a nomination without being certain of the consent of the civil power.[28] The post of coadjutor fell to an Alsatian, Franz Ludwig Fleck, the vicar general at Metz. An imperial decree of 25 June 1881, approved publication in Germany of a papal bull recognizing Fleck as bishop *in partibus*, and granting him canonical sanction as coadjutor. In his decree, however, the emperor carefully protected the rights of the state in the area of church law. The decree explicitly declined to recognize anything in the papal bull which might contradict existing religious laws in Alsace-Lorraine, or which might prejudice the emperor's sovereign rights in the Reichsland.[29] The imperial decree concerning Fleck made the status of the Concordat even more questionable. The government implied that while it was willing to accept the person named by the pope as coadjutor in Metz, it did not necessarily recognize the method by which the nomination had been made.[30]

While Church and state negotiated the appointment of a coadjutor in Metz, a deeper controversy erupted in Strasbourg. Bishop Raess wanted no coadjutor, but the Vatican doubted the eighty-seven-year-old bishop's ability to handle the affairs of his diocese. Pressured from Rome, Raess consented to the naming of a coadjutor in 1881, but stipulated that the post go to Felix Korum, an Alsatian already being considered for the bishopric of Trier. The circumstances of Korum's appointment to Trier, considered one of the most important German bishoprics, remain uncertain. Edwin von Manteuffel told Count Bogdan von Hutten-Czapski in 1881 that he had used his influence to secure the seat at Trier for Korum in order to promote good church-state relations in both Germany and the Reichsland; the appointment proved that the most important bishopric in the empire could be held by an Alsatian. But Manteuffel's successor as governor, Prince Chlodwig zu Hohenlohe-Schillingsfürst, told papal nuncio Cardinal Antonio Agliardi in 1890 that Manteuffel had proposed Korum for Trier in order to keep him out of Alsace.[31] Whatever Manteuffel's motives, he did reject Korum for Strasbourg, and instead suggested Peter Paul Stumpf, another Alsatian priest who had just demonstrated his loyalty to the regime by running as a government-backed candidate in the 1881 Reichstag election. Stumpf won the nomination, and in 1883, aided by Manteuffel's influence, he received full administrative powers in the Strasbourg diocese.[32]

Stumpf's death on 10 August 1890 provided the government with an opportunity to act decisively against the continuing clerical opposition in the Reichsland. Stumpf had been unable to control the anti-German elements of the lower Alsatian clergy; perhaps a German bishop could. In discussions concerning Stumpf's successor held with the papal nuncio Cardinal Antonio Agliardi in October, Hohenlohe-Schillingsfürst made it clear that the nationality issue was of primary importance. Emperor Wilhelm II, Chancellor Leo von Caprivi, Hohenlohe-Schillingsfürst, and German public opinion united on this issue; the next bishop of Strasbourg must be a German.[33] A few opposition voices in Germany warned that a German bishop would alienate the Reichsland's Catholics from the Church and leave them easy prey for the socialists, but no one took this threat seriously.[34]

Berlin authorities seemed unconcerned with filling the Strasbourg seat promptly. Two months after Stumpf's death, on 10 October, Hohenlohe-Schillingsfürst held preliminary conversations with the papal nuncio, and the following day sent a lengthy report on those talks to the kaiser. When Hohenlohe still had not received permission to begin talks with prospective candidates a month after submitting his report, he finally went on 11 November to Caprivi, who promised to take up the matter with the kaiser. Hohenlohe wished to send his own special envoy directly to the Vatican to negotiate the bishop's appointment; his choice for the mission was Count Bogdan von Hutten-Czapski, who appeared to hold the necessary qualifications. The count's service as adjutant to Governor Manteuffel from 1883 to 1885 had rendered him familiar with territorial affairs, and his successful negotiations with Pope Leo XIII in 1879 on procedures for appointing priests established his diplomatic credentials.[35] Caprivi, with less than eight months' experience as imperial chancellor, was a relative neophyte in such matters. He first rejected Hohenlohe's proposal, then changed his mind and accepted it. Caprivi was concerned by what he considered the incompetence of the Ministry of Ecclesiastical Affairs in filling the bishopric at Posen; with Hohenlohe's plan, he could circumvent the ministry and keep it out of the Strasbourg case.[36] On 19 December Hohenlohe finally received the emperor's permission to send Count Czapski to Rome.

Negotiations with the Holy See lasted far into January 1891. Although the Vatican bargained hard, most of the delay stemmed from utter confusion in the German camp. From the beginning, the kaiser had preferred to handle the negotiations through normal diplomatic channels, that is, through the Prussian ambassador to the Vatican, Kurt von Schlözer. Arguing for the mission of Count Czapski, Hohenlohe had contended that in serving Prussia, Schlözer

could not do justice to the interests of Alsace-Lorraine. Furthermore, the Vatican would prefer proposals made by the territorial
administration of Alsace-Lorraine to nominations from the Prussian
foreign office.[37] Schlözer resented Count Czapski's presence in
Rome, and intrigued to sabotage his negotiations with the papacy.
According to Czapski's account, Schlözer had powerful allies. Caprivi's opponents, led by Army Chief of Staff Count Alfred von
Waldersee, joined the opponents of Czapski and forced the kaiser
to dismiss the count early in January 1891 and turn the negotiations
over to Schlözer. The Vatican feared Czapski's removal presaged
an attempt to impose a "Prussian" solution in Alsace-Lorraine.[38]
    Personality conflicts and jurisdictional disputes merely added to
a basic confusion on the substantive issue facing the German government. It was a simple matter to decide that the next bishop of
Strasbourg would be a German; it was nearly impossible to decide
which German would receive the post. Nearly everyone in Berlin
had his favorite candidate, and of course Hohenlohe had his own
preference. The governor instructed Czapski to propose the Freiburg professor Franz Xaver Kraus, a liberal Catholic and an old
friend of both Hohenlohe and the grand duke of Baden. If he failed
to win consent for Kraus, Czapski was to nominate Hohenlohe's
second choice, Adolf Fritzen, a native of Cleves then serving as
director of the seminary at Montigny in Lorraine.[39] While insisting
on a German bishop, Hohenlohe would accept an Alsatian suffragan
bishop (distinguished from a coadjutor, who has the right of succession to a vacant bishopric); for the auxiliary position he recommended either Léon Dacheux, the superior of the seminary at
Markolsheim with whom Hohenlohe had established a close working
relationship, or the Strasbourg canon, Straub.
    According to Czapski, neither the kaiser nor the pope shared
Hohenlohe's enthusiasm for Kraus. Papal secretary of state, Cardinal Mariano Rampolla del Tindaro, told Czapski that the pope
considered the Freiburg professor's liberal teachings to be theologi-
cally unsound. The pope would have none other than Mathias
Hoehler, then serving under the bishop of Limburg. Hohenlohe had
already placed Hoehler on his "unacceptable" list, and Czapski
characterized him as a Jesuit-trained supporter of the Alsatian anti-
German extremists. Both sides eventually compromised and agreed
on Adolf Fritzen, though the Vatican held deep reservations about
appointing to such a demanding position a philologist and historian

who had never served as an active priest. Chosen as suffragan bishop was Carl Marbach, the penitentiary priest of the Strasbourg cathedral.[40]

Fritzen's elevation to the bishopric produced a new conflict between church and state as they searched for Fritzen's successor as director of the seminary at Montigny. Bishop Fleck, who as coadjutor had succeeded to the Metz bishopric upon the death of Paul Dupont des Loges in 1886, nominated an Alsatian. The government agreed, but only on the condition that the seminary relinquish its right to confer certain types of diplomas. When Fleck rejected the government's conditions, "it was necessary to look for a German" to fill the post. After a lengthy search and prolonged negotiations, a German lay professor at Montigny named Rech received the appointment. Rech's dedication as a seminarian hardly served as a praiseworthy example to the novices. Using his office as the springboard to a political career, he became mayor of the town of Sablon, lost a bid for a seat in the lower house of the territorial committee, but later entered the upper house of the territorial assembly as a government appointee.[41]

Fleck's death on 27 October 1899 touched off the most bizarre episode in the history of episcopal appointments in the Reichsland. For two years the bishopric of Metz remained vacant as controversy raged between the government, the Vatican, and local anti-German priests led by Nicolaus Delsor, a Reichstag deputy from the district of Molsheim. The government supported Franz von Bulach, brother of the undersecretary of state for agriculture in Alsace-Lorraine, Hugo Zorn von Bulach (younger). Pope Leo XIII opposed Bulach because he felt his appointment would place too much power in the hands of one family. Delsor and his followers considered Franz von Bulach a renegade, just like his father and brother.

The kaiser finally agreed to the German Benedictine Willibrod Benzler, and on 28 October 1901, Metz at last had a bishop once more. To counteract the widespread belief that he had capitulated to Alsatian opposition to Bulach, the kaiser proceeded to appoint Bulach suffragan bishop of Strasbourg. This nomination would not have been noteworthy, except for the fact that Strasbourg already had a suffragan bishop, Carl Marbach, who had been appointed along with Fritzen in 1891. To make way for Bulach, Fritzen was forced to resign. Bulach served until opposition forces compelled him to withdraw as French troops occupied Strasbourg in 1918.

His career as suffragan bishop ended as it had begun, determined solely by the dictates of raw political power. In this respect, Bulach's story recapitulates church-state relations in the Reichsland between 1871 and 1919.[42]

Influence over episcopal appointments facilitated government control over all Church-related activities in the Reichsland. The major thrust of the government's anti-Catholic campaign attacked clerical influence in education. During the regime of Napoléon III, the Church had gained power in all levels of education. Many communities hired members of religious teaching orders simply because they cost less than lay teachers. The Germans considered education to be the responsibility of the state, not the Church. In April 1871 the occupation government of Bismarck-Bohlen imposed compulsory education on boys up to age fourteen and girls to age thirteen. Two years later, all elementary and higher education came under state supervision; teaching, hiring a teacher, or opening a school now required state sanction. The chancellor or his representative inspected all schools in the Reichsland, and closed any which did not meet his standards.[43] Contradiction and vacillation marked early German educational policy in the Reichsland. During the occupation period, Civil Commissar Kühlwetter tried to please the Catholics by segregating the confessionally mixed teachers' colleges. In 1870 the normal school at Strasbourg enrolled sixty-four Catholics, twenty-six Evangelicals, and four Jews. Kühlwetter reserved the Strasbourg institution for Catholics, and restricted the teachers' college at Colmar to Evangelicals. Jewish students could attend either the Strasbourg or Colmar college.[44] Bismarck found Kühlwetter's educational policy incompatible with his emerging anti-Catholic program, and quickly reestablished all of the normal schools on a nonconfessional basis.

Anxious to rid the schools of Jesuit teachers, Bismarck closed all teachers' seminaries run by Jesuits in the Reichsland before the imperial order expelling the Jesuits was handed down.[45] Teaching orders headquartered in France lost their operating privileges in Alsace-Lorraine, and public schools were required to hire lay teachers. By prohibiting the segregation of boys and girls in separate elementary schools, the Germans ingeniously forced nuns to give up teaching, since the nuns refused to teach in schools where the sexes were mixed. Integration of the sexes in elementary schools produced angry charges that the government was encouraging promiscuity among the children.[46]

Curtailment of the religious teaching orders created a drastic shortage of teachers. The government found itself in a difficult position. Bismarck had warned that for the time being, the political and military security of the empire would take precedence over education in the Reichsland. The chancellor argued that the temporary shortage of teachers was far more preferable to the harm done by the religious teaching orders.[47] But since the schools were an important part of the government's Germanization plan, the state had to maintain an adequate supply of teachers. Recognizing the need for qualified teachers, the government in 1875 began to permit nuns to take the required state teaching examinations. Although the examinations were usually administered in a state institution, nuns whose vows restricted them to the cloister received permission to take the examinations in their convents. To encourage more lay Catholics to enter the teaching profession, High President Möller established a teachers' seminary for women at Sélestat.

Relaxation of some of the restrictions on the education of Catholic teachers coincided with a tightening of restrictions on the education of Catholic priests. Article eleven of the Concordat granted each bishop the right to maintain a seminary under his own personal control. Prior to 1871 French authorities had understood this clause to apply not only to the *grand séminaire* for candidates for the priesthood, but also the *petit séminaire* (*Knabenseminar*), the pre-preparatory school for the *grand séminaire*. The Germans, however, considered the *petits séminaires* as ordinary secondary schools, requiring them to follow the state teaching plan and submit to state inspection. When they refused to comply with state regulations, most of the *petits séminaires* were closed in 1874.

Not all Alsace-Lorrainers viewed the removal of clerical influence from education as an evil. The autonomists, anticlerical by their own admission, welcomed the turn of events. Religious opposition generated by German educational policy was counterbalanced by real benefits for the people of Alsace-Lorraine. While the Germans immediately introduced compulsory education, France did not require school attendance until 1882. The deficiencies of the old French educational system stand out sharply in education and literacy statistics. In 1875, 3.5 percent of the Reichsland army recruits had received no formal education; by 1910, this figure had been reduced to 0.02 per 5,000. Secretary of State Herzog commented that if the state compelled children to attend school, then the state was also obliged to insure that they received a good education.[48] His statement cannot be dismissed as merely an attempt to justify unpopular government policies.

Manteuffel's appointment as governor in 1879 brought a significant improvement in church-state relations. As Bismarck was now liquidating the *Kulturkampf* in Prussia, the clericals hoped the government would relax restrictions against Catholics in Alsace-Lorraine as well. Manteuffel came to the Reichsland pledged to a policy of conciliation; he would make a genuine effort to win respect and acceptance for the German regime. The success of Manteuffel's conciliation policy depended on the support and cooperation of the bishops of Strasbourg and Metz, Raess and Dupont des Loges. Manteuffel established a rather intimate relationship with Dupont, but only by making concessions to the Church. Because he regarded the clergy, even the Catholic clergy, as a bastion of political stability, Manteuffel was willing to make concessions. On the basis of suggestions he solicited from Dupont, Manteuffel established the normal schools on a confessional basis, reopened the *petits séminaires*, reopened the convent of the Sisters of the Sacred Heart of Jesus, permitted nuns to teach in schools segregated by sex, and authorized the teaching of the catechism in the lower grades of elementary schools.[49]

Manteuffel, in fact, introduced basic legislation aimed at tightening clerical control over elementary education. In a regulation which stood until 1908, the governor ordered special consideration be given to Catholics in the appointment of elementary school teachers. To end the practice whereby communes dominated by "liberals" had established nonconfessional elementary schools free from clerical influence, Manteuffel's decree of 4 December 1880 created a new administrative body, the district educational council (*Bezirks-Unterrichtsrat*) to screen all applications for confessionally-mixed schools. Membership on the council included a bishop, another Christian priest, and a representative from the Israelite consistory. The council worked effectively; in 1912 Alsace-Lorraine counted only fifty-six confessionally mixed elementary schools in a total of 2,850.[50]

Prince Chlodwig zu Hohenlohe-Schillingsfürst, a south German liberal Catholic, sought to continue Manteuffel's conciliatory policy

after 1885. Like Manteuffel, Hohenlohe established close relations
with certain members of the Catholic clergy, although he aimed a
bit lower than his predecessor. Whereas Manteuffel preferred to deal
with the bishops of Metz and Strasbourg, Hohenlohe adopted as his
confidante Léon Dacheux, superior of the *grand séminaire* at
Markolsheim. A chronic complainer, Dacheux found a sympathetic
listener in Hohenlohe. The priest, in fact, while assuring Hohenlohe
he had no ambition for high Church office, least of all a bishop's seat,
used his position of trust with the governor for his own gain. In one
private talk with Hohenlohe, Dacheux accused his own coadjutor
bishop of discrimination in failing to promote him to the canonical
status generally held by all superiors of seminaries. But Dacheux also
used his intimacy with the governor to point out numerous injustices
against the Church in general; the drafting of seminarians into the
army, improper instruction and organization in the seminaries
(which were regulated by the state), lack of a Catholic theological
faculty at the Strasbourg university, and repressive actions against
nuns all came under attack from Dacheux. Hohenlohe listened
sympathetically, but seems to have taken little action during his first
two years as governor. On one matter, however, he was obstinate;
the Jesuits must never be permitted to return to Alsace-Lorraine
and spread their anti-German propaganda.[51]

Demands for repression after the 1887 *Septennat* election destroyed any hope for Catholic reconciliation. In 1888, under pressure from the government, the bishops of Strasbourg and Metz
ordered the use of French discontinued in their seminaries, and
replaced French-trained instructors with personnel educated in
Germany.[52] Hohenlohe's willingness to establish a Catholic theological faculty at the university lost all significance as the university
itself was nearly destroyed in the tide of repression. Many of the
best professors resigned when their professional organizations were
banned; Hohenlohe tried to persuade them to stay on, even those who
had taken antigovernment positions.[53] It was not until 22 October
1903, under the governorship of Hohenlohe-Langenburg and his
secretary of state, Ernst Matthias von Köller, that the Catholic
theological faculty opened its doors.

Creation of a Catholic theological faculty involved some difficult
questions of church-state relations requiring lengthy negotiations
with the Vatican. The Germans had planned to establish a Catholic
theological faculty when the university was founded in 1872, but a

dispute over procedures for faculty appointments delayed these plans for thirty years. Catholic priests were ordinarily educated in seminaries under a bishop's control. Displeased with what they considered the pro-French attitude of the seminaries in Metz and Strasbourg, the Germans strongly favored a more easily controlled Catholic faculty at the university. Under the French Concordat of 1801, which presumably still held good in Alsace-Lorraine, bishops retained the right to make faculty appointments to their seminaries, and they now claimed the same right to appoint professors to any Catholic theological faculty at the university. The government rejected the Church's position, and there the matter lay until it was revived by Friedrich Althoff in 1898. Formerly a professor and administrator at the Strasbourg university, Althoff now served as an expert advisor on university matters in the Prussian ministry of education. Technically, the affairs of the Strasbourg university lay outside his official domain, but with the consent of the chancellor, Count Bernhard von Bülow, Althoff opened talks with Center party leader Count Georg von Hertling.

Hertling went to Rome for discussions with the Curia; the talks immediately bogged down on the matter of appointments. The Vatican refused to trade its seminaries, theoretically controlled by the bishops, for a state-controlled theological faculty at the university. Althoff finally agreed that in addition to establishing a Catholic theological faculty, he would appoint Catholics to the history and philosophy faculties as well. Demonstrating his good will, Althoff secured an appointment to the historical faculty for Martin Spahn, a twenty-six-year-old Bonn-educated historian. Spahn's history of Alsace-Lorraine, published in 1919, remains a standard work; but in 1898 the young historian had still to make his mark. Lacking impeccable academic credentials at the time of his appointment, Spahn owed his selection to two other factors. He was a Catholic, and he was the son of a prominent Centrist Reichstag deputy, Peter Spahn. Hoping to please the Catholics, Althoff merely succeeded in raising a storm of protest in both Strasbourg and German academic circles. The academicians resisted an appointment based on political and religious factors rather than demonstrated competence. Negotiations with the Curia threatened to collapse. Althoff made more concessions. Although the bishops would not receive the right to make appointments to the university faculty, they could continue to operate their own seminaries; the Catholic university faculty would thus supplement, rather than replace, the seminaries. The bishops and university faculty could nominate professorial candidates, and the prior agreement of the Strasbourg bishop would be sought before the government actually made appointments to the Catholic theological faculty. Technically, the arrangements at Strasbourg did not officially concern the bishop of Metz, but a special arrangement was made whereby the Metz bishop could send young theologians to study at Strasbourg. There is no evidence that the bishop ever availed himself of this privilege.[54]

With the agreement on the Catholic theological faculty in December 1902, church-state relations appeared to lose their crisis atmosphere. But there was always some problem, sometimes minor as when Bishop Benzler of Metz tried to prevent the burial of a Protestant in a traditionally Catholic cemetery, sometimes serious as when the bishops of Metz and Strasbourg advised Catholic school teachers against joining the General German Teachers' Association in 1909. Believing the General Association to be anti-Catholic, the bishops urged the interconfessional Territorial Union of Alsace-Lorraine Teachers to affiliate with the Catholic German Teachers' Association. Local liberals, annoyed by this clerical intervention in what they considered an educational matter, pressured the governor, Count Karl von Wedel, to intervene. In a letter to Bishop Benzler, Wedel warned that the Church had overstepped its competence by interfering in a purely educational matter properly regulated by the state. The bishops rejected Wedel's position, and appointed the suffragan bishop of Strasbourg, Franz von Bulach, whose brother was now secretary of state, to conduct conversations with Wedel and Chancellor Theobald von Bethmann Hollweg in an effort to lay the matter to rest. The affair ended when Berlin authorities told Wedel to drop the whole question. Wedel complied, but made his position clear in 1912 when he wrote that as a warm friend of the teachers, he would always try to protect them from "unjust clerical interference."[55]

While the endless conflicts between a Protestant state and the Catholic Church in the Reichsland were predictable, no one foresaw that a similar fate awaited relations between the Evangelicals and the state in Alsace-Lorraine. The Protestants looked forward to a privileged position after the annexation, but their illusions soon dissipated as they faced attacks from both the Catholics and the government. With the development of political Catholicism, and the

introduction of universal suffrage in 1911, the minority of politically
fragmented Protestants lost its political voice. The government gave
the territorial Protestants little support, and considered the Evangelicals no less subject to state control than the Catholics. As early as
1871 Governor General Bismarck-Bohlen had proposed to abolish
the Protestant Directory and the Protestant church parliaments, but
local opposition forced the chancellor to quash the plan. The Directory continued to function during the German regime, but a government representative frankly told the territorial committee that the
Directory was nothing more than an organ of the state. Until 1910
the state appointed the lay members of the Directory, who more
often than not were Germans. The extent of state control became
clear in 1881, when the Directory attempted to appoint a new pastor
for the town of Hatten. Governor Manteuffel, citing powers held
under a French law of 26 Messidor, Year Ten, refused to confirm
the nominee on the grounds that he was not sufficiently orthodox.
To the Protestants, such action was indistinguishable from the *Kulturkampf* against the Catholics. In the long run, however, it was the
majority Catholics rather than the minority Protestants who held
the key to the government's success in the Reichsland.[56]

No one has expressed the dilemma of governing Alsace-Lorraine
more precisely than Prince Alexander zu Hohenlohe-Schillingsfürst,
when he warned that the greatest problem facing any government,
whether it be French or German, was the overwhelming influence
of the Catholic clergy over the spirit of the people.[57] Lacking an
understanding with the Church, no Germanization program could
succeed. Manteuffel and Hohenlohe-Schillingsfürst did indeed bring
to their office a sense of duty to attempt to reconcile the Catholics
to the German regime. The founding of the Catholic theological
faculty under Hohenlohe-Langenburg represented another official
attempt to placate the clericals. These attempts to bridge the confessional gap in the Reichsland coincided with periods of radical
anticlericalism in France. Catholics in Alsace-Lorraine naturally
tended to compare their situation with what it might have been had
they remained with France. At its best, German policy in Alsace-
Lorraine compared favorably with the treatment French Catholics
were getting from their government. While Manteuffel was courting
the bishop of Metz, France appeared to take up the *Kulturkampf*
just as the Germans were dropping it. Expulsion of the Jesuits and
dissolution of all religious teaching orders followed the resignation

of the Catholic French President Marshal Patrice de MacMahon in 1879. The Ferry laws of 1882 banned all religious education from public schools. Conservative Robert von Puttkamer observed in the Reichstag that the closing of the German *Kulturkampf* and the eruption of French anticlericalism might produce more friendly relations between the German government and the Alsace-Lorraine Catholics.[58] Manteuffel took advantage of the repression in France to demonstrate to the Reichsland Catholics that they could expect better treatment from a German administration. A similar opportunity presented itself between 1903 and 1905, when the French government legislated against the authorization of religious congregations and definitively separated church and state.

Despite outwardly favorable conditions, attempts at Catholic conciliation produced meagre results. Does this prove that the people of Alsace-Lorraine were simply irreconcilable, that nothing the Germans might have tried would have won them over? No, it simply forces us to look deeper for the causes of continuing Catholic opposition. Reasons for the failure of the government's Catholic policy are really not far to seek. In Manteuffel's case, he was plagued by subordinates who sabotaged his program by refusing to implement many of his concessions to the clericals. Manteuffel's rank of fieldmarshal may have insured the cooperation of his military subordinates in Alsace-Lorraine, but it cut no ice with the Protestant Prussian bureaucrats who had no desire to appease Catholics. The governor's habit of excluding lower administrative officials from his discussions with the bishops widened the breach between Manteuffel and his staff. In both Berlin and Strasbourg, his "notable policy" stirred resentment long after Manteuffel's death in 1885, and future governors would have to think twice before attempting to deal with the territory's leading religious and political figures. Hohenlohe's flirtation with the seminary director Dacheux hardly compared with Manteuffel's relations with the bishops and coadjutors.

More basic in the failure of attempts to conciliate the Catholics was the fact that these attempts were neither systematic nor enduring. The government subordinated its Catholic policy to broader political considerations; defeat of government-supported candidates in the Reichstag elections of 1881, 1884, and 1887 transformed conciliation into repression. The military party in Berlin dictated Hohenlohe-Schillingsfürst's shift from conciliation to coercion in 1887; Manteuffel created his own difficulties with little help from anyone. As a fieldmarshal inexperienced in politics, he failed to realize that his interference in the local Catholic political movement would destroy the effectiveness of his official programs. His attempts to exert political pressure through the bishops cost Manteuffel the support of the lower clergy as well as that of his own subordinates.

Catholics in the Reichsland could not count on a consistently conciliatory policy from the government. Elections unfavorable to the government might call forth new demands for repression. Even during periods of relative political calm, disputes such as the teachers' association controversy of 1909–10 constantly reminded the Catholics of their vulnerability. In an imperial territory where the *Kulturkampf* never really ended, Catholics looked increasingly to political action as the best defense against Prussian anticlericalism. Borrowing Friedrich the Great's dictum that the best defense is a good offense, the Catholics of the Reichsland followed their German coreligionists in the development of a new style of political Catholicism.

6

COUNTERATTACK:
POLITICAL CATHOLICISM
CONFRONTS THE STATE
AND THE SOCIALISTS

Discarding Metz Bishop Dupont des Loges' early nonpolitical stance in response to German anticlericalism, Alsace-Lorraine's Roman Catholic clergy emerged as the strongest political force in the Reichsland between 1871 and 1918. But despite their deep political involvement, the clericals established no regular party organization until the 1890s, refusing even affiliation with the Center party formed by their German coreligionists in 1870. Catholic reluctance to create a strong party apparatus encouraged German officials to play one Catholic faction against another, hoping to split the Catholic vote and secure the election of government-supported Reichstag candidates. Although clerical leaders recognized the government's attempts to exploit the unorganized Catholic political movement, they never regarded government interference as sufficient reason to form a cohesive party. It was the challenge of social democracy during the 1890s which finally drove the Catholics to form a regular political organization.[1]

The government actively discouraged Catholic political organization. Led by Ignace Rapp, vicar general of Strasbourg, the Catho-

This chapter is a revised and expanded version of the material contained in my article, "Political Catholicism and Social Democracy in Alsace-Lorraine, 1871–1914," which appeared in the *Catholic Historical Review* (April 1966). Reprinted by permission.

lics organized a "Committee for the Protection of Catholic Interests." The committee's main function was to pay fines incurred by Catholics who refused to send their children to Protestant schools. The government claimed, with some justification, that the committee was engaging in political agitation on the eve of the 1874 Reichstag election.[2] High President Möller suppressed the committee and ordered Rapp to leave Alsace-Lorraine within forty-eight hours. Swift and decisive government action against this early attempt at political activity discouraged later attempts to establish a Catholic party. It was, however, a turning point in relations between Catholics and the government. The wait-and-see attitude of many Catholics now turned to outright opposition as the Reichsland prepared for its first Reichstag election in 1874.

Germany regarded the 1874 election as the first real test of public opinion in Alsace-Lorraine. Public opinion, however, found no solid political parties around which it could rally. True political parties had not yet developed, but three clearly defined movements shared the territorial political arena. The so-called protesters refused to accept the fact that Alsace-Lorraine was now part of the German empire. Refusing to participate in German public affairs, they sought places in the Reichstag only because the rostrum of the German parliament provided an excellent propaganda platform. Opposing the protesters were the "autonomists." Resigned to the fact of annexation, they were willing to work with the Germans and try to make the best of the situation. The autonomist goal was self-government for the Reichsland, within the context of the German imperial structure. In practical terms, the autonomist program demanded that the seat of local government be located in Strasbourg rather than in Berlin, and that the people legislate for themselves through a territorial assembly. In national politics, the autonomists associated with the National Liberal party, and openly supported Bismarck's anticlerical policies. The third and most powerful political group was the Catholic movement. Formed in response to repressive measures, the main concern of the Catholic political movement was the protection of Church interests.

The shock of annexation failed to break local political tradition. The configuration of protesters, autonomists, and Catholics merely represented old political movements under new names. The autonomists, for example, included many former Bonapartists and others who supported the French imperial regime in the 1870 plebiscite.

The radical, republican opposition of the later years of the Napoleonic empire gravitated toward the protester movement after 1871.[3] The Catholic movement reflected the continuation of heavy clerical involvement in the French parliamentary election of 1869. The old issues of empire against republic, clericalism versus liberalism, continued to color local politics long after the annexation. The position a candidate had occupied in French politics before 1871 often determined his fate in the 1874 Reichstag election. The *Elsässisches Volksblatt*, a democratic and moderately protester newspaper in Mulhouse, refused to support Ferdinand Schneegans, whose "worst offense was that he supported the Empire; he was a plebiscite man."[4] Jean Schlumberger, another autonomist leader, encountered opposition in his bid for a territorial committee seat because he was a known Bonapartist. The *Volksblatt*'s support went not to the candidates who were most outspokenly anti-German, but rather to those who had opposed the imperial regime of Napoléon III. Ernst Lauth, the Strasbourg mayor whom the Germans removed from office in 1873, received the *Volksblatt*'s support in 1874 because he had "faithfully worked to bring about the fall of the December Emperor." The choice, according to the *Volksblatt*, was between "the party of progress, which includes liberals, democrats, and radicals, and the party of reaction, whatever they may call themselves."[5] Politics, rather than pure nationalism, guided the opposition after 1871. The people objected to the new regime not simply because it was German, but because it represented a continuation of the hated French imperial system.

All of the fifteen Alsace-Lorraine Reichstag delegates elected in 1874 were either clericals or protesters.[6] Although the government ascribed its total defeat to a coalition of Catholics and protesters against the autonomists, there was no genuine alliance between the two victorious groups. The relationship between Catholics and protesters in the 1874 campaign was complementary rather than cooperative. Catholic candidates stood for election in districts where Catholic registration was high and where no protester candidate was on the ballot.[7] Each of the two camps had its own objectives; "the lay and republican party provided the negative cry of protest, while the Catholic party provided the positive element of the defense of the rights of the Church, plus organization. Protestation captured the votes, but the Catholic party was the chief beneficiary."[8] The Mulhouse industrialist Auguste Lalance claimed the French republican leader Léon Gambetta advised the protesters to make maximum use of the Catholic priests during the campaign.[9] Any cooperation which did result from Gambetta's advice occurred on a purely practical level. The intellectual bond between the Catholics and protesters was minimal. The sole aim of the protester Henri Haeffely was to protest the annexation. He deplored the raising of religious issues in the campaign, and explicitly withheld his promise to support Church interests.[10] In sharp contrast, the priest Landolin Winterer told his constituents that, "priests must appear in political assemblies because political assemblies make religious laws."[11]

The appearance of a coalition between protesters and Catholics resulted not from any common positive goals, but from the negative grounds of common opposition to the autonomists. The autonomists parted with the protesters when they accepted the annexation as a *fait accompli*; then they alienated the Catholics with anticlerical propaganda. Their common focus of opposition gave the appearance of an alliance between Catholics and protesters, and the election results reinforced that impression. Clericals, including two bishops and five priests, captured eleven Reichstag seats, while protesters won the remaining four.

Continuing repression of the Church in the Reichsland produced a semblance of unity between Catholics and protesters, but the arrival in 1879 of a governor pledged to conciliation raised the possibility that the Catholics might desert the protesters. Governor Manteuffel did indeed hope to split the Catholics from the protesters, but because he failed to recognize the deep gulf separating the upper and lower clergy in Alsace-Lorraine, his attempts to influence local politics failed. While winning the support of the two bishops, Andreas Raess and Paul Dupont des Loges, he lost the confidence of the lower clergy.[12]

Priestly obedience to the authority of the pope and bishops in the areas of faith and morals found no counterpart in political matters, where the lower clergy acted with great independence. The bishops of Strasbourg and Metz were more willing to cooperate with the Germans than was the lower clergy. Even more pro-German than the bishops were the coadjutors appointed in 1880 and 1881. Coadjutor Franz Ludwig Fleck of Metz backed the government candidate Father Jacques in the 1884 Reichstag election. The priesthood stood divided between the supporters of Coadjutor Fleck and the followers of Bishop Dupont des Loges.[13]

In Strasbourg, relations between Bishop Raess and his coadjutor, Peter Paul Stumpf, were never cordial. Stumpf received the coadjutor's post only with Governor Manteuffel's help, and promptly demonstrated his loyalty to the regime by running as the "official" candidate in the 1881 Reichstag election. Antagonism between Raess and Stumpf destroyed ecclesiastical authority in the Strasbourg diocese. Believing Stumpf to be nothing more than Manteuffel's agent, the opposition clergy led by Landolin Winterer, Igance Simonis, and Joseph Guerber buried their differences with Raess and supported him against Stumpf. Although Manteuffel claimed he wanted nothing to do with internal Church disputes, he did aid Stumpf indirectly whenever possible.[14]

Manteuffel's interference in Church affairs crippled his program of conciliation. His support of certain members of the higher clergy cost him the cooperation of other members of the upper clergy and their followers among the lower clergy. It is impossible to exonerate Manteuffel, as some have attempted, by claiming that he was unaware of the variety of political views represented by the Catholic priesthood.[15] Manteuffel's personal report to the emperor on the 1881 election emphasized the lack of political discipline among the clergy. Depicting Simonis and Winterer as the leaders of the opposition, he acknowledged Stumpf as being friendly to the regime. The governor pinpointed Raess' 1874 Reichstag speech as the source of the breakdown of Catholic political discipline; the bishop's attempt to disassociate the clergy from the annexation protest cost him the respect of the entire lower clergy.[16] Manteuffel recognized the political schism in the Catholic movement, and tried to take advantage of it by encouraging progovernment Catholic candidates.

While it is doubtful that any type of government manipulation could have produced election victories for the German regime during the 1880s, Manteuffel was a particularly inept politician. Having devoted his entire life to a military career, he admitted shortly before the 1881 campaign that he had absolutely no previous experience with elections. Inexperience, however, proved no deterrent to his involvement in the 1881 Reichstag campaign. He placed the reputation of his entire administration on the line by announcing that the outcome of the vote would determine whether or not Alsace-Lorraine was prepared for more self-government. The governor's proclamation turned the election into a plebiscite which, according to most observers, the government had no chance of winning.[17] Manteuffel used his official position to support government-backed candidates. His chief objective was to defeat the protester Jacques Kablé in Strasbourg. Failing to persuade either the Alsatian bishop of Trier, Felix Korum, or the German commissar in Strasbourg, Otto Back, to oppose Kablé, Manteuffel finally induced Coadjutor Stumpf to enter the race against the protester.

Had Manteuffel left the election to the Alsace-Lorrainers, the Catholic-protester alliance might have broken down in 1881. The Catholic newspaper *Union von Elsass-Lothringen* broke its ties with the protesters early in the campaign, retaliating against the resurrection of anticlericalism in the protester camp. Manteuffel's attempt to influence the election came as an unwelcome intrusion; the Catholic press regarded Stumpf's candidacy as an attempt to split the Catholic vote. As the campaign progressed the Catholics re-established contact with the protesters, and the *Union*, along with the Catholic *St. Odilienblatt*, eventually endorsed Kablé. Stumpf polled only 657 votes against 6,874 for Kablé. The Reichsland once again sent a solid delegation of Catholics and protesters to the Reichstag.

Learning nothing from the 1881 debacle, Manteuffel again used his official position to attempt to influence the 1884 election. His efforts focused on defeating the veterinarian Jules Antoine, elected to the Reichstag in 1882 to fill the vacancy at Metz created by the death of Paul Bezanson. A true protester, Antoine had led an Alsace-Lorraine delegation to the funeral of the French republican leader Léon Gambetta. Manteuffel's tactics against Antoine duplicated those which had failed against Kablé. Under official pressure, Etienne Jacques, editor of the Catholic newspaper *Lorraine* and a former military chaplain, agreed to challenge Antoine. As in 1881, the Catholic press and clergy generally refused to support the "official" Catholic candidate, and Antoine easily defeated Jacques.

Manteuffel's lack of success in manipulating elections failed to deter similar attempts by his successor as governor, Prince Chlodwig zu Hohenlohe-Schillingsfürst. The governor became involved in Bismarck's attempt to secure passage of a seven-year military budget. When the Reichstag rejected the *Septennat*, Bismarck called for elections to try to create a sympathetic parliamentary majority. Crucial in the construction of any parliamentary majority was the attitude of the German Center party. In an instruction to Mgr. di Pietro, the papal nuncio at Munich, the papal secretary of state,

Cardinal Jacobini, urged the Center to support the military bill. Catholic backing for the *Septennat* was to be Bismarck's reward for ending the *Kulturkampf*.[18] Ludwig Windthorst, however, refused to subordinate the independence of his Center party to the dictates of the pope, and the Center continued to oppose the *Septennat*. In Strasbourg, however, coadjutor Stumpf issued a pastoral letter asking his priests to refrain from all electoral agitation which might be "compromising" to the clergy.[19] Disregarding Stumpf's directive, Simonis strongly denounced the military bill. Stumpf countered with a declaration that Simonis' manifesto failed to conform to the instructions of the Holy Father, and warned his priests against supporting Simonis' candidacy.[20] Before the campaign ended, Hohenlohe-Schillingsfürst had injected the government into the controversy through a public letter addressed to the voters of Alsace-Lorraine. The governor warned of the need for a strong military deterrent to forestall French aggression. Alsace-Lorraine would bear the brunt of devastation in another Franco-German war. A vote for the *Septennat*, argued Hohenlohe, would be a vote for peace.[21] Papal and government pressure had no effect on the outcome of the election in the Reichsland; all of the Alsace-Lorraine Reichstag deputies elected in 1887 opposed the seven-year military bill. The immediate result was the suspension of civil rights in Alsace-Lorraine under a new wave of government repression described in Chapter 3.

Caprivi's army bill of 1892 threatened to re-create the crisis of 1887, a prospect which thoroughly frightened Hohenlohe. While Caprivi's military bill differed in details from Bismarck's, it had about the same impact on the Reichstag. To counterbalance the Franco-Russian August Convention of 1891, Caprivi proposed to increase the size of the army by expanding military conscription. To pacify the opposition, he conceded reduction of military service from three to two years, and shortening of the military bill itself from seven years' duration to five. The chancellor won support only from the Conservatives, the National Liberals, and the Poles; the Reichstag voted down the army bill, and Caprivi ordered new elections for 15 June 1893.

The 1881 and 1884 elections had destroyed Manteuffel's program, the 1887 election had nearly wrecked Hohenlohe's career, and now it was going to happen all over again. Hohenlohe could plainly read the handwriting on the wall. The Alsace-Lorraine Reichstag delegates had lined up solidly against Caprivi's bill, and

the repercussions were not long in coming. Holstein wrote Hohenlohe 9 May 1893 that an unnamed General Staff officer had suggested
Hohenlohe resign in view of his inability to keep the Reichsland
politicians in line. Holstein counseled Hohenlohe to accuse Winterer,
Simonis, and Guerber of making seditious campaign speeches, and
then expel them.[22] Hostile press reaction in Berlin forced Hohenlohe to defend himself. The ultranationalists singled out the Alsace-
Lorraine deputies in particular; *their* vote against the military bill
constituted a threat to the stability and security of the Reich, an
attempt to weaken Germany's military position against France. Why,
argued Hohenlohe, attach so much significance to the Alsace-
Lorraine deputies? The territorial administration could not control
their votes any more than the governments of the other south German states could force their deputies to vote for Caprivi's bill. The
Alsace-Lorraine clericals merely voted along with the majority of
Reichstag deputies. Did the Bavarian and other south German clericals demonstrate any greater concern for the security of the Reich?
The deputies from Alsace-Lorraine, reasoned Hohenlohe, were no
worse than the other enemies of the Reich on the east bank of the
Rhine.[23]

Hohenlohe had no doubt made a telling debating point, but he
perceived the basic truth in the dictum attributed to Bismarck: "Not
through speeches and majority decisions are the great questions of
the day decided—that was the great mistake of 1848 and 1849—
but through iron and blood." The governor recognized his real
enemy, the generals surrounding Wilhelm II. He had barely saved
himself in the aftermath of the 1887 election; he was determined not
to repeat the experience in 1893. Hohenlohe devised a seemingly
radical, but from his point of view a most realistic, plan. He proposed to suspend the 1893 election in Alsace-Lorraine. What better
way to avoid anti-German agitation, what better way to satisfy the
generals? After all, the ultranationalists themselves had originally
proposed depriving the Alsace-Lorrainers of their Reichstag representation after the 1887 election.

Hohenlohe unfortunately failed to understand that a perfectly
good plan proposed by ultranationalist militarists immediately became unacceptable when proposed by the governor of Alsace-
Lorraine. When he went to Berlin to defend his plan, Hohenlohe
met nothing but icy silence. His interview with the kaiser went badly.
Describing it in his diary, Hohenlohe wrote, "He said nothing about

my proposal . . . On taking leave I asked him if he had read my report, and he said, 'I shall consult with the Imperial Chancellor on the matter.' " Hohenlohe had already seen Caprivi, who "had great scruples of a political nature." After eight days of discussions with cabinet officers and imperial legal experts, a dejected Hohenlohe confided to his diary that, "The authorities will have nothing to do with my proposal. Lucanus [Chief of the Civil Cabinet Hermann von Lucanus] spoke very disapprovingly. Caprivi fears that a little stratagem of this sort would make a bad impression on the Center and the Liberals, and thus spoil the election, while reasonable, sober-minded persons believe it would make the best possible impression."[24]

Caprivi's position was indeed difficult, and it would be unjust to minimize the political dilemma he faced. Another parliamentary defeat might finish his career; he had already lost the Zedlitz-Trützschler school bill before the Reichstag defeated the 1892 army bill. The chancellor clearly had to avoid any action which would alienate potential support. The question was to determine from which quarters he was most likely to receive support. The bewildering complexity of Caprivi's situation comes through clearly in J. Alden Nichols' *Germany After Bismarck*. The Center remained on the fence; a *coup* against the clerical deputies from Alsace-Lorraine would have forced the German Center to vote against the government. On the other hand, a *coup* in Alsace-Lorraine might bring Caprivi widespread gains among arch conservatives who would support the army bill. But the Conservative agrarians, alienated by Caprivi's tariff policy, were at the moment the chancellor's worst enemies and not likely to rally to his support. Caprivi could conceivably push through his army bill and then be overthrown by conservative opposition. Agrarian discontent was compounded by the opposition of many generals who disliked the provision for two-year military service.[25]

Caprivi managed to piece together a shaky coalition after the 1893 election, and guided his army bill through the Reichstag by a sixteen-vote margin. The mainstays of the clerical opposition in Alsace-Lorraine, Winterer, Guerber, and Simonis, won reelection, but Hohenlohe's fear of wild antigovernment agitation failed to materialize. Lorraine's four districts returned Catholic priests, but voters in Alsace gave the government some reason for optimism. Johannes Hoeffel, an adherent of the *Deutsche Reichspartei* first elected in the Zabern district in 1890, won reelection, as did Baron Hugo Zorn von Bulach (younger), the progovernment Alsatian whose loyalty won him the post of undersecretary for agriculture in 1895. In a hotly contested race in Schlettstadt, the county director, Otto Pöhlmann, a Conservative, won a disputed victory; three years later his election was invalidated and he lost his seat in a by-election to a clerical, Ignaz Spies. The administration's most stunning achievement, however, was the election of Hohenlohe's son Prince Alexander in Hagenau.

Alexander was in Russia as the election campaign began. His father asked him to return to help elect progovernment candidates, but before he could reach Alsace-Lorraine, he learned that "liberal anticlerical elements" had nominated him for the Reichstag. Alexander bound himself to no particular platform, but it was understood that he was the liberal, anticlerical candidate. Although he was a Catholic (a "liberal" Catholic), he received wide support from Protestant farmers as well as Jews. Alexander did no campaigning himself, leaving the actual electioneering to the county director of Wissembourg, Julius Sengenwald, an Alsatian who had married a Berliner. His margin of victory on the first ballot was quite comfortable, 13,699 to 5,449 for the clerical candidate.[26]

The administration did receive some disquieting news in 1893. Emil Petri, the Alsatian National Liberal who later headed the department of religion in 1899, lost his Strasbourg Reichstag seat to the Social Democrat August Bebel, and Jean Ruhland, also a National Liberal, lost to the independent Jacques Preiss in Colmar. Another Social Democrat, Ferdinand Bueb, won a seat in Mulhouse. While the socialist victories posed a threat to the government, they portended even more trouble for the clericals. On one issue, the government and the Social Democrats could agree; they both hated the clericals. When the socialist candidates in 1893 used Coadjutor Stumpf's support for the *Septennat* in 1887 as proof that the clericals were tools of the government, they grossly misrepresented the clerical position, for Stumpf certainly was not a typical political Catholic in Alsace-Lorraine.

In 1893 the battle lines between political Catholicism and social democracy began to form clearly. Attempts by Manteuffel and Hohenlohe to exploit the Catholic vote had failed. The Catholics, of course, invited exploitation by their inability to establish a disciplined party. A strong, united Catholic party would have discouraged Stumpf's attempt to split the movement in 1881 and 1887.[27]

Although the weakness of the Catholic political movement was obvious, government interference had failed to impel the Catholics to establish a tighter organization. Only when social democracy gained a strong foothold in Alsace-Lorraine after 1890 did the Catholics feel the need for a political machine capable of meeting the socialist threat.

Catholics held the government responsible for socialist gains in the Reichsland. They claimed that while the government had blindly persecuted the Church during the *Kulturkampf*, the socialists had quietly put down roots in Alsace-Lorraine.[28] The truth of this accusation against the government is doubtful. Until 1890 German antisocialist laws made socialist agitation difficult; when the antisocialist laws were dropped in 1890, the government continued to suppress the socialist movement in the Reichsland under the "dictatorship paragraph" or by appealing to old French antisocialist legislation which remained valid in Alsace-Lorraine.

Although Social Democrats were active in local politics as early as the 1874 Reichstag election, they had little success until 1890. Lacking native leaders, the socialists were forced to nominate Germans in 1874. A group of Strasbourg workers nominated August Bebel, while a faction in Mulhouse espoused Karl Liebknecht's candidacy. Although Bebel and Liebknecht had received prison sentences for their opposition to the annexation, their outspoken support of the local cause failed to win them many votes. Liebknecht received 388 votes, and Bebel polled only 168. Social democracy found little support in Alsace-Lorraine because it was a foreign product. The Social Democratic party was a German party, and Bebel and Liebknecht were Germans. Workers in the Dollfus-Mieg textile plant in Mulhouse refused to vote for a German, contending it was the duty of Germans, not Alsace-Lorrainers, to deliver Liebknecht from prison and elect him to the Reichstag.[29] The Social Democrats flourished only after 1890, when they were able to produce local candidates. Until that time, socialist activity in the Reichsland remained minimal. The 1876 German Social Democratic party congress debated ways of enhancing socialist strength in the Reichsland. Pointing to the illegality of the annexation, a visiting delegation of French socialists argued that the German Social Democratic party had no right to send agents into the territory. Settlement of the jurisdictional dispute came when both sides recognized that Alsace-Lorraine promised few rewards for either French or German socialists. The congress decided to discontinue formal operations in the Reichsland. If local Social Democrats wished to nominate their own candidates, the national SPD would support them; but the national party would exert no pressure of local socialists to campaign for public office.[30] The virtual abandonment of Alsace-Lorraine by the national SPD proved to be a fateful decision. During the critical years on the eve of World War I, when socialist unity was most needed, the feeling of kinship between the local Social Democrats and the SPD was lacking.

In the 1893 Reichstag election the Social Democrats made their first substantial gains in Alsace-Lorraine. Strasbourg returned August Bebel, and Mulhouse elected Ferdinand Bueb. Traditional explanations attribute these socialist victories to the dropping of the antisocialist laws in 1890, and outright support lent to the socialist movement by Governor Hohenlohe-Schillingsfürst, who allegedly viewed the socialists as a counterweight to the clericals and pro-French bourgeoisie.[31] Neither of these explanations is satisfactory. The territorial government found other means of repressing socialist agitation after the imperial antisocialist laws expired in 1890, and the charge of coddling socialists lodged against the governor has not been substantiated. Socialist victories reflected profound changes in the local political situation which traditional analyses have failed to recognize. The territorial Social Democratic movement no longer suffered because it was "German"; Bebel's socialist ideas were now considered more significant than his German nationality. The continuing immigration of Germans undoubtedly aided Bebel's cause in the Reichsland, but his victory should not obscure the essential fact that the Social Democrats were able to nominate an Alsace-Lorrainer in each of the fifteen constituencies.

The emergence of territorial leadership immensely strengthened the popular appeal of the socialist movement. With the development of new leaders came a new set of issues which captured the popular interest. For the new generation of political leaders, simple protest of the annexation did not constitute a real program. Nor was it merely a case of electing men who promised to represent territorial interests in the Reichstag, for until 1893 those interests had been defined by priests and industrialists. The socialist vote was not just another form of protest vote; it reflected the exclusion of the working class from the fruits of capitalist prosperity.

The spirit of protest had been replaced by a new set of political and economic issues by 1893. As the problem of achieving social and economic justice became the key political issue, even clerical politicians felt compelled to drop the religious issue in favor of social reform and taxation policy. The very survival of political Catholicism was at stake; it all depended on whether the Catholics really had anything to offer the working class. Catholic social and economic doctrine in the Reichsland borrowed heavily from the ideas of the German Bishop Emanuel von Ketteler and the guidelines of Pope Leo XIII's encyclical, *Rerum Novarum*. Claiming that God ordained the system of private property, the clericals conceded that justice toward others and love for one's neighbor should characterize the use of private property. Priests such as Landolin Winterer admitted that some property owners failed to live up to their social responsibilities, and that society had been slow to recognize the undesirable effects of rapid industrialization. Emphasizing as it did the greatest production at the lowest unit cost, the capitalist system had neglected the welfare of the working people. While social problems created by industrialization had to be solved, and just complaints had to be dealt with, the capitalistic order established by God must not be destroyed in the process of reform.[32]

Priests such as Cetty believed only the Church could provide the leadership necessary for reform, although Cetty himself rejected the dream of some clericals for a total resurrection of the Middle Ages. The medieval Church with its vast territories and enormous political power was inappropriate for an age facing new problems requiring new remedies. Basic to the clerical solution of the social problem was the development of a corporative system forming a moral bond between the owners and the workers. Modern industrial capitalism would give way to a system of Christian workers' unions (*Christliche Arbeitervereine*), closely resembling medieval guilds. Based on the rather questionable premise of identity of interests between workers and owners, the corporations would join both parties of their own free will, and would operate under the Christian principles of charity and love. The expansion of big capitalist industry (the priest Victor Guerber referred to it as the *Judenindustrie*) must end.[33] Reduction in the size of the great factories would permit a new balance between the factory system, handicrafts, and agriculture. Modern industry, merely the creation of man, must bow before the system of handicrafts and agriculture ordained by God.[34]

Modern large-scale capitalistic industry had destroyed the old

corporate society based on the "Christian handicrafts," and had
contributed greatly to the moral decline reflected in the growth of
socialism. Jewish industrialists were forcing artisans out of business,
and it was these displaced artisans, claimed the clericals, who became converts to socialism. Society was disintegrating into two
camps; the small group of millionaire industrialists, and the poverty-
stricken proletariat. In the process, the middle class, "the solid
foundation of human society," was being destroyed.[35] Concern for
the *Mittelstand* was by no means confined to the clericals. Heinrich
Meyer, director of both the Territorial Commercial Bank and the
Alsace-Lorraine Association of Factory Inspectors' Unions, claimed
that the *Mittelstand* formed the backbone of German society, and
warned that its destruction prevented the economic rehabilitation
which could assure integration of Alsace-Lorraine into the Reich.[36]

No less hard-hit by industrialization was the working-class family.
The priest Heinrich Cetty complained that the moral level of
working-class society had declined in direct proportion to the rate
of economic "progress." The evidence for moral decline was every-
where; rising alcoholism, concubinage, illegitimate births, rising rate
of stillbirths, vice, gross language, lack of respect for women, and a
generally cynical attitude, all pointed to a crisis of the spirit. "The
language of materialism," warned Cetty, "has been carried into the
sacred domain of the family." At the root of the evil Cetty detected
the modern system of economic liberalism, that "economic science
which . . . proclaimed its independence from religious as well as
political society and established the liberal industrial regime." Under
the liberal approach, problems of the production and distribution
of wealth have been resolved by the application of natural laws in
the name of individual liberty. The result has been the creation of
glaring inequalities in the condition of men, and the socialists have
been the ultimate beneficiaries.[37]

Catholic politicians gave only limited support to social legislation
in Alsace-Lorraine. The priest Emile Wetterlé was far ahead of most
of his colleagues when he advocated extension of insurance benefits
to the elderly and orphans in 1898.[38] The clericals feared state
socialism would reduce the Church's influence over the masses by
shifting responsibility for the poor to the state.[39] The state's only
legitimate role consisted of negative action against the enemies of
Catholicism. Socialist demonstrations should be banned, taverns,
regarded as "schools for socialists," should be closed down, restric-

tions should be placed on the foreign and local press, "which has become in large measure an instrument of perversion and corruption," and libraries which served as "veritable sinks of corruption" should be outlawed. The Germans had introduced a particularly dangerous new kind of publication, the pagan classics.[40] The workers, argued the clericals, needed no help from the state; all they required was the freedom to form their own unions and negotiate their grievances with the factory owners.[41] Catholic advocacy of freedom of association carried the risk that the workers would form socialist unions. The Catholics were prepared to form their own unions to combat the socialists. In Mulhouse the clericals founded the *Christliche Textilarbeiterverband* to counter the socialist *Elsass-Lothringischen Textilarbeiterverband* formed in 1897. Admitting that their program was moderate, the clericals warned that the "all or nothing" platform of the Social Democrats would indeed achieve nothing.[42]

In his work on the social condition of the Mulhouse textile workers, Anton Krieger has charged the clericals with deliberate neglect in forming Christian unions. He accused the priest and Reichstag deputy Landolin Winterer of collaborating with factory owners such as Jean Schlumberger to thwart the establishment of any workers' organizations. Krieger attributed Winterer's electoral defeat in 1903 (he had held the seat from Altkirch since 1874) to Catholic workers who established their independent Catholic electoral committee and nominated the successful candidate, Eugen Ricklin, a Catholic physician. Membership in Alsace-Lorraine's Christian unions reflected the alleged lack of proper support from the clergy, who did not care for the idea of organized labor.[43] Krieger uses the fact that membership in Christian textile unions in Mulhouse dropped from 1,500 in 1906 to 1,100 in 1911 to demonstrate the clergy's lack of support for unionization. While the clergy may indeed have been cool toward organized labor, these figures alone fail to prove that contention. As Laufenburger and Pflimlin have shown, the free unions experienced the same fluctuation in membership, an indication that the nonsocialist unions were suffering from a combination of government interference, socialist competition, conflicts between Alsatian and immigrant German workers, and the large number of women in the textile industry who generally stayed out of the unions.[44]

Raw statistics fail to reveal the problems encountered by all unions, including socialist, Christian, and free organizations, in recruiting members in Alsace-Lorraine. The government used the antisocialist laws, and after 1890 the dictatorship paragraph, to suppress organized labor. Between November 1898 and December 1899, police intervened sixty times against free unions alone in Alsace; socialist organizations were tolerated only in Strasbourg and Mulhouse. The unions imposed restrictions on themselves which tended to limit membership. The socialist *Elsass-Lothringischen Textilarbeiterverband* at first admitted only men over age twenty-one, even though women and children comprised a large proportion of the textile industry labor force.[45] When the Mulhouse branch of the German Textile Union opened in 1900, the district president ruled that membership must be confined to men and women age eighteen or over. The Christian textile workers challenged this ruling in 1902, when they admitted sixteen-year-olds. Partly as a result of labor union problems, the government introduced the imperial law on associations into Alsace-Lorraine in 1905. As the government interpreted this law, the unions constituted *sozialpolitische Vereine*, and as such could admit no one under twenty-one.[46]

Alsace-Lorraine's Protestant minority demonstrated the same reticence in attacking social problems as did the Catholic majority. The treatment of the Protestant approach to the social question in Otto Michaelis' history of the Alsace-Lorraine Evangelical Church is both forthright and honest.[47] Michaelis recognized that socialism, with its alleged leaning toward atheism and materialism, threatened the spirituality of both Protestantism and Catholicism. Why, then, did the Protestants and Catholics fail to unite against the common enemy? Michaelis has found a number of reasons, ranging from failure to recognize the danger of socialism until it was too late, to outright lack of concern for working-class welfare. The German *Völkstum* felt smugly secure, refusing to recognize the ultimate significance of the materialistic movement. The Protestant church, tied as it was to the propertied classes and the state, demonstrated little concern for urban social problems. Factory owners, small businessmen, and farmers held very strong influence over the church, and the antireligious agitation of the Social Democrats reduced the church's interest in the workers' legitimate complaints. Only a few within the Protestant church understood the importance of winning the working class away from social democracy. When toward the end of the German regime the Social Democratic party had become so strong that no one could ignore it, both the church and the state finally showed some interest in welfare reform. The high rate of stillbirths in working-class quarters, and the increasing incidence of alcoholism finally did stir the Protestant church into very limited action. The Strasbourg Pastoral Conference, however, was sixty-four years old before it finally heard an authoritative report on alcoholism in 1898. Only two years previously, when Pastor Dietz of Mundolsheim had attempted to secure the concensus of the Conference for a resolution asking the imperial chancellor to establish a state liquor monopoly as a means of controlling alcoholism, the Conference reminded the good pastor that churchmen did not meddle in political questions.[48] The Catholic priests had never held such a naive view. The Protestants, however, could fall back on one argument which did not apply to the Catholics; as a minority group in the Reichsland, the Protestants could hardly expect to solve social problems on their own. Michaelis goes so far as to argue that the introduction of universal, direct, equal suffrage for the *Landtag* in 1911 silenced the Protestants in politics, left the Catholics free to legislate as they pleased, and increased the bishops' influence in politics.[49]

By 1893, the political focus in Alsace-Lorraine centered on the struggle between political Catholicism and social democracy. The liberal parties, observed the Social Democratic *Elsass-Lothringische Volkszeitung*, were dead. The "middle" parties had been pushed aside by the progressive SPD and the reactionary clerical party.[50] As the socialist movement gained momentum, controversy over the question of party organization intensified within the clerical movement. In an 1878 memorandum titled, *Ce qu'il est urgent de faire*, a Father Guthlin felt it unnecessary to establish a formal Catholic party, since God, the Church, and the bishops already provided ample political leadership.[51] The 1890s witnessed the coming of age of a new generation of priests, attended by the inevitable conflict between the younger generation and the old. The older generation remained unconvinced of the need for organized political action, since the Catholics had always done well at the polls without benefit of party organization. They hesitated to risk another *Kulturkampf* by alarming German authorities with organized political action. Younger priests led by Nicholas Delsor, Emile Wetterlé, and Charles

Sipp, out of sympathy with the doubts of their elders, took control
of the *Revue Catholique d'Alsace* and voiced their demand for
Catholic organization.

Organization did not necessarily mean formation of a true political
party. In 1890 Ludwig Windthorst, the German Center party leader,
had founded a *Volksverein*, a Catholic popular association encom-
passing all social classes. Catholics in Strasbourg established a
similar organization in 1892. Continuing Social Democratic electoral
advances forced the Catholic leadership to consider more effective
political action. Some believed joining the German Center party was
preferable to creating an independent Catholic party in the Reichsland. Relations between the Alsace-Lorraine Catholic Reichstag
deputies and the Center party deputies had never been close. Identi-
fying the Alsace-Lorraine Catholics with the protesters, the Center
deputies feared recriminations from Bismarck if they consorted with
"anti-German" forces in the Reichsland. The Alsace-Lorraine
Catholics, on the other hand, feared their local interests would be
ignored if they subordinated themselves to Center party discipline.[52]
One final consideration may have prejudiced the Alsace-Lorraine
Catholics against joining the German Center party. Prince Alexander
zu Hohenlohe-Schillingsfürst had accused Ernst Matthias von Köller,
Alsace-Lorraine undersecretary of state for the interior from 1889
to 1894, then secretary of state between 1901 and 1908, of attempting to "use Beelzebub to drive out the Devil; that is, attempting
to persuade the Alsatian Catholics to unite with the German Center
party in a joint effort against the socialists."[53] Köller was making one
more attempt in the Manteuffel-Hohenlohe tradition to manipulate
the Catholics for the benefit of the government. While the Catholics,
on their part, certainly had no objection to fighting the socialists,
they did not want to be tools of the government.

As the Center improved its relationship with Bismarck and gained
more influence over the chancellor's legislative program after 1879,
pressure on the Alsace-Lorraine Catholics to join the Center
mounted. The larger the membership of the Center, the more seats
it would hold on Reichstag committees. A group led by Emile Wetterlé, claiming that Center leaders Count Georg von Hertling, Ernst
Lieber, and Martin Spahn had become "government men" and supporters of German imperialism, resisted merger with the Center.
Although the details of the friction between the Alsace-Lorraine
Catholics and the German Center party remain obscure, the op-

ponents of merger clearly prevailed. According to one account, the Alsace-Lorraine Catholic Reichstag deputies became *Hospitants* of the German Center party; they became party members, but reserved their independence on certain local questions which were agreed to in advance. A subsequent Center demand that the reservations be dropped was rejected. Center promises of support for Alsatian autonomy failed to lure the Catholics into the party, whereupon the Center threatened to oppose Alsatian demands for equal status with other German states, and ran four of its own candidates against Alsatian clericals in the 1903 Reichstag election.[54]

Alsatian Catholics who favored closer ties with the German Center recognized the need to create a unified Alsace-Lorraine Catholic party prior to unification with the Center. In 1893 the Catholic priest Dr. Paul Muller-Simonis established the *Katholische Volkspartei*, whose influence hardly extended beyond the Strasbourg area. The party was expanded in 1897 and renamed the *Elsass-Lothringische Landespartei*. The Catholic *Landespartei* made its most profound impact in the urban areas, but due to financial difficulty and political splits it barely functioned in Lorraine. Lorraine's Catholics posed a particular problem in any plan for Catholic unity and association with the German Center. They resisted attempts to enroll them in a German Catholic party, and rejected just as vigorously any attempt to integrate them into an Alsatian Catholic party. On no other issue are the political differences between Alsace and Lorraine so clear. The conservative Lorrainers cared little for the Alsatian radical-democratic-protester-clericals. The Alsatian clericals were always talking about Alsatian culture, Alsatian particularism; but what about Lorraine? On a more personal level, the Lorraine clericals resented the personal domination of strong Alsatian personalities such as Winterer, Guerber, Simonis, and Delsor. In a unified territorial Catholic party, the Alsatians would run the show.[55]

To supplement the *Landespartei*, Catholics in major cities formed *Zentrumsvereine*, which gradually superseded the *Landespartei*. In 1906 the Catholics used the *Zentrumsvereine* as the basis for establishing the *Elsass-Lothringische Zentrum*.[56] But even now, the Lorraine Catholics remained aloof. In 1902 they had formed their own *Bloc Lorraine*, and ran their own candidates in Reichstag and territorial elections. After the 1907 Reichstag election, four Catholic deputies from Alsace-Lorraine, led by Dr. Leo Vonderscheer, joined

the German Center party, but the Alsace-Lorraine Center as a whole
remained independent of the German Center.[57] The continuing
failure of the Catholics to establish a close relationship with the
German Center party produced serious consequences when the
Reichstag considered the new Alsace-Lorraine constitution of 1911.
The German Center refused to support liberal amendments proposed
by Catholic deputies from Alsace-Lorraine. In retaliation, the
Alsace-Lorraine Center vowed never to join the German Center,
and declared its support for a new "national party" in Alsace-
Lorraine whose sole aim would be to protect local interests.[58]

Establishment of the Alsace-Lorraine Center in 1906 resulted
from a combination of internal pressure from within the Catholic
movement itself, and external pressure from the rising power of the
social democratic movement. Like the Catholics, the Social Democrats admitted the need for strict discipline and organization with
great reluctance. Under prodding from men like Bernhard Bohle, a
prominent socialist Reichstag deputy who warned of the threat posed
by Catholic political organization, the socialists established the
Sozialdemokratische Partei Elsass-Lothringen in May 1905. The
new socialist party controlled three newspapers, the Strasbourg
Freie Presse, the *Mulhauser Zeitung,* and the St. John *Saarwacht.*
Hoping to preserve their competitive positions, democrats led by
Daniel Blumenthal and Jacques Preiss formed the *Elsass-Lothringen
Volkspartei* in 1897, and liberal supporters of the German National
Liberal party organized the *Liberale Landespartei von Elsass-
Lothringen.* Dissatisfied with the *Volkspartei's* anticlerical tendencies, Preiss soon left the ranks to form an alliance with the clericals
under the leadership of Emile Wetterlé. Organization in the liberal
camp was no stronger than it was in the democratic group. Only
after their survival was threatened in the 1903 Reichstag election
did the liberals establish their *Liberale Landespartei,* and not until
1906 did the liberal party create such vital apparatus as a party
secretariat.

The so-called middle parties never fared well in the Reichsland.
The more conservative liberals often refused electoral alliances
with the less conservative democrats. Native-born liberals refused
to cooperate with the German merchants, artisans, and bureaucrats
who comprised the major share of liberal party membership. Wilhelm Kapp attempted to solve the latter problem in 1909 with the
founding of the *Elsass-Lothringische Vereinigung,* a nonpolitical

organization dedicated to the task of reducing tension between the Germans and natives who wished to see their territory develop within the framework of the German Reich.

By 1910, just prior to the introduction of a new "constitution" in Alsace-Lorraine, the political contest in the Reichsland had narrowed to a struggle between political Catholicism and social democracy. Reichstag election results indicated a steady growth of Social Democratic support from 19,157 votes in 1890 to 81,589 and two seats in 1907. Between the 1907 and 1912 Reichstag elections, the Social Democratic growth rate gained remarkable momentum. With 31.7 percent (102,500 votes and four seats) of the vote in the 1912 election, the Social Democrats were closing the gap with the Alsace-Lorraine Center, which now held thirty-four percent of the vote. The liberals and democrats, capturing only 19.5 percent of the ballots, formed a significant but hopelessly outnumbered bloc. Until the 1907 election, the Catholics remained uncertain whether their prime target should be the Social Democrats or the anticlerical liberal-democrats. With the clericals warning the voters against casting their ballots for a liberal, Bernhard Böhle became the socialist deputy for Strasbourg in 1907 with local Center support on the run-off ballot. This Catholic-socialist alliance quickly collapsed in the wake of charges that "the red flag now flew atop the Strasbourg cathedral."[59]

Socialist gains became manifest on a smaller scale in the territorial elections as well as the Reichstag contests. Only one socialist, Joseph Emmel of Mulhouse, ever won a seat in the territorial committee; he was elected by the Mulhouse municipal council, which before the 1908 municipal elections included fourteen socialists. In 1909, six of the ninety-three members of the three general councils in Upper Alsace, Lower Alsace, and Lorraine were socialists, with three each in the two Alsatian districts and none in Lorraine. The *Bloc Lorraine* performed very effectively against the socialists, even in the Reichstag elections. The only socialist ever elected to the Reichstag from Lorraine during the entire German regime was Georges Weill, elected in Metz in 1912. Territorial elections, however, provided a very imperfect representation of socialist strength in the Reichsland, because the government made efforts to reduce socialist representation by manipulating and gerrymandering election districts. The 1908 municipal elections showed how successful the government was. In 1902 Strasbourg elected sixteen Social Democrats to the council with 6,450 votes; in 1908 the socialists polled 8,545 votes but won no seats. The Social Democrats also lost their fourteen seats on the Mulhouse council, as well as their places in Colmar. Social Democrats after 1908 held only seventy-eight municipal council seats in twenty-five of the territory's 1,705 communes.[60]

In assessing the success of German attempts to integrate Alsace-Lorraine into the empire, the history of political Catholicism and social democracy assumes critical importance. Resistance to integration cannot be ascribed solely to obtuse Prussian bureaucrats and repression from Berlin. The two major parties in the Reichsland, the Alsace-Lorraine Center and the Social Democrats, never achieved a close working relationship with their counterparts in Germany. Mutual suspicion among the local parties, and between the local parties and the national German parties constituted a factor detrimental to integration over which the government had little control. There was one problem, however, over which the government held absolute veto power, and that was the granting of real self-government to the Reichsland on a basis of equality with the other federal German states. By 1911 Alsace-Lorraine hovered on the brink of political maturity. The Reichsland had become politicized to a large extent. Out of a very amorphous political configuration in 1871 there had emerged true political parties differentiated by a new set of political, social, and economic issues. If this process of political maturation were to achieve its final consumation, the government in Berlin would have to grant the territory greater control over its own destiny. For reasons of his own, the imperial chancellor, Theobald von Bethmann Hollweg, arrived at the same conclusion, and with great difficulty Alsace-Lorraine won a new "constitution" in 1911.

7
CONSTITUTION-MAKING IN 1911

Only if Alsace-Lorraine were granted self-government could the development of Catholic, Social Democratic, democratic, and liberal parties proceed to its logical conclusion of thorough politicization. In view of the repression following the 1887 *Septennat* election, prospects for liberalization appeared bleak during the regime of Governor Prince Chlodwig zu Hohenlohe-Schillingsfürst (1885–94). Upon Hohenlohe's elevation to the chancellorship in 1894, his successor, Prince Hermann zu Hohenlohe-Langenburg (1894–1907), abandoned most of his functions to his secretary of state, Max von Puttkamer, a holdover from the previous administration who continued the program of repression. Only with the replacement of Puttkamer with Ernst Matthias von Köller in 1902 did the outlook for constitutional reform brighten.

As high president in Schleswig-Holstein and Prussian minister of the interior, Köller developed a reputation as a tough Prussian bureaucrat. But during his tenure as secretary of state in Alsace-Lorraine, several important reforms such as the repeal of the dictatorship paragraph and establishment of a Catholic theological faculty at the Strasbourg university, both in 1902, paved the way for the resumption of political development. Personnel changes reflected the government's willingness to permit more self-administration— the governor appointed two Alsatians to his cabinet. Baron Hugo Zorn von Bulach received the post of undersecretary for agriculture in 1895, and Emil Petri, a Protestant, became undersecretary for religion and justice in 1898.

Repeal of the dictatorship paragraph opened the way to the de-

velopment of modern political parties in Alsace-Lorraine. The 1903
and 1907 Reichstag elections produced contests livelier than any
since the 1887 *Septennat* election. Although their ideologies differed,
the new parties were capable of forming alliances, especially when
the government tried to influence the elections. In 1903 liberals and
clericals combined against Social Democratic and democratic candidates, while Social Democrats and democrats joined forces to prevent the election of liberal and clerical candidates.[1] During the 1907
campaign, the Catholic *Mülhauser Arbeiterfreund* published Chancellor Bernhard von Bülow's letter to the *Reichsverband gegen die
Sozialdemokratie*. Here Bülow expressed the hope that the Right,
the National Liberals, and the *Freisinnigen* would gain enough
ground to give the government a majority against the Center and
Social Democrats.[2] Bülow's tactics backfired in the Reichsland,
where he only provoked a surprising unnatural alliance between the
clericals and socialists. The liberals and democrats, bitter opponents
in 1903, now found themselves joined in the embarrassing position
of supporting the government.

The 1907 election demonstrated the weakness of the liberal-
democratic movement in the Reichsland. The antigovernment
parties, including the clericals, Social Democrats, and independent
Lorraine Bloc, swept to victory. Although they received 17.2 percent
of the vote, the liberal-democratic candidates won no seats.[3] While
the Social Democrats made substantial gains on the clericals between
1907 and 1912, the liberal-democratic parties increased their share
of the popular vote by only two percent during the same period.
The annexation unfortunately introduced the element of nationalism
into the local liberal movement. The resulting split between followers
of the German National Liberals on the one hand, and those who
took a more democratic line on the other, condemned the local
liberal movement to perpetual impotence during the German
regime.

While the new parties contested Reichstag elections vigorously,
they seldom showed much interest in local elections for the county
councils, district councils, and the territorial committee. The law
prohibited the district and county councils from discussing "political" matters, and members of these councils were required to take
an oath of allegiance to the emperor. Men willing to take such an
oath were regarded as opportunists willing to compromise local interests. The territorial committee, composed of members elected

from the three district councils, suffered from the same deficiency. When the constitution of 1879 gave the reconstructed territorial committee wider powers, including the right of initiative, protesters who had previously refused to participate in local politics were forced to reconsider their position. The new protester program, personified in Jacques Kablé, was one of "protest and action." While continuing to repudiate the annexation, the protesters would engage in local politics when the interests of Alsace-Lorraine were at stake. The composition of the territorial committee reflected the modified protester position during the 1879–80 session, when five opposition deputies took seats. Even Jules Antoine, notorious for his anti-German views, took the oath to the emperor and served in the territorial assembly. The government looked unfavorably upon this development in the protester movement, and used extreme forms of pressure in local elections. Antoine was eventually arrested and charged with treason.[4]

When Alsace-Lorraine received greater self-government under the new constitution of 1911, local elections assumed added importance. The development of political parties inevitably produced the desire for a territorial parliament through which the parties could direct local affairs. The territorial committee, with its limited powers and indirect method of election, failed to meet the needs of modern political parties. Few people in Alsace-Lorraine had accepted the constitution of 1879 as the final word; the Federal Council and emperor still held ultimate control over the territory, and the emperor appointed the higher administrative officials. On 17 December 1910, the German government introduced two bills in the Reichstag, one proposing a new constitution for Alsace-Lorraine, the other outlining procedures for electing the lower chamber of an Alsace-Lorraine *Landtag*. The government's sudden desire for reform in the Reichsland was rooted in general political developments in the empire.

German politics in 1910 witnessed mounting demands for an end to the emperor's "personal rule," coupled with parliamentary responsibility for government ministers, democratic control of foreign policy, abolition of the Prussian three-class voting system, and self-government for Alsace-Lorraine. Although the liberals alone could not muster a parliamentary majority for such reforms, they received strong reinforcement from the burgeoning Social Democratic movement. The "Bülow bloc" formed during the 1907 Reichstag campaign held the Center and SPD in check for a time. When Conservatives, joined by members of the Center, defeated an inheritance tax bill in June 1909, the bloc dissolved and Bülow resigned the chancellorship. His successor, Theobald von Bethmann Hollweg, found that political anarchy had replaced bloc politics. When the SPD emerged from the 1912 election as the strongest party in the Reichstag, Bethmann Hollweg recognized that a stable order could be constructed only if the Social Democrats were recognized as legitimate members of the German community. To continue the government's antisocialist policy was impractical. "The adaptation of the labor movement to the existing order of society," wrote the chancellor, "was the most important task of our time." Conflict with the Social Democrats was incompatible with the pursuit of a conservative and constructive program.[5]

A government genuinely seeking to integrate the socialist movement into German society had to grant some concessions to the demands for constitutional reform and public control over public affairs. Impelled by a combination of public pressure and personal predilection, Bethmann Hollweg obtained improvements in the industrial code, and won passage of an imperial insurance code in 1911. As Prussian minister-president, he tried unsuccessfully to enact a Prussian electoral reform bill. In the matter of constitutional reform for Alsace-Lorraine, however, the chancellor scored a significant victory. From a purely political viewpoint, leaving aside military considerations, the Reichsland was the ideal place for the government to make concessions; it was the one part of the Reich where constitutional reform would alter neither the basic structure of the empire nor that of any of the German states.

Although few high German officials regarded the Alsace-Lorraine administration as satisfactory, even fewer advocated reform. Even among those who might have been willing to consider reform, the Reichsland's position on the list of political priorities was rather low. When, for example, Hohenlohe mentioned to Caprivi the possibility of granting Alsace-Lorraine votes in the Federal Council, the chancellor expressed his willingness to consider the matter, but added, "Not just yet; let's wait until the Reichstag debates [on the military bill] are finished."[6] Caprivi already had enough trouble on his hands with the military's coolness toward his army bill; proposing concessions for Alsace-Lorraine at this time would only raise the level of conservative hostility.

When, asked the people of Alsace-Lorraine, would the time be "ripe" for reform? Only when the people of Alsace-Lorraine had met a list of conditions set down by the government. The nature of the conditions was left rather vague, probably deliberately, so that the government could always claim they had not been met. Chancellor von Bülow indicated how the government would respond to a specific demand for reform when in 1903 the territorial committee proposed a very modest program which the Abbé Emile Wetterlé, a clerical Reichstag deputy, labeled as merely an "installment payment."[7] In Strasbourg the secretary of state, Ernst von Köller, agreed to lay the proposals before the imperial chancellor. Bülow, however, approached the reform proposals like a man walking on eggs. "I want to examine whether this is the right moment to attempt anything," said the chancellor. "There are certain political and constitutional questions which require further investigation . . . I am not sure of the appropriateness of the measure . . . and it is not certain whether the measure really expresses the wishes of the people of Alsace-Lorraine." In his touching concern for the wishes of the people of Alsace-Lorraine, Bülow managed not to lose sight of the real issues. Constitutional development in the Reichsland must be compatible with the security and integrity of the Reich, and must promote Germany's diplomatic aims on the Continent. Additionally, reform must strengthen, rather than weaken, the ties between Reichsland and Reich. Such were the government's conditions for any change in the Alsace-Lorraine constitution.[8]

While Secretary of State Köller went along with the moderate reform proposals of 1903, in 1907 he warned that the government would not discuss any proposal to remove the kaiser from his commanding position in territorial affairs, and intimated he might resign rather than approve a resolution recommending universal suffrage. Köller's removal was the prerequisite to any meaningful reform. The secretary of state was indeed dismissed 21 October 1908, and replaced by Baron Hugo Zorn von Bulach (younger), a native Alsatian. The new secretary of state complemented a new governor, whom the kaiser had appointed exactly one year earlier.

Although no one realized it at the time, the drama culminating in the constitution of 1911 began in September 1907 when Chancellor Bernhard von Bülow asked for the resignation of the seventy-five-year-old governor, Prince Hermann zu Hohenlohe-Langenburg. The relative quiet which had marked Langenburg's thirteen-year term as governor of the Reichsland came to an abrupt end. His successor, General Count Karl von Wedel, assumed the governorship in the midst of rising demands for Alsace-Lorraine autonomy, and increasing Franco-German tension on the diplomatic front. Every appointment to the governorship carried major political implications, and Wedel's was no exception. A Frisian noble, Wedel had entered the Hanoverian military service and had won a decoration for his part in the Hanoverian "victory" over Prussian forces at Langensalza in the Austro-Prussian war of 1866. With Hanover's annexation to Prussia after that war, Wedel offered his services to the Prussian army, rose to the rank of cavalry general, and became one of Wilhelm II's closest adjutants. The general served as military attaché in Vienna between 1877 and 1887, ambassador to Rome in 1899, and ambassador in Vienna in 1902. In the crisis over his mother's visit to Paris in 1891, the kaiser threatened to replace Münster as ambassador in Paris with Wedel, but eventually satisfied himself with tightening the passport restrictions.[9] Wilhelm's biographer, Michael Balfour, claims Wedel refused the chancellorship in 1909; the offer of such a position would ordinarily indicate the great trust the kaiser placed in Wedel, but Balfour implies that Wilhelm hoped Wedel would decline because he thought the count would be "too obstinate."[10] Bülow admitted to Holstein at the time of Wedel's appointment to the governorship that Wedel "may some day become Reich Chancellor . . ."[11]

Holstein found it inconceivable that the kaiser could entrust the strategic Reichsland to a man who had won the Langensalza medal. Holstein also suspected that Wedel was "perhaps even an Alsatian home ruler."[12] Aside from objections concerning Wedel himself, Holstein and many others in Germany were becoming increasingly concerned with the kaiser's "sultanesque methods of rulership." All too often, wrote Holstein to Bülow, matters were decided "according to the by no means infallible political instinct of the Kaiser," a situation which might lead to domestic crises as the people began to lose confidence in the system.[13]

Bülow would "not deny the drawbacks of Wedel," but defended him as the best available choice for the governorship. Other contenders such as Prince Hermann von Hatzfeldt, a Free Conservative Reichstag deputy and former head of the administration in Silesia, and Joseph Maria von Radowitz, the ambassador in Madrid, would have been inclined to "foster a policy of conciliation towards France from the banks of the Ill." Bethmann Hollweg (Prussian minister of the interior, 1905–7, state secretary of the Reich ministry of the interior, 1907–9) was indispensable in Berlin. Bülow thought that "the selection of a general was indicated," and of the four who came under consideration, Wedel was the ablest and most qualified. The chancellor pointed to what he considered Wedel's greatest asset for the position; "he has dignity. He will not run after the French. He is too reserved to do that," wrote Bülow. Wedel's other major asset for Bülow was the general's apparent disinterest in the chancellor's position. Bülow was careful to appoint no one who might wish to use the governorship as a stepping-stone to the chancellorship.[14]

Wedel's political aims in Strasbourg indicate that the new governor understood the political situation in the Reichsland. This in itself was a novelty in German policy. One of the most controversial matters in the territorial administration since the Manteuffel era had been the questionable usefulness of the so-called notable policy, under which the administration attempted to hold the population in check by granting concessions to the leading religious and economic interests. The generals in Berlin generally regarded the notable policy as a sign of weakness against the demands of pro-French agitators. To be accused of following the notable policy was to be damned, and not even the supposedly typical Prussian bureaucrat, Secretary of State Ernst Matthias von Köller, escaped the stigma. Wedel's successor, Hans von Dallwitz, labeled Köller's repeal of the dictatorship paragraph in 1902 and the establishment of the Catholic theological faculty at the university as concessions to the pro-French notables.[15] On the other hand, the administration had made only minimal efforts to organize government supporters in a liberal middle party, leaving the field to the antigovernment socialists and clericals.

Wedel understood all of this, and set out on his own "New Course." "I regard it as my mission," wrote the governor, "to politicize and mobilize the *Mittelstand* which previously has stood passively and indifferently beside the 'Notable' leadership." Wedel never doubted that, "to accomplish this, it was necessary to change the electoral law."[16] The governor could not realize his political aims in the Reichsland without basic constitutional reform, but he had to convince Berlin that reform would not simply please the people of Alsace-Lorraine and the governor of the moment, but would also prove beneficial to the empire as a whole.

As soon as he had had an opportunity to acquaint himself with conditions in the Reichsland, Wedel reported to the kaiser on the need for reform. It was time, said Wedel, to show Alsace-Lorraine some trust. The governor's specific reform proposals generally followed the more moderate territorial committee resolutions. These included raising the territorial committee to *Landtag* status, giving it the right of interpellation, excluding the Reichstag from any role in territorial legislation, and granting Alsace-Lorraine three votes in the Federal Council. The Federal Council delegates would be appointed by the kaiser and instructed by the governor in accordance with the emperor's orders. At this time (27 February 1908), Wedel made no mention of granting universal suffrage.[17] Two years later, the governor recognized that moderate reform was not commensurate with his own political objectives. Regardless of his personal tastes, Wedel realized that the 1879 system with its rigged suffrage entrusted political power to the upper bourgeoisie and Catholic prelates, men whose position guaranteed them relative immunity from government intimidation. In his 10 April 1910 report to the kaiser, Wedel argued that a territorial parliament elected by universal suffrage would embarrass the government less and produce more fruitful legislation than the existing territorial committee. Admitting that he was certainly not advocating universal suffrage for Prussia, the governor believed it would work in Alsace-Lorraine, where the way had been prepared by a long democratic tradition.[18]

In a December 1908 memorandum to Bülow, Minister of the Interior Bethmann Hollweg supported Wedel's original, moderate proposals for constitutional reform in the Reichsland. Bülow found little support for reform in the Prussian ministry, however, and dropped the matter quickly.[19] Prussian conservatives such as Hans von Dallwitz opposed any reform in Alsace-Lorraine because they recognized it as the first step in a liberal campaign to overturn the Prussian three-class voting system.[20]

Wedel could not strongly advocate constitutional reform until he was certain of support in Berlin. His own secretary of state, Ernst Matthias von Köller, who had been retained from the Hohenlohe-Langenburg administration on Bülow's advice, fought against reform, even though it was under his regime that the dictatorship paragraph had been repealed.[21] Köller's dismissal in October 1908 smoothed the way for implementation of Wedel's reform proposals. When Bethmann Hollweg assumed the chancellorship in 1909, prospects for a new constitution in the Reichsland brightened further. As minister of the interior, Bethmann Hollweg had already recognized the need to make Alsace-Lorraine a true *Bundesstaat*; failing to achieve that goal immediately, he was willing to accept a provisional solution. As chancellor, Bethmann Hollweg recognized that provisional solutions no longer sufficed. Action to achieve the complete, definitive integration of the Reichsland into the empire had to be taken at once.[22]

The chancellor hoped the government could initiate proposals before the Reichstag suggested reforms more radical than the government was willing to grant. His plans for orderly reform controlled by the government were jolted when, during the session of 14 March 1910, three Lorraine deputies introduced a resolution asking that Alsace-Lorraine be raised to the status of a true *Bundesstaat*, with a territorial legislature elected by equal, direct, universal manhood suffrage, under a system of proportional representation. Jacques Preiss, an Alsatian deputy, introduced a second resolution which merely asked for constitutional reform, without demanding extension of the suffrage.[23] Attempting to forestall any precipitous move by the Reichstag, Bethmann Hollweg told the deputies that the government had already prepared a proposal for constitutional and electoral reform.[24] Although it is doubtful that the government proposals were actually completed by 14 March, the chancellor wished to avoid the embarrassment of unacceptable proposals from the Reichstag. He was even willing to risk a clash with the emperor, who was not yet convinced of the need for immediate reform. When the emperor announced his support for the government reform plans at Metz on 30 April 1910, the last obstacle had been overcome.[25]

Under the government plan, the emperor, as agent of the Federal Council, continued to exercise sovereign powers in Alsace-Lorraine. The senior administrative official in Strasbourg was still the governor, appointed by the emperor. Although a local *Landtag* was to be established to legislate for the Reichsland, no law could take effect without the emperor's sanction. Deputies in the *Landtag's* lower chamber were to be elected by secret, direct, universal suffrage, under conditions to be defined in a separate electoral law. The emperor and each chamber of the *Landtag* could initiate legislation, and each chamber had the right of interpellation and petition. The Reichstag and Federal Council, with the emperor's consent, possessed sole right to amend the new constitution. Thus, if the experi-

ment with self-government proved unworkable, the imperial government could scrap it.[26]

Having granted universal manhood suffrage, the government tried
to dampen its effects by adding a number of special restrictions in
the electoral law. A three-year residence requirement discriminated
against lower-class transient workers, and a system of plural voting
based on age favored the older, presumably more conservative
generation. Electoral districts were to be fixed by imperial decree,
raising the possibility of gerrymandering by the government. Supported by the smaller German states, the government refused to
grant Alsace-Lorraine Federal Council votes. Her votes, it was
argued, would always be cast for Prussia, since the emperor, who
was also the king of Prussia, named the governor who would instruct
the Alsace-Lorraine Federal Council delegates.[27]

Wilhelm Kapp, founder of the liberal, government-oriented
Elsass-Lothringische Vereinigung, has attributed the technical drafting of the 1911 constitution to Karl Wilhelm Mandel, Alsace-
Lorraine undersecretary of state for the interior since 1906. Kapp
claims that although Mandel drafted the provisions, he did not approve of the reforms, especially the provision for a *Landtag* elected
by universal suffrage. If Mandel could be forced to draft a set of
reforms in which he did not really believe, how seriously should one
take any of the territorial administrators? Are they really important
historical figures? All of the territorial administrations demonstrated
uncertainty and vacillation in their implementation of official programs. Should this be interpreted as weakness and incompetence on
the part of the bureaucrats themselves? Kapp argues rather con-
vincingly that neither Mandel nor even Wedel set their own course
in the Reichsland; they simply followed orders from Berlin. They
of course might influence the final decisions handed down in Berlin,
and in this respect the opinions of the territorial administrators did
count. But the winds from Berlin were constantly changing; the
chancellor's political requirements at any moment might dictate
either a forceful show of strength, or a conciliatory program to coax
his opposition into line. Either way, the impact was likely to be felt
in Alsace-Lorraine. In 1911, Bethmann Hollweg had decided on a
"final solution" to the Alsace-Lorraine problem. Wedel was pleased
that Berlin saw things his way, and Mandel, the professional bureaucrat, executed his orders with precision.[28]

Among the Progressives, National Liberals, Center, and SPD, the government proposals received strong support. Some members of the *Reichspartei* expressed reservations, while the Conservatives and *Wirtschaftliche Vereinigung* viewed any reform as dangerous. In the Reichsland, most local politicians found the government plans unacceptable in their original form, but optimistically believed they could be amended in the Reichstag constitutional committee. While all political leaders desired constitutional reform, they disagreed on the substance of those reforms. Some demanded a republic, some denounced the provision for the upper chamber of the *Landtag*, some objected to certain provisions of the electoral law, and some held out for votes in the Federal Council.

Local Social Democrats and democrats leveled the most severe criticism against the government bills. Claiming a long republican tradition for Alsace-Lorraine, Social Democrats Joseph Emmel and Bernhard Bohle, joined by the democrat Daniel Blumenthal and the Catholic priest Emile Wetterlé, demanded a republic.[29] Most parties, however, rejected the republican idea. Leaders of Wetterlé's own party, Georg Ricklin and Karl Hauss, denied the existence of majority support for a republic; at any rate, intransigence on the issue was foolish, because the government would never concede. Hauss and his colleagues found themselves in a dilemma. While they preferred monarchy to a republic, they nevertheless disliked the particular Prussian brand of absolutism and militarism. Searching for a compromise, Hauss eventually recommended the appointment of a lifetime governor or regent, free from the influence of Berlin.[30] From a democratic camp, Daniel Blumenthal criticized Hauss's halfway solution; since the government would accept neither a republic nor a nonremovable governor, it made little sense to compromise one's principles by giving up the demand for a republic.[31]

When the Reichstag committee rejected the proposal to establish a republic, the Social Democrats suggested that the governor be elected for a five-year term by the Alsace-Lorraine *Landtag*. The committee turned down this proposal for an elected governor, and finally adopted a Center recommendation for a governor appointed for life, named by the emperor upon the recommendation of the Federal Council. Although the committee had rejected all of the more radical suggestions, it was not acting as a tool of the government, for, as Blumenthal had predicted, the government had already informed the committee that a lifetime governor was unacceptable.[32]

With the issue of the governorship presumably settled, the attack

now turned to the government's insistence on an upper chamber for
the *Landtag*. The Social Democrats and democrats, demanding a
unicameral legislature, considered the upper chamber as a device
for thwarting the will of the people. The socialist Joseph Emmel
charged the government and liberals with using the upper chamber
as protection against the strong possibility of a clerical, nationalistic
majority in the lower chamber.[33] On the question of the upper chamber, the Alsace-Lorraine Catholics were willing to compromise. Recognizing that the government was determined to have an upper
chamber, the clericals merely wished to assure the adequate representation of Catholic interests. Only the bishops of Strasbourg and
Metz received seats in the upper chamber under the government
plan; the Alsace-Lorraine Center argued that the Catholics were
entitled to at least two additional seats on the basis of the large
Catholic population.[34]

While the dispute over the upper chamber became heated, it was
the bill concerning elections to the lower chamber of the *Landtag*
which created the loudest dissent. None of the local parties accepted
the provision fixing electoral districts by imperial decree, rather than
delimiting them in the pending electoral law. Districting plans designed by the emperor might discriminate against parties considered
unfriendly to the government, and in the Reichsland, all of the
major parties might conceivably be considered unfriendly. When the
government steadfastly refused to fix the electoral districts by law
rather than by decree, the orderly progress of the government bills
through the Reichstag was threatened. Hoping to reassure all parties
that the emperor's districting plan would be fair, the government
unofficially leaked its plan to the Reichstag committee. There would
be sixty electoral districts, each having a population between 25,000
and 30,000. The government's disclosure of its scheme merely added
fuel to the controversy, for the parties could now attack specific
provisions of the plan.

The Alsace-Lorraine Center claimed the government districting
plan was designed to reduce Catholic political influence. Because
Catholics comprised a majority of the territorial population, they
claimed the right to a majority in the *Landtag*. The government assured the Reichstag committee that the districting plan carried no
intent to deprive any party of a legitimate parliamentary majority;
it merely sought to insure adequate minority representation in the
Landtag. "Since when," inquired the Catholic Georg Ricklin, "is it

the duty of the state to assure parties of representation in parliament? This is the business of the parties themselves."[35] Georg Wolf, a liberal, advanced proportional representation as the solution to the districting impasse. While some Social Democrats supported Wolf, the clericals rejected any system which threatened to weaken the expected clerical majority in the *Landtag*. Ricklin and his colleague Karl Hauss argued that while proportional representation was acceptable in principle, political parties in the Reichsland were too rudimentary to enable such a system to function.[36]

The electoral law offered Alsace-Lorraine in 1910 was in some respects more liberal than those prevailing in some of the other German states. A study made by the *Strassburger Post* in March 1910 found that many states did not have universal manhood suffrage, tied the right to vote to the payment of taxes, and insured election of conservative candidates through indirect balloting. Prussia, with its famous three-class voting system, still did not have the secret ballot. Although the electoral law proposed for Alsace-Lorraine was in many respects liberal, it nevertheless contained such provisions as plural votes based on age, which the Social Democratic *Freie Presse* denounced as reactionary, class legislation. The *Freie Presse* went much further, claiming the government soon hoped to secure a Conservative-National Liberal majority in the Reichstag, in order to recast the Reichstag electoral law in the restrictive mold now being proposed for the Reichsland.[37] With a "Red scare" sweeping many areas of the German empire, such fears of reaction were justified. To preserve the old order against social democracy Saxony had implemented a new *Landtag* electoral law in May 1909. The former three-class system bowed to one based on factors of income, education, profession, land ownership, and age. Under the new regulations, some balloters could cast as many as four votes. Studying the results of the October-November 1909 *Landtag* election in Saxony, the *Frankfurter Zeitung* found the new election law benefited the middle-class parties at the expense of the Social Democrats. Social Democrats won twenty-five of the ninety-one contested seats; had the election been conducted under equal suffrage, they would have won sixty-eight seats.[38] Under mounting pressure from the Social Democrats, the Reichstag committee discarded the government plan for plural voting in Alsace-Lorraine, and reduced the proposed residence requirement.

Debate on the specifics of the government proposals had thus far overlooked one major problem; the government bills lacked any explicit statement concerning the exact legal status of Alsace-Lorraine under the new constitution. Was the territory still a Reichsland, or was it now a true *Bundesstaat*? Nicholas Delsor, an Alsace-Lorraine Center leader, offered a clarifying amendment stating that Alsace-Lorraine was an independent *Bundesstaat* with three votes in the Federal Council. Despite government warnings that it was not acceptable, the Reichstag committee approved Delsor's amendment. Having been overruled by the Reichstag committee on two important issues, lifetime appointment for the governor and Federal Council votes for Alsace-Lorraine, the government was now thoroughly confused. Clemens von Delbrück, imperial secretary of the interior, asked the committee to adjourn while the government decided what to do. Hans von Dallwitz's reaction to the demand for *Bundesstaat* status makes the government's paranoia on this issue more understandable. Dallwitz discounted the sincerity of Alsace-Lorraine's demand for legal and political equality. When they spoke of equality, warned Dallwitz, the Alsace-Lorrainers really were talking about an initial step toward eventual reunification with France. By implementing French linguistic and cultural programs, they would use their "autonomy" to prepare for the first opportunity (by this he undoubtedly meant a French military victory over Germany) to rejoin France.[39] No German administration was going to permit the Alsace-Lorrainers to use constitutional reform as a cloak for anti-German activities.

When the committee hearings resumed, Delbrück outlined the government's revised position. Alsace-Lorraine could have three Federal Council votes so long as there was no reduction in the powers of the emperor and governor. To protect the interests of the other states, Alsace-Lorraine's votes would not be counted if they provided a majority for Prussia. Alsace-Lorraine could be considered as a *Bundesstaat* (without actually being one) in the sense of articles six, seven, and eight of the imperial constitution.[40] Accepting the government compromise, the Reichstag committee dropped both the Delsor amendment explicitly granting Alsace-Lorraine *Bundesstaat* status and the amendment providing for a governor appointed for life.

When the bills came up for debate in the Reichstag, the Conservatives demanded to know why they were being asked to give Alsace-Lorraine Federal Council votes which, in their view, would be counted only when cast against Prussia. The granting of voting rights in the Federal Council was a vital ingredient in Bethmann Hollweg's plan to bind the Reichsland closer to the empire. The sacrifice this entailed was more apparent than real, for the powers of the emperor and governor in Alsace-Lorraine remained undiminished. The general demand for reform was being satisfied with a minimal change in the German political system. While the chancellor sympathized to some extent with conservative fears that any reform was dangerous, he believed failure to take any action could have even graver consequences.[41] The Reichstag agreed with the chancellor, approving the new constitution and electoral law on 26 May 1911 by a vote of 202 to 94. The conservatives, the Alsace-Lorraine Social Democrats, and the Alsace-Lorraine Center provided most of the negative votes. The split between the territorial parties and their German counterparts came into the open, as the German SPD supported the bills, and the affirmative vote of the German Center delegation consisting of 105 members provided the winning votes. The SPD justified its support of the measure with the expectation that the introduction of universal suffrage in Alsace-Lorraine might be the first step toward suffrage reform in other German states. This was certainly an overly optimistic calculation.[42]

In Alsace-Lorraine, the desire for real self-government remained unsatisfied. The inadequacy of the reform was felt not only by natives of the territory, but also by Germans who had migrated to the region since 1871. They were all treated as second-class citizens in the German empire, and after waiting forty years, they were keenly disappointed with the government's reform offer in 1911.[43] Because of ambiguities in the constitution, not even the legal experts were certain of the meaning of the reform. Between 1911 and 1919, a deluge of legal studies sought to define the legal position of the emperor in territorial affairs, the relationship of Alsace-Lorraine to the rest of the empire, and the status of the governor and *Landtag*. To this day, no one has a clear idea of what the 1911 constitution accomplished. Widely used histories continue to make vague and inaccurate statements. The *Encyclopedia of World History* states that, "a law was passed organizing Alsace and Lorraine as a state, with a two-chamber legislature and a large measure of autonomy."[44] Koppel S. Pinson recently wrote incorrectly that "legislation was passed in 1911 converting Alsace-Lorraine from an imperial domain to a separate state."[45] In a study which for many years served as a standard work on the Bismarckian empire, W. H. Dawson concluded enigmatically that, "by the constitution given to Alsace-Lorraine in 1911, the Province became for most practical purposes an autonomous federal state, though without political independence."[46]

Most German legal scholars agreed that Alsace-Lorraine did not become a federal state under the 1911 constitution. The territory lacked the sovereign powers, such as amending her own constitution and appointing her own officials, which characterize most sovereign states. The emperor, as agent of the Federal Council, still exercised sovereign power in Alsace-Lorraine. Granting of Federal Council votes did not, in itself, confer statehood on Alsace-Lorraine. While the 1911 territorial constitution no longer referred to the region as a "Reichsland," Article One of the imperial constitution never listed Alsace-Lorraine among the federal states.[47] The constitutional position of Alsace-Lorraine remained as confused after the 1911 reform as before. Friedrich Koenig's unintentionally muddled conclusion indicates the futility of trying to convince the Alsace-Lorrainers that they had made greater gains than was the case. "In practice," Koenig wrote, "it has become just like every other *Bundesstaat* in the German Empire, although theoretically a few important questions remain unresolved."[48] Otto-Günther von Wesendonk came much closer to the truth when he concluded that, "even after the reform of its constitution, the Reichsland retains a special, abnormal position within the Reich."[49]

No less vague than the status of the territory was the position of the governor under the new constitution. Because the emperor could delegate sovereign powers to the governor, the governor served as both an ordinary government official at the head of the territorial administration, and as executor of the emperor's sovereign powers. The dual nature of his office inevitably raised questions concerning the governor's "responsibility," questions for which the 1911 constitution provided inconclusive answers. When he countersigned decrees issued by the emperor, the governor assumed responsibility for them. When the governor issued decrees under the sovereign powers delegated to him by the emperor, the secretary of state added his signature and thereby assumed responsibility for the measures. The constitution, however, furnished no definition of "responsibility."

The German concept of responsibility has drawn the attention of numerous legal experts. Wilhelm Lepsius made one of the most detailed studies of the problem. The monarch, he wrote, is above the law. Although he can commit improper acts, he cannot be punished for them under the law. The monarch is, in short, not responsible. In constitutional monarchies, the responsibility of the chief minister usually compensates for the monarch's freedom from responsibility. Lepsius distinguished several types of responsibility, which he classified as general, particular, moral, political, parliamentary, constitutional, juristic, and disciplinary. Political and parliamentary responsibility were often identical. In his role as chief minister, the governor of Alsace-Lorraine bore a political responsibility; he was required to furnish explanations of official policy by answering parliamentary criticism and interpellation.[50] Lepsius complicated his argument by claiming that the governor was responsible to both the territorial *Landtag* and the imperial Reichstag. This idea of duel responsibility was not universally accepted by German legal scholars. Alfred Döring, for example, noted that the 1911 constitution described the governor as standing at "the head of the territorial government"; his sole responsibility was thus to the territorial legislature, the *Landtag*.[51]

Beneath the confusion about the 1911 constitution, one point was clear; the dream of self-government remained unfulfilled. Secretary of State Hugo Zorn von Bulach had reminded the territorial committee during the constitutional debate that politics is the art of the possible. This often-used phrase is meaningless, since one never knows what is possible until he has tried all of the alternatives. If the constitution was not what many had hoped for, the local political leadership of Alsace-Lorraine must share some of the blame. The reform movement lacked unity, and in the end the constitutional debate degenerated into political squabbles among the territorial political parties. Each party blamed the others for the shortcomings of the reform bills. The clerical Karl Hauss pointed to what he called the "transparent double game of the liberals," who made radical demands in Strasbourg but went along with the government at the moment of decision in Berlin.[52] The Social Democrats charged the Alsatian Catholic Leo Vonderscheer and the German Catholic Count Georg von Hertling with selling the German Center party vote to the government in return for additional Catholic representation in the upper chamber of the *Landtag*.[53]

Amicable relations among the parties might have helped the Alsace-Lorrainers in their struggle for self-government. Daniel

Blumenthal, the democratic leader, sought to form a Constitutional party devoted to the single cause of obtaining a satisfactory constitution. United in a single party, argued Blumenthal, the Reichsland deputies would have greater influence in the Reichstag. The Constitutional party would retain complete freedom of action and avoid compromising on key demands by rejecting affiliation with any other party.[54] Liberals and clericals rejected Blumenthal's call for a Constitutional party, which they feared would only isolate the Alsace-Lorraine deputies and weaken their influence in the Reichstag.[55]

Blumenthal's idea for unity deserved more consideration than it received. It is interesting to speculate on what might have happened had the territorial parties united behind a single constitutional program and refused to compromise with the government. The results might still have fallen short of expectations. Perhaps, as some believed at the time, the government would have withdrawn its reform proposals from the Reichstag.[56] Retreat on the constitution would have marked a grave defeat for the government, and Bethmann Hollweg might not have survived the crisis.

The tenuous relationship between parties in Alsace-Lorraine and their counterparts in Germany may hold the key to the failure to achieve satisfactory reform in 1911. Blumenthal was indeed misguided in advising that a unified Constitutional party should refuse any connection with the larger Reichstag factions. With her fifteen votes, Alsace-Lorraine could never hope to command a parliamentary majority. Only with steady support from the German Center, SPD, and liberals could the Reichsland obtain an acceptable constitution. Such cooperation failed to materialize in 1911. The constitutional debate only increased the existing tension between the Alsace-Lorraine Center and the German Center. The Reichsland Social Democrats and the German SPD also went their separate ways on the constitutional vote. Never had there been much cooperation between the major parties in Alsace-Lorraine and the corresponding parties in Germany. When cooperation was needed in 1911, the historical basis for it was lacking. In an ironic twist of fate, the struggle to preserve Alsace-Lorraine's individualism and autonomy contributed to the failure to achieve self-government in 1911.

8
UNDER THE CONSTITUTION: TURN TOWARD THE REICH

Its deficiencies notwithstanding, the 1911 constitution ushered in a new era in territorial politics. The quickening pace of politicization witnessed the formation of new parties, modified combinations of old parties, and indicated a growing willingness to look beyond purely regional issues to larger national questions. Alsace-Lorraine, observed a prominent liberal leader, was at last emancipated from irresponsible clique politics.[1] The new politics tested its wings in the first *Landtag* election in 1911 and the last Reichstag election in 1912.

As the shortcomings of the constitution became apparent, Daniel Blumenthal's previously rejected idea of a constitutional party gained wider acceptance. In June 1911 a small group of influential politicians met in Strasbourg and established the *Nationalbund*, a new party dedicated to the protection of regional interests. The *Nationalbund* asserted that, "the people of Alsace-Lorraine have other things to do besides representing the political goals and ideas of German parties which developed under entirely different circumstances." The Alsace-Lorrainers should pursue their own special interests, which included the following:

1. full political autonomy and equality with the other federal states
2. Alsace-Lorrainers in all important administrative positions
3. more instruction in French in the elementary schools
4. greater concern for territorial agricultural and industrial interests
5. amnesty for pre-1890 draft dodgers

6. reduced spending, rejection of increased appropriations for the army, navy, and bureaucracy.[2]

Founded by men such as the Catholic priest Emile Wetterlé, the once anti-Catholic Blumenthal, and the independents Jacques Preiss and Ludwig Pierson, the *Nationalbund* was broadly based. Although the Catholics found the alliance with anticlerical democrats somewhat distasteful, they saw no other way to achieve meaningful reform. The Alsace-Lorraine Center expelled from its ranks Leo Vonderscheer, who had served as chairman of the Reichstag constitutional committee; having purged the party, the clericals condemned the German Center party for having sold out on the constitution, and adopted a resolution urging cooperation with the *Nationalbund*.[3]

Many democrats shrank from a coalition with clericals like Wetterlé. Blumenthal assured his followers that joining the *Nationalbund* did not involve giving up the democratic party program; it was simply a matter of giving priority to the most important problems. The issue of self-government took precedence over religious and educational questions.[4] Blumenthal hoped to re-create the atmosphere of the 1874 Reichstag election, when the clerical issue had been kept out of politics and party differences were laid aside as the people united in protest against the annexation. The *Nationalbund* resembled the earlier coalition of Catholics and protesters, but the times had changed. Social, political, economic, and religious questions that so preoccupied the electorate in 1911 could not be put aside until autonomy had been achieved. The *Nationalbund* claimed it stood above party politics. While such a lofty stand placed the new party in a strong moral position, it left the *Nationalbund* tactically defenseless. Whether they supported the *Nationalbund's* specific program or not, all of the older territorial parties eventually joined against it. Though theoretically "above" politics, the *Nationalbund* in effect threatened to replace all of the other parties. The Social Democrats, Alsace-Lorraine Center and liberal-democrats all regarded the new organization as unwanted competition.[5]

Anticlericalism, more than any other factor, rendered impossible the achievement of regional unity. Representing the 1911 *Landtag* election as a battle between political Catholicism and Social Democracy, the socialists expressed willingness to ally with bourgeois liberals, democrats, and anyone else willing to combat clericalism.[6] Because many Catholics were associated with the *Nationalbund*, the

Social Democrats and liberals considered the new party as nothing more than a branch of the Alsace-Lorraine Center.[7] Laurent Meyer, a Social Democratic candidate in the 1911 *Landtag* election, characterized the *Nationalbund* as "wolves in sheepskins, the *Schwarzen* who employ their Jesuitical cunning to drape themselves with the red-white flag to disguise their black deeds."[8] There was, in fact, no formal relationship between the Alsace-Lorraine Center and the *Nationalbund*, even though a few candidates ran on both tickets. The Alsace-Lorraine Center's 11 June resolution to support the *Nationalbund* never received full implementation. Nor could the Alsace-Lorraine Center endorse the *Nationalbund*'s plea to ignore the religious issue in a time of rising anticlericalism.[9]

The *Nationalbund*'s vigorous espousal of the nationalist-particularist position forced all of the other parties to take a stand on the same issue. In every case, the decision was a difficult one, involving severe conflicts between principles and tactics. The threat to world peace precipitated by the second Moroccan crisis focused attention on the national question. Liberals and Social Democrats, accusing the *Nationalbund* of "demagogic nationalism," warned that this was an inopportune moment for a nationalistic outburst from the Reichsland. In 1916 Solomon Grumbach, a German member of the Colmar SPD branch who had lived in the Reichsland for twelve years, explained the socialist position on nationalism between 1911 and 1914. "We opposed the nationalist movement in Alsace-Lorraine," recalled Grumbach, "because in view of rising international tension, it would have provided ammunition for the German war party." The war party hoped to provoke the Alsace-Lorrainers into actions which would have to be "corrected" through a "preventive war." At an SPD conference at Colmar 6 August 1911, nationalists and anti-nationalists disagreed on what stand to take toward the *Nationalbund*, but when the vote was taken, the nationalists lost out. From that day until August 1914 the Alsace-Lorraine Social Democrats waged a two-front war against both the nationalists and the government. At this point in his argument Grumbach encountered that painful situation where lofty principle must be reconciled with political reality. As the results of the 1911 *Landtag* election amply demonstrated, no candidate could win an election solely on the basis of a nationalist-particularist platform. But on the other hand any candidate who explicitly repudiated Alsace-Lorraine's particular interests was also committing political suicide. As a purely tactical matter, parties looking for election-day victories had to support Alsatian "nationalism" in some form. Grumbach and the Social Democrats recognized this fact of life, for after severely criticizing the nationalistic excesses of the *Nationalbund,* Grumbach hastened to add that it was the middle-class parties, not simply the socialists, which defeated the nationalists in the 1911 *Landtag* election and again in the 1912 Reichstag election. Every party wished to be rid of the *Nationalbund*'s competition, but no one wanted to assume responsibility for defeating its program of defending territorial interests.[10]

Grumbach had every right to point to the liberals' role in defeating Alsatian nationalism in 1911, but the liberals, too, had difficulty reconciling principles and tactics. Most liberal support came from German immigrants, whose interest in Alsatian nationalism was certainly minimal. Despite their large numbers, the immigrants commanded nothing like a majority in the Reichsland; unless they could form a coalition with the native middle-class elements, the liberal parties were doomed to minority status and political impotence. Wilhelm Kapp founded his *Elsass-Lothringische Vereinigung* in 1909 for the express purpose of bringing together the German and native liberal elements. To accomplish such a fusion, the liberals had to virtually ignore the nationalistic question. This they tried to do by fighting the *Nationalbund* in the 1911 *Landtag* election. The results were hardly encouraging; on the first ballot, the liberal-democratic coalition won only one seat out of sixty. With Social Democratic help against the clericals on the second ballot, the liberal-democrats won another eight seats. After the 1911 election, Kapp admitted that if the liberals hoped to mobilize the Alsatian middle classes, they would probably have to adopt a more particularist program stressing the defense of the interests of Alsace-Lorraine, within the framework of the German Reich.[11]

For the clericals, too, the nationalist-particularist issue produced a good deal of hedging. As a competitor of the *Nationalbund,* the Alsace-Lorraine Center considered itself a "national" party, striving to "centralize and harmonize the demands and interests of all walks of life." Embracing all social and economic classes, the Center saw no need for another party of unity.[12] The nationalist-particularist program, however, did not endear any territorial party in the eyes of the government, and the government's attitude weighed heavily for a party still nursing painful memories of the *Kulturkampf.* Still more important was the attitude of the socialists and liberal-democrats, who denounced the clericals along with the *Nationalbund* for their nationalist-particularist stand. Center apologists argued that the clericals really did not believe in their own particularist propaganda. Circumstances beyond their control, so they maintained, forced the Alsace-Lorraine Center candidates to adopt nationalism as an electoral tactic, without accepting it in principle. The anti-Catholic attitude of many German immigrants obliged the Center to insure its standing with the native voters by espousing nationalist slogans. For their effect on the voters, the Center even employed French clichés, but no one except the government took them seriously. Nationalism verging on a pro-French attitude was nothing more than a vote-getting tactic employed by any intelligent politician.[13] Such attempts to explain away the Alsace-Lorraine Center's nationalism in 1911 ignore the historical role in the clerical movement of such men as Winterer, Guerber, Simonis, and Wetterlé, whose sympathies lay more with France than Germany. They also ignore the Alsace-Lorraine Center's expressed desire in 1911 to play the role of a "national" party embracing all social, economic, and religious interests.

The *Nationalbund*'s nationalistic program became a matter of international as well as domestic concern. The French socialist newspaper *L'Humanité* considered Blumenthal's defeat essential to any Franco-German understanding.[14] The semiofficial *Strassburger Post* warned that a sizable vote for the *Nationalbund* would encourage the war party in France. The Catholic *Elsässer Kurier* (Colmar) countered that the real warmongers in Alsace-Lorraine were the liberals, not the *Nationalbund*.[15]

Although the issues of clericalism and nationalism provoked the most spectacular campaign oratory, they shared the stage with a growing concern with economic and social questions. The democrats advocated abolition of the death penalty and the extension of suffrage to women. All parties conceded the need for reform of the tax structure; all parties advocated repeal of the liquor license tax and direct taxes which burdened the poor. On the proposal to introduce a progressive income tax, however, disagreement was sharp. Totally involved in the struggle for a new constitution, the *Nationalbund* sidestepped the whole tax question by suggesting fiscal economy as a means of avoiding higher taxes. Labeling it the "indisputable and indispensable backbone of any modern tax system," the *Liberale Landespartei* supported the progressive income tax.[16] The Social Democrats also supported it, and managed to tie the issue to their anticlerical campaign. The clericals took an ambiguous position on the progressive income tax. The Social Democrats contended that the Alsace-Lorraine Center no longer stood behind its original endorsement of the tax. In December 1910 Anselm Laugel, chairman of the Alsace-Lorraine Center group in the territorial committee, had published a pamphlet in which he argued the incompatibility of a progressive income tax with universal suffrage. The have-not masses, he contended, would use their voting power to dispossess the propertied classes. The people could have either universal suffrage or a progressive income tax, but not both.[17] Since the new *Landtag* was elected by universal suffrage, the Social Democrats assumed that the clericals no longer supported the progressive income tax. This was an incorrect assumption, for the clericals did in fact favor the progressive income tax as a means of improving the condition of the working class without attacking private property; Laugel's warning was not taken seriously by other Catholic politicians. Both the Alsace-Lorraine Center and the liberals, however, felt it was the task of the imperial government, rather than local authorities, to take care of the working class. Recognizing the inadequate representation of labor in the territorial legislature, the Alsace-Lorraine Center advocated creation of a regional *Arbeiterkammer* which would send delegates to the upper chamber of the *Landtag*. The Alsace-Lorraine Center's main concern, however, was with the small businessmen who were being squeezed out by big industry. The state had a duty to protect the petty bourgeoisie by providing legal privileges, technical education, and cheap credit.[18]

The *Landtag* election took place 22 October 1911. Numerous complaints charged the government with what was termed *Kaiserliche Sozialdemokratie*, official support for Social Democrats against clericals and nationalists. Of the cases tried before the *Oberlandesgericht* at Colmar, convictions were sustained only against several members of the Catholic clergy accused of election abuses, prompting the *Oberelsässische Landeszeitung* to comment that the court had in effect created a new anticlerical law on election abuses.[19] Accusations of foul play notwithstanding, the voters clearly repudiated the *Nationalbund*. The first ballot produced victors in only thirty-five of the sixty electoral districts. *Nationalbund* candidates received only 9,476 votes, 3.2 percent of the total. Clerical candidates, including several in the Lorraine Bloc, took twenty-eight of the thirty-five seats decided on the first ballot; the *Nationalbund* failed to win a single contest.[20]

Facing possible clerical control of the *Landtag*, the Social Democrats and liberal-democrats combined forces on the second ballot, held 29 October. The socialists withdrew seventeen candidates, while the *Liberale Landespartei* and the *Demokratische Partei* together dropped seven candidates. The coalition parties also agreed on a common platform, including proposals for lowering the voting residence requirement, abolishing direct taxes on food and luxuries, enacting progressive income and property taxes, extending factory inspection laws, securing the right of association for all workers, and combatting clerical influence in schools and other state institutions. Exhorting its followers to vote for liberal-democratic candidates, the Social Democratic committee in Strasbourg reassured them that, "you are not voting for liberalism, you are voting against clericalism."[21]

The alliance between socialists and liberal-democrats failed to dislodge the clericals from their commanding position taken on the first ballot. Although the Alsace-Lorraine Center gained only six seats on the second ballot, the damage had already been done on the first. The final count gave twenty-four *Landtag* seats to the Alsace-Lorraine Center, eleven to the Social Democrats, eleven to the liberal-democrats, ten to the predominantly clerical Lorraine Bloc, and two to independent candidates. Repeating its dismal performance on the second ballot, the *Nationalbund* failed to gain a place in the territorial parliament. The second ballot alliance between socialists and liberal-democrats proved ineffective against the clericals. Since the Alsace-Lorraine Center, Social Democrats, and liberal-democrats each won six additional seats of the second ballot, the clericals did as well as any other party. Although the Social Democrats, liberal-democrats, and independents won a larger percentage of contests entered on the second ballot than they did on the first, so did the clericals. The Alsace-Lorraine Center elected thirty-one percent of its candidates on the first ballot, and 54.5 percent on the second.

Clerical control of the *Landtag* was assured by a coalition between the Alsace-Lorraine Center and the Lorraine Bloc. Although the Lorraine Bloc was technically independent, it received strong support from the Center. About 16,000 votes for the Lorraine Bloc went to candidates backed by the clerical party. With thirty-four votes in the *Landtag*, the Center-Lorraine Bloc coalition held a workable Christian-conservative majority.[22] Although the *National-bund* attributed the clerical majority to government interference in the election, the 1911 *Landtag* election simply proved that the clericals had lost little of their political strength since the first Reichstag election in 1874.[23] The Social Democrats had made their spectacular gains mainly at the expense of the liberal-protester group.

Table 3.   *Landtag* Election of 1911[a]

	Candidates	Elected	Vote
ALSACE-LORRAINE CENTER			
1st ballot	42	18	93,101
2nd ballot	11	6	
SOCIAL DEMOCRATIC			
1st ballot	60	5	71,476
2nd ballot	8	6	
LIBERAL-DEMOCRATIC			
1st ballot	34	1	47,759
2nd ballot	12	6	
LORRAINE BLOC			
1st ballot	18	9	39,374
2nd ballot	2	1	
NATIONALBUND			
1st ballot	11	0	9,476
2nd ballot	4	0	
INDEPENDENTS[b]			
1st ballot	24	2	30,472
2nd ballot	9	6	

a. Sources: *A.D.B.R.*, AL 27, paquet 57, no. 246; Rossé et al., *Das Elsass*, 4: 73.
b. "Independents" includes candidates supported by the liberal-democrats, but who preferred to run as independents.

Analysts have variously interpreted the 1911 *Landtag* election. Some saw it as proof of a growing mood of separatism in Alsace-Lorraine, a growing estrangement from the Reich. This argument was bolstered by the absence of some of the German parties such as the German Center, *Deutsche Reichspartei, Deutsche Volkspartei,* and *Freisinnige Vereinigung,* which had played minor roles in recent Reichstag elections in Alsace-Lorraine. Instead, the Alsace-Lorraine Center, the territorial Social Democratic party, the *Liberale Landespartei,* the *Elsass-Lothringische Demokratische Partei,* the *Bloc Lorraine,* and the *Nationalbund* emerged as territorial parties rather than German national parties.[24] One certainly cannot argue against the fact that these were territorial parties, but the existence of territorial parties in itself does not prove a growing estrangement from the Reich. In the first place, this was a territorial *Landtag* election, not a national Reichstag election, and the first territorial election based on universal suffrage. One would expect greater emphasis on territorial issues and a greater focus on strictly territorial parties. What happened in Alsace-Lorraine was really no different from what ordinarily occurred in other German states such as Bavaria, where there were numerous territorial parties. The only difference was, as Hohenlohe-Schillingsfürst had pointed out, that when an ordinary event occurred in the Reichsland, German ultra-nationalists always managed to attach some sinister importance to it. Those who argue that the election indicated an alarming growth of separatism conveniently forget that the *Nationalbund,* the one party totally dedicated to a nationalist-particularist program, suffered a crushing defeat. Being a new party, the *Nationalbund* naturally lacked an expert organization; but as one proponent of the separatist argument himself has admitted, the *Nationalbund* also lacked a precise legislative program. No candidate campaigning solely on a particularist platform won a seat in the *Landtag.* The people wanted more than just nationalistic slogans; they wanted candidates who promised to deal with concrete issues such as tax policy. The parties may have been territorial parties, but the issues of taxation and foreign policy were questions of concern to all German citizens.

The *Landtag* election pointed up the particularly complex political situation in Lorraine. The Lorrainers used the right of universal suffrage to express their conservative and clerical sentiments. But the vote was not uniform throughout Lorraine; it generally followed linguistic and cultural lines. By 1911 Lorraine consisted of three parts, including the old French and German cultural and linguistic areas, and an additional "foreign" German enclave which had grown up around Metz since the turn of the century. The Lorraine Bloc took the ten districts on the French (west) side of Lorraine, the Alsace-Lorraine Center won the seven districts in the old German-speaking area in the east, while the liberals captured the three Metz districts heavily populated with German immigrants.[25] To speak of the "Alsace-Lorraine political situation" in 1911 is clearly impossible, since the situation in Lorraine alone displayed major variations.

Finally, one might argue that the 1911 *Landtag* election proved nothing at all, because the electoral districts were gerrymandered. The Reichstag districts had not been altered since 1874, so that population shifts could explain the fact that districts such as Colmar, Ribeauville, and Schlestadt had less than 70,000 inhabitants, while Mulhouse, Strasbourg-Ville, Metz, and Thionville had over 160,-000. But the *Landtag* districts were brand new in 1911, so why should the Niederbronn and Busendorf districts have 20,000, while Molsheim-Wasselone had 35,000, and the two Thionville districts in Lorraine had 44,000 inhabitants each?[26]

Only three months after the *Landtag* election, the 1912 Reichstag election challenged territorial parties to another test of strength. Still exhausted from the *Landtag* election, the major parties in Alsace-Lorraine conducted a rather subdued campaign. The liberal-democrats, whose organization was particularly weak, barely functioned at all, and received sharp criticism from the Social Democrats for doing so little to combat the clerical "reactionaries." Although there were only fifteen Reichstag electoral districts in Alsace-Lorraine compared to the sixty *Landtag* constituencies, the liberal-democrats were unable to nominate candidates in several districts, and entered other races so late as to make their appearance virtually worthless.[27]

Continuing the trend set in the *Landtag* election, national issues outweighed regional questions in the 1912 Reichstag election. Discussions of war and peace, the size of the military budget, and democratic control of foreign policy dominated the political debate. Emphasizing the need for amicable relations between Germany, France, and Great Britain, the Social Democrats campaigned for parliamentary control over foreign policy and a reduction of the military budget. Funds diverted from the military budget could be spent on socially useful projects. The socialists complained that irresponsible fiscal policies of the German Center and Conservatives had raised the imperial debt from 267,786,000 RM in 1890 to 4.9 billion in 1910.[28] Joining the Social Democrats in calling for reduced military expenditures, the *Liberale Landespartei* further urged the creation of a "people's army," and the establishment of true parliamentary government by making the chancellor responsible to the Reichstag. Blumenthal's democratic party also backed candidates pledged to oppose increases in the military budget.[29] Local concern for national German political and economic affairs in the 1912 campaign indicates that on the eve of World War I, the people of Alsace-Lorraine were willing to assume the role of full citizens in the German empire. As good citizens, they saw their role as one of responsible criticism.

Results of the Reichstag election in Alsace-Lorraine closely reflected the trend of national politics. As the national SPD increased its strength in the Reichstag from 43 to 110, the territorial Social Democratic organization raised its vote from 81,589 (23.7 percent) in 1907 to 110,695 (31.7 percent) in 1912. Although the Alsace-Lorraine Center won seven seats against the socialists' five, the percentage of votes going to the Center dropped from 41.9 in 1907 to 34 in 1912.[30] The socialists elected three of their deputies on the second ballot, with help from the liberal party in Strasbourg, Colmar, and Metz.[31] Metz was a particularly significant victory for the Social Democrats; Georges Weill was the only socialist ever elected to the Reichstag from Lorraine during the German regime. His victory indicated that the Lorraine Bloc was beginning to crack under the strain of continuing German immigration spurred on by Lorraine's burgeoning iron and steel industry.[32]

The 1911 *Landtag* election and 1912 Reichstag election provided catalysts for further political transformation in Alsace-Lorraine. Shocked by their disappointing performance in the elections, the bourgeois parties reorganized for more effective action. Amidst rumors of disorder within the liberal movement, Georg Wolf offered assurances that the old German dualism between National Liberals and Progressives would not be reproduced in Alsace-Lorraine.[33] Two months later, in March 1912, the liberal and democratic parties joined to form a new Alsatian *Fortschrittspartei*. The party platform, which made no mention of the traditional democratic demand for a republic, reflected the liberal point of view. Throughout 1913 and 1914, the liberal and democratic wings of the party threatened to split apart; in July 1914 several German newspapers reported the imminent creation of a new *Deutsche-Elsässischen Partei*, composed of liberals from the progressive party, moderate monarchists, and the *Wirtschaftlichen*.[34]

Responding to the progressives, the right wing of the liberal movement established the Alsace-Lorraine *Mittelpartei* in May 1912. The *Mittelpartei* charged other parties with selling out their principles in efforts to win votes among the newly enfranchised electorate. By uniting with democrats and independents in the progressive party, the left-wing liberals had made concessions to local nationalism and aided democratic attempts to establish a republic.[35] While claiming to support Alsace-Lorraine's struggle for equality, the *Mittelpartei* stressed the need for "a closer bond with the German empire and her monarchical institutions, protection of the Reich from both external and internal forces, and the preservation and strengthening of her world position."[36] Although regional interests must not be forgotten, they must be secured in conjunction with the interests of the empire. The *Mittelpartei*'s influence is difficult to estimate, since no major election took place between its founding and the outbreak of the Great War. Like the earlier *Nationalbund*, the *Mittelpartei* viewed itself as a party of national conciliation, bringing together the "nationally oriented elements of Right and Left." The *Mittelpartei* probably would have fared better than the *Nationalbund*, for it did not repeat the mistake of emphasizing "local nationalism" or particularism. The *Mittelpartei*'s attempt to align regional policy more closely with that of the empire, its desire to narrow the distance between Alsace-Lorraine and the empire, struck a responsive chord. The *Mittelpartei* offers further evidence that by 1914, the process of politicization was leading the territory toward a closer relationship with the German empire.

The magnetism of the Reich affected the major parties as well as lesser forces such as the *Mittelpartei*. Introduction of universal suffrage in the 1911 *Landtag* election produced splits in most of the territorial parties, as factions sympathetic to Germany began to assert an independent line. In April 1913 several German newspapers commented on the "crisis" within the Alsace-Lorraine Center. The crisis involved a struggle for leadership between a democratic-particularist wing led by Emile Wetterlé, Anselm Laugel, and Nicolas Delsor, and a more conservative German-oriented group including Karl Hauss, Georg Ricklin, Charles Didio, and Martin Spahn. Hauss finally gave up the Center chairmanship amid rumors that he would establish a separate Catholic party sympathetic toward Germany and attached to the German Center party. Political observers regarded Didio's 1913 *Landtag* candidacy as evidence of increasing support for the German cause in Alsace-Lorraine.[37]

Implementation of the 1911 constitution produced a general realignment in regional politics. While the basic dualism between political Catholicism and Social Democracy continued to dominate regional politics, there was also a significant tendency toward closer political integration with the rest of the German empire. Concern with imperial, national issues as well as traditional local questions, the emphatic rejection of the particularistic *Nationalbund*, the founding of the *Mittelpartei*, and the development of a pro-German wing of the Alsace-Lorraine Center all indicate that on the eve of World War I, prospects for the successful political integration of Alsace-Lorraine into the German empire were by no means dim.[38] At least one French observer in 1910 pointed to the growing success of Social Democracy as proof that the Germanization program had at last succeeded in imposing on Alsace-Lorraine the "German spirit, which as we know is much more inclined than ours to adopt socialist-collectivist ideas."[39] In a post-war reflection on the situation at the close of the German regime, the former territorial liberal leader Wilhelm Kapp maintained that the Franco-German conflict in the Reichsland had faded away, replaced by the struggle for internal political power within Alsace-Lorraine itself.[40]

Kapp's assessment may sound unduly optimistic, but it reinforced the view of Governor Wedel himself. The German ultranationalist press loudly assailed Alsace-Lorraine's particularism, to the point where Wedel complained that the German press was causing him more trouble than Abbé Wetterlé and his pro-French friends. Wedel considered the development of a "healthy" particularism as the surest, perhaps the only means of integrating the Reichsland into the Reich. As Alsace-Lorraine became more conscious of its individuality, it would naturally draw away from France and gravitate toward Germany, where her economic and political interests were more fully represented. Since Wedel's opinion carried little weight with the German nationalists, the governor cited the infallible Bismarck, claiming that the Iron Chancellor himself had counted on the

development of "German particularism" when he created the territory of Alsace-Lorraine. In the summer of 1912 Wedel held high
hopes for the successful integration of Alsace-Lorraine into the
empire. "In any case," wrote the governor, "I have great optimism
concerning the present situation, though admittedly tempered with
skepticism that a sudden change could bring about a set-back."[41]
Then came the Zabern affair.

9
POLITICAL ECONOMY IN THE REICHSLAND: THE ECONOMIC SUBVERSION OF POLITICAL INTEGRATION

Political and cultural Germanization programs promised little success without the corresponding integration of Alsace-Lorraine into the German economy. The enormity of the economic crisis facing the Alsace-Lorrainers in 1871 possibly outweighed the political disaster. Their land was not only detached from France in a political sense, but was also torn from the French market and tariff system and incorporated into the foreign world of the German *Zollverein*. The result was a forty-seven-year period of economic "adjustment" which pointed toward the economic subversion of political integration.

In 1871 the focal point of Alsace-Lorraine's economy was the cotton textile industry centered in Mulhouse. The industry was significant both qualitatively and quantitatively, producing at the time of the annexation nearly as much cotton goods as the entire German *Zollverein*. The achievements of the Alsatian textile industry represented the fruits of decades of technical innovation and farsighted business decisions. Its success also depended upon favorable government tariff policies. During the Restoration, Alsatian

Portions of this chapter have appeared in my article, "The Economic Consequences of Annexation: Alsace-Lorraine and the German Empire, 1871–1918," and are reprinted with permission from *Central European History* 4, no. 1 (March 1971), 34–53.

commerce and industry suffered from the government's discriminatory and protectionist policies. The law of 28 August 1816
favored the seaports of southern and western France over Strasbourg
as the entry point of goods destined for Swiss and German markets.
The government steadfastly refused any concessions which might
shift some of the overseas trade toward the Rhine and Strasbourg.[1]
The Alsatian economic center began to shift from Strasbourg to
Mulhouse, as the textile industry challenged the transit trade for
supremacy. The developing textile industry soon became the center
of controversy between free-traders and protectionists. The protectionist French government rejected opportunities to join the
Prussian *Zollverein* despite indications that Bavaria, Baden, and
Württemberg would have preferred French leadership to Prussian.
While the Upper Alsatian textile manufacturers found a steady
market in Paris for their quality products, the more commercially-
oriented region around Strasbourg encountered serious economic
difficulties through the mid 1850s. Economic stagnation in Bas-Rhin
accompanied a population loss of 23,579 between 1851 and 1856.[2]

With the signing of the Chevalier-Cobden Treaty, 23 January
1860, France and Britain embarked upon a course which virtually
established all of Europe as a free-trade zone for a number of years.
Between 1861 and 1867, France concluded additional tariff reduction agreements with Belgium, the German *Zollverein*, Italy, Switzerland, Norway, Sweden, the Hansa cities, Spain, the Netherlands,
Austria, Portugal, and the Papal States. Just as the impact of the
trade agreements was about to be felt, the Civil War erupted in the
United States. The regular supply of raw cotton from the American
South suddenly dried up, forcing the Alsatians to seek substitutes
from all parts of the world. Mulhouse textile mills continued operating at a reduced pace, but only at substantial cost to the owners.
The leading new import was Egyptian cotton, which required the
conversion of machinery originally designed to accommodate short-
staple American cotton.

Ignited by the 1860 trade agreement with Britain, controversy
split the Alsatian textile industry. The most explosive aspect of the
pre-1870 tariff controversy concerned "temporary admissions" (*admissions temporaires, appreture Verfahren*). An 1836 French law
authorized temporary duty-free import of raw materials destined
to be manufactured into finished products, or products intended for
additional processing in France. So it would not compete with

French goods on the domestic market, material entering under temporary admission had to be processed and reexported or placed in bond within six months. When imperial decrees of 1861 and 1862 revived the temporary admission system, critics claimed the 1836 law had not envisaged importing cotton goods for the purpose of printing them. Nevertheless, during the 1860s the government permitted temporary admission of both low grade cottons produced more cheaply in Britain, and fine grades which printers could have purchased just as reasonably from French producers.[3]

Temporary admission of textiles produced serious division in the Alsatian textile industry. Cotton spinners and weavers generally opposed the practice while textile printers, seeking the least expensive source of cotton goods, favored it. One of the most powerful Alsatian proponents of temporary admission was Jean Dollfus, owner of some of the largest textile printing factories. Dollfus had collaborated with his British friend Richard Cobden to help consummate the 1860 trade agreement. In Mulhouse the 1869 parliamentary election pitted the free-traders represented by Jean Dollfus against protectionists led by Pierre-Albert Tachard. Dollfus lost, for although the textile printers supported him, most of the spinners and weavers opposed him.[4] A most interesting aspect of the campaign was the solidarity between protectionist factory owners and their workers who, "eagerly joined their bosses in the demonstrations under the illusion that protection would somehow produce better working conditions."[5]

On the eve of the Franco-Prussian War, the tariff controversy still boiled in Alsace. Fighting for higher tariffs, owners of spinning and weaving mills in Haut-Rhin formed the Syndicat cotonnier de l'Est. Pressure from this group led to the discontinuance of temporary admissions by an imperial decree of 10 January 1870. A rival Syndicat des Imprimeurs then secured a parliamentary hearing resulting in restoration of temporary admission in a modified form making it slightly less advantageous to the printers.[6]

The annexation of 1871 created an entirely new situation for both the Alsatian and German textile interests. While the loss of the French market represented a disaster to the Alsatian textile industry (of the 18,410,000 kilograms of cotton thread produced in Haut-Rhin in 1869, all but 2,000 kilograms were sold in other parts of France), the competitive threat from Alsace represented a potential disaster to the relatively undeveloped German textile industry.

French factories consumed 128,000 tons of raw cotton in 1869, while their counterparts in the entire German *Zollverein* consumed an average of only 68,000 tons annually between 1866 and 1870. A German textile industry still relying on manual equipment in 1870 faced Alsatian textile factories utilizing modern power-driven equipment manufactured locally by the Alsatian machinery industry. Recognizing the probability of stiff competition from the Alsatian textile industry, the Committee of South German Industrialists petitioned King Wilhelm of Prussia to renounce annexation of the upper Alsatian industrial region.[7] Other south German industrialists pressured the French and German governments to give the Alsatian industrial region to Switzerland; as compensation to Germany, Switzerland would transfer territory to the German empire. Bismarck did suggest such a plan during the 1870–71 Brussels negotiations with France, but the Swiss government refused to embroil itself in the Franco-German dispute.[8]

Failing to prevent annexation, the south German textile manufacturers felt the government at least ought to protect German businesses from Alsatian competition. Such protection, they argued, could be achieved only through guaranteeing the Alsatians their traditional French markets by maintaining low tariffs between Germany and France. One German proposal envisioned a twenty-year transition period, during which the German government would pay all or part of the tariff on Alsatian goods exported to France, while France and Germany simultaneously reduced general tariff rates.[9]

Annexation also threatened the Alsatian industrialists' heavy capital investment; production for a new German market would require major expenditures for new equipment. Faced with a political and economic crisis of major proportions, the Alsatian textile industry demonstrated remarkably little solidarity. While some promoted the anti-German League of Alsace, others sought an accommodation with the Germans.

The varied reactions of Alsatian industrialists to the German regime become more understandable in the context of the long-standing dispute over tariff policy. The post-1871 schism among industrialists was still based on different approaches to the tariff question; but the incorporation of Alsace-Lorraine into the German customs union occasioned a realignment of opposing factions. Most Alsatian industrialists became free-traders, even if they had been protectionists before 1870. They recognized that only a free-trade agreement between France and Germany could guarantee Alsatian access to the traditional French market. Those who remained protectionists after the annexation were businessmen who believed they could transfer most of their operations to French branch factories, thereby maintaining contact with regular customers without the benefit of a Franco-German trade agreement. When it became clear that no permanent economic agreement concerning Alsace-Lorraine would materialize, the tariff and temporary admission issues came alive once again.[10]

Efforts to reach a Franco-German agreement on special arrangements for Alsace-Lorraine's foreign trade began in 1871 while peace negotiations were still in progress. The burden of the effort rested with the Alsace-Lorrainers themselves, since Adolphe Thiers, elected chief of the French executive power by the Bordeaux National Assembly, believed direct overtures by the Alsatians in Berlin or at the Brussels peace talks would produce the best results.[11] To strengthen their hand before negotiating with Bismarck, owners of Alsatian spinning and weaving mills formed a *Syndicat Industriel Alsacien*, the textile printers formed a committee, and the Mulhouse industrial society created a "Committee for the Protection of Alsatian Interests." Part of the Mulhouse committee, led by Auguste Dollfus, held conversations with Bismarck at Versailles beginning 23 February 1871. Another segment of the Mulhouse group, headed by Jean Dollfus, consulted with officials in Berlin. The committee hoped to conclude an agreement permitting Mulhouse industrialists to sell existing stocks of goods under prewar tariff conditions, an objective which they partially achieved. During April 1871 Colmar and Strasbourg followed the lead of Mulhouse in forming committees to protect local economic interests, and also sent delegations to Berlin.[12] For a few brief months, the threat of annexation compelled the Alsatian textile interests to unite. As planned by the Germans, the new Franco-German boundary would separate the various segments of the industry by tariff barriers. Spinning and weaving operations would be denied free access to the finishers, dyers, and printers. The industry would be destroyed unless the French and German governments reached an agreement protecting the economic interests of the territory.

Considerable suspicion surrounded the negotiations at Versailles, Brussels, and Berlin. Many people believed the industrialists were simply trying to protect their own interests at the expense of the rest of the people, and others questioned the propriety of any loyal Frenchman dealing with German authorities. Politically oriented Catholic priests such as Landolin Winterer and Joseph Marbach took a particularly dim view of negotiations between Protestant industrialists and German officials. Some Catholics claimed that "anti-Catholic liberal" delegations encouraged the Germans to introduce anticlerical measures in Alsace-Lorraine. Some priests disagreed with Winterer and Marbach. Joseph Guerber commented that, "in my opinion, they [the delegations] are doing the sensible thing, and the Catholics might learn something from them."[13]

The industrialists' delegations in the spring of 1871 achieved limited success. In political matters, the talks failed completely. Bismarck made vague promises about regional self-government, promises which were never honored. He refused to postpone introduction of German military conscription. Although Bismarck promised that the Alsace-Lorrainers would "be consulted on everything that happens," the Organic Laws for the Reichsland were framed by the imperial government without consultation with territorial representatives.[14] There was, of course, some question as to who really represented the people. The League of Alsace would have refused to meet with the Germans, and branded the industrialist delegations as traitors. In defense of the German government, it must be admitted that lack of any political consensus in the Reichsland made it difficult to consult local representatives prior to introducing the new regime.

Although they failed on the political front, the delegations did secure important economic concessions. The 12 October 1871 additional act to the Frankfurt Treaty permitted Reichsland products to enter France duty-free until 31 December 1871. After that date, the tariff was to be increased gradually until it reached the full normal rate by 1 January 1873. French products and raw material entering Alsace-Lorraine received a reciprocal low tariff rate.[15] Although the additional act did not provide the twenty-year transition period desired by some German and Alsatian industrialists, it was nevertheless a worthwhile achievement. The German government was not completely insensitive to economic dislocation caused by the annexation. Negotiations on the German side were carried out by no less a personage than Count Harry von Arnim, the German plenipotentiary in Paris. Arnim's reports to Bismarck indicate willingness to make rather significant concessions to France in order to win a period of economic grace for Alsace-Lorraine. The French insistence upon reciprocity for French goods entering the Reichsland received recognition. Even more surprising in view of the militaristic foundation of the German Empire was the agreement to reduce by 50,000 the number of German occupation troops in six eastern departments in return for French tariff concessions for Alsace-Lorraine. As Arnim reported to Bismarck, the advantage to France in reducing her occupation costs was greater than the cost of the tariff concessions she was making; but he never made clear how Germany was to benefit from the agreement.[16] The French bargained hard, and Arnim had trouble nailing down a firm agreement. In his 14 September 1871 report to Bismarck, Arnim indicated a "final agreement" setting 1 July 1873, as the concluding date of the transitional tariff period, but the actual additional act of 12 October extended only to 31 December 1872.[17]

The special tariff arrangements for Alsace-Lorraine granted the Alsatian textile interests a reprieve from immediate loss of their French markets, and gave the German industry some time to prepare its market for Alsatian competition. This was only a temporary situation, however; the special tariff arrangements expired 31 December 1872, although provisions for the temporary admission of partly finished products from French Lorraine were extended through 30 June 1873. Under the agreement Alsace-Lorraine manufacturers could receive special tariff rates only for the amounts of goods they had sent to interior France in 1869. After all of Arnim's hard bargaining, the Alsatian textile manufacturers were unable to take full advantage of the treaty provisions. In 1872 the only full year during which the special provisions operated, they exported 66,177,807 meters of unprinted cotton fabric, against a permissible total of 150,026,630 meters. Out of an authorized total of 67,713,-198 meters of printed and dyed cotton material, they exported to France only 18,321,757 meters, and an additional 27,137,671 meters of goods finished under the temporary admission provision, for a total of 45,459,428 meters. The relatively high figure for temporary admissions indicated that a large number of spinners and weavers on the French side of the Vosges mountains continued to have their finishing work performed in Alsatian plants until new facilities could be readied in France.[18] A special *Syndicat Industriel Alsacien* supervised all exports to France during the transition period; they, rather than German authorities, were charged with preventing fraud in determining the amounts of exports. Despite their failure to reach their legal quotas, the Alsace-Lorraine industrialists under the *Syndicat* exported products valued at 350 million francs to France, against only 1,449,330 francs to Germany during 1871–72. Toward the end of 1872, however, the value of exports to France began to decline, as the Alsace-Lorrainers prepared to enter the German market and tariff system.[19] As they finally felt the full impact of the economic consequences of annexation in late 1872, how would the Alsatian industrialists react to their new German fatherland?

Financial considerations, rather than patriotism or lack of patriotism, determined the attitude toward the German regime taken by Alsatian industrialists. Over the years, the Alsatian textile industry had tended to disintegrate; that is, in the interests of efficiency, firms specialized in spinning, weaving, bleaching, dyeing, and printing, rather than attempting to combine all operations in a single unwieldy factory complex. Only spinning and weaving remained closely connected in a common plant, largely because the spinners preferred not to risk selling their products on the open market. The effect of the annexation was to sever the Alsatian textile industry, the brain resting at Mulhouse, from the rest of the body in what was now France.[20] The new political boundary confronted the Alsatian industrialists with a dilemma which taxed their financial genius far more than their patriotism. Some Alsatian companies continued operations within the French market and tariff system by transferring the bulk of their operations to factories within France. Other firms lacking the necessary capital and flexibility continued to operate in Alsace-Lorraine, and tried to adjust to the German market structure. At Mulhouse, for example, operators began to manufacture worsted, which was preferred on the German market. Such adjustment generally required extensive, costly modification of production techniques; and rapid price increases in the construction and metallurgy industries after 1871 forced the cost of retooling out of reach of many firms. German tariff policy, however, provided continuing pressure for production modification. Before annexation, much of the cotton thread spun in Alsace was number 40 or above, very fine thread for the French luxury market. The progressive *ad valorem* tariffs of 1860 guaranteed adequate protection for the fine threads, but after 1871 the German flat rate produced much greater protection for coarse than for fine numbers.

New German tariffs amounted to about twenty percent for coarse numbers, but only about one-half percent for fine thread. Production statistics soon reflected German tariff policy, as the average thread number declined from 38 in 1869 to 30 in 1877.[21]

Firms capable of shifting operations to France held a distinct advantage over those which could not. It is unclear how many companies moved across the Franco-German border after 1871, but it seems to have been a fairly large-scale movement. Henri Laufenburger and Pierre Pflimlin have pointed to "a veritable migration of our industry to nearby departments which remained French," and J. H. Clapham wrote that, "many Alsatian manufacturers refused to accept German citizenship and made a fresh start on the French side of the Vosges."[22] Clapham's implication that French patriotism accounted for the departure of Alsatian industries is overdone. By moving to France, Alsatian industrialists could take advantage of both French and German markets; German tariffs remained low until 1879, while French tariffs protected domestic producers from foreign competition.[23]

Few factory owners closed their Alsace-Lorraine operations and constructed new plants in France. Firms generally established branch factories in France and continued to direct business from a home office in Alsace-Lorraine. The important Wesserling finishing establishment of Gros, Roman, and Marozeau, cut off from its normal source of fabric on the French slope of the Vosges, moved part of its bleachery to Thaon (department of Vosges), where it developed into an operation of considerable proportions. While Alsace thus lost significant capital, labor, and management resources after 1871, the gain to France was considerable. The number of cotton spindles in the department of Vosges alone jumped from 366,148 in 1871 to 451,800 in 1879. The *Groupe cottonier de l'Est*, which dominated cotton production in the five eastern departments, controlled 627,200 spindles in 1879, 720,000 in 1889, and nearly three million, or forty percent of the French total, in 1912. The same process occurred in the weaving industry as the number of looms in the department of Vosges rose from 13,183 in 1871 to 16,450 in 1879; for the five eastern departments, the number of looms increased from 21,180 in 1879 to 23,000 in 1889, and 50,000 in 1912. Alsatian interests controlled much of the new plant in eastern France; 978,000 spindles and 15,330 looms in the five eastern departments remained under Alsatian direction in 1908.[24]

There is no reliable estimate of the total loss suffered by Alsace-
Lorraine through industrial migration to France; the impact in
various parts of the territory was very uneven. One of the more
extreme cases often cited is that of Bischwiller, a leading center for
the manufacture of cloth before 1870. Between 1869 and the beginning of 1874, Bischwiller's population dropped from 11,500 to
7,700; her labor force from 5,000 to 1,800; the number of weaving
machines from 2,000 to 650; the number of spindles from 56,000 to
22,000; and the amount of annual business from 18–20 million
francs to only 5–6 million francs.[25]

The declining health of the textile industry led to decreased prosperity for its main supplier, the machine industry. In the long run,
the Alsatian machine construction industry managed to survive and
even expand on the basis of orders from the German railways and
developing electrical industry. In the short run, however, the machine makers experienced serious reversals. The French government granted export subsidies to French machinery manufacturers,
enabling them to compete favorably with the Alsatians even within
the German tariff union; thus the smaller Alsatian firms experienced
great difficulty. Hoping to gain strength through merger, André
Koechlin and Company joined with a Graffenstaden firm in 1872
to form the *Société Alsacienne de Constructions Mécaniques*. Merger failed to keep the firms afloat, and the *Société* finally established
a French branch at Belfort in 1879. The Alsatian factory continued
to produce textile machinery, while locomotive production went to
the Belfort works.[26]

Like the machinery manufacturers, the Alsatian chemical industry
depended largely on the local textile industry for its market. Annexation made little difference, since the chemical manufacturers
sold most of their production to local printers, dyers, and finishers.
Development of artificial colorants during the 1870s caused some
factory closings in Alsace, but this type of technological unemployment can not be ascribed to either the annexation or subsequent
government policy. Although the Alsatian chemical industry did
not participate in the tremendous upsurge experienced by the German chemical industry as a whole prior to 1914, it did remain strong
enough to supply the Alsatian textile industry and thereby retarded
the economic integration of the textile industry with the German
economy.[27]

A few firms in the Lorraine iron industry, despite extremely high plant construction costs, established branch operations in France. Particularly hard hit by the annexation, the Lorraine iron industry was cut off from the French market by tariff barriers and suffered in the German market owing to high German railway rates. The German iron and steel industry in the Rhine-Westphalia region already supplied the nation with much of her requirements at lower cost than the Lorraine plants; nevertheless, the Lorraine iron industry held up surprisingly well during the early 1870s despite the 1873 crash. Speculation in Lorraine had not been so rampant as in the rest of Germany, and orders from expanding railways and heavy industry in Germany and the United States kept the Lorraine mills going. Eventually the depression of the 1870s took its toll in Lorraine too, but the German tariffs of 1879, coupled with the new Thomas-Gilchrist process for smelting phosphorous iron ores, ultimately revived the Lorraine iron industry.[28]

War, annexation, and emigration disrupted traditional Alsatian family businesses, most of which could not raise the capital required for retooling and establishment of branch factories in France. As a means of surviving, many firms established themselves as joint stock companies—the *Société Alsacienne de Constructions Mécaniques,* for example—as a means of raising capital without sacrificing company control to the bankers. Alsatian industrialists who did turn to the banks found it advantageous to build new factories in France, since French discount rates and interest rates were lower and more stable than German rates. At a time of general abundance of free-market capital during the 1870s, Germany suffered from a continuing outflow of gold, and was forced to protect its gold supply with a high discount rate.[29] Not only did German loans cost more than French, but labor costs were also higher in Germany, due to German restrictions on child labor, and a labor shortage caused by emigration. The construction of branch factories in France in part represented a search for cheap, plentiful labor.[30]

The Alsatian industrialists who could afford to retool or establish branch factories in France possessed a formidable advantage over their less fortunate Alsatian competitors. They could well afford to be anti-German, since they did not depend on a Franco-German tariff agreement to preserve their share of the French market. Charges by the League of Alsace that the 1871 delegations to Berlin hoped to protect their own interests were true; but the industrialists opposing negotiations with the Germans had just as much at stake.

Some industrialists protected their interests through large capital investment in new plants. Others had to turn to the German government for a tariff agreement which would enable them to remain competitive.

The expiration of the special tariff arrangement with France at the end of 1872 forced the Alsatian industrialists into the open market without any type of protection. Although the general European depression of the 1870s undoubtedly accounted for a major portion of their difficulties, the Alsatians, along with other German industrialists, blamed the government's free-trade policy for the decline in business activity. The damage done to manufacturers of fine cotton products is indeed incontestable, and the story appears similar in other industries. It has been plausibly argued that French locomotives, backed by government export subsidies, commanded a larger share of the Alsatian market than engines built in the local factories in Graffenstaden. There was little justice in a system which permitted French locomotives to enter the Reichsland duty-free, while the Graffenstaden manufacturers paid approximately 3,000 francs duty on each locomotive exported to France. It was no consolation that some of the French competitors were former Alsatian manufacturers who had moved their operations to the French side of the border.[31]

From 1873 to 1878 Alsatian industrialists led the fight for protective tariffs in Germany. Largely as a result of pressure brought by the *Syndicat industriel alsacien*, government inquiries in 1877–78 produced evidence of the need for higher tariffs to protect all German industries. These findings fortunately coincided with Bismarck's shift from free trade to protection as a means of finding new revenues for the imperial government. The year 1879 thus brought some relief to Alsatian interests in the form of higher tariffs. In the case of cotton thread in particular, a new progressive system, ranging from 15 centimes per kilogram on coarse numbers to 45 centimes on fine, assured the Alsatian textile industry's survival without complete retooling.

Within two years of Bismarck's resignation in 1890, Germany under Caprivi had embarked on a most ambitious series of trade agreements whose effect was to reduce German tariffs just as the French were raising theirs under the Méline legislation.[32] Hoping to secure concessions for German manufactured goods in return for reductions in German agricultural tariffs, the Caprivi government between December 1891 and February 1894 signed trade agreements valid until 1903 with Switzerland, Belgium, Italy, Austria-Hungary, Serbia, Rumania, and Russia. Agricultural interests in Germany reacted violently to what they regarded as an attack on the integrity of the landed aristocracy. Alsace-Lorraine had no landed aristocracy, but it did account for 26.19 percent of Germany's wine-growing acreage in 1898, more than any other German state. It was the German-Italian trade agreement which most directly affected the Alsatian wine industry. Caprivi made important concessions to the Italians, ostensibly because he hoped to drive French wine off the German market by introducing stiffer Italian competition. Getting squeezed in the middle, without much concern from Caprivi, was the Alsatian wine industry, which seems to have suffered most from the Italian trade agreement. As Caprivi expected, Italian wine imports did rise after 1892, but imports from France also held steady, leaving the Alsatians with more competition than before 1892.[33]

The trade agreement which most concerned the Alsace-Lorrainers was the pact with Switzerland. The Swiss agreement directly affected the Alsatian textile industry, already hard-pressed as a result of the French Méline tariffs. The French tariffs of 1892 unwittingly accomplished what Bismarck had hoped to accomplish with the passport regulations a few years earlier; they severed nearly all remaining economic ties between Alsace-Lorraine and the French market. Indeed, the French 1892 tariff may have been as much of a shock to the economy of Alsace-Lorraine as the annexation itself in 1871. It produced many of the same effects, including renewed interest in the establishmnet of branch installations across the French border. [34] In addition to losing what was left of her French market, Alsace-Lorraine now faced increasing competition from British textile manufacturers, who had also been driven from the French market by the Méline tariffs and sought to replace their losses in Alsace. Caprivi disregarded Alsatian textile interests when he negotiated the Swiss trade agreement. The Swiss made few concessions, and in some cases the new Swiss tariffs on Alsatian textile products were higher than before the agreement. For the Alsatian manufacturers of fine cottons, the Swiss agreement brought no improvement at all. In 1870 they had produced about 2,250,000 kilograms of fine cotton thread (numbers 60–79); between 1887 and 1892, the average was 838,600 kilograms; and by 1899, production of

fine cotton thread had fallen to 361,506 kilograms. Using 1891 as
the base year (100), imports of numbers 60–79 rose to 162.5 by
1898.[35] In defending the Swiss trade agreement, the government
argued that no German textile interests would be harmed, since none
of them manufactured fine thread above number 60.[36] One can
hardly blame the Alsatian textile manufacturers if they refused to
think of themselves as Germans, because the government apparently
did not consider them to be Germans either.

Viewed as a whole, German tariff policy after 1872 did little or
nothing to help integrate the Alsatian economy into the imperial
structure. In fact, German tariff policy consistently sacrificed Alsatian interests to those of the Reich, under both Bismarck and Caprivi.
One must, however, take care not to attribute all of the Reichland's
economic problems to German tariff policy. The French tariffs of
1892 did their share of damage, too. And if the Swiss agreement opened Alsace to foreign competition, it is equally true that
the agreements with Italy, Austria-Hungary, Belgium, and Russia
opened new markets for the Alsatian textile industry. Finally,
Alsace-Lorraine's economic vitality depended on factors other than
German tariff policy, as important as that tariff policy might have
been. In the general European depressions of the 1870s and 1890s,
Alsace-Lorraine suffered as did every other state, and for this type
of general slump the German government cannot be held responsible.

When government financial and economic policy did happen to
coincide with the interests of Alsace-Lorraine, German business
interests, fearful of competition from the Reichsland, usually managed to find enough Reichstag votes to defeat the government's
programs. Alsace-Lorraine played a major role in the execution of
Bismarck's imperial financial policy. The chancellor used the Reichsland as a testing ground for programs he hoped to apply to the entire
empire, and in cases such as the proposed imperial tobacco monopoly, the interests of the Reich and the Reichsland were identical.
Critics have accused Governor Manteuffel of using Alsace-Lorraine
as a battering ram for Bismarck's imperial financial program.[37]
When he learned that Bismarck desired to establish an imperial
council on political economy (*Volkswirtschaftsrat*), Manteuffel set
up such a council in the Reichsland. The governor also collaborated
in using Alsace-Lorraine for experiments with liquor taxes and an
imperial tobacco monopoly.

In the case of the liquor taxes, imperial and Prussian interests overrode regional interests. One of the most controversial measures introduced in the Reichsland, the liquor tax was not simply a financial matter; it affected the growing social problem of alcoholism. Alcoholism ranked as a major cause of death in Alsace-Lorraine after 1870 because people were consuming excessive amounts of inferior liquor. The annexation cut Alsace-Lorraine off from the normal supply of French wines, and the resulting shortage was met by importation of low grade liquor from north Germany, Silesia, and Pomerania, where landowners produced alcohol from potatoes.[38] Territorial committee debates on alcoholism indicated that a solution might lay in reform of the liquor tax laws; higher taxes would reduce consumption of inferior German alcohol. The imperial government, however, which legally held sole responsibility for liquor taxes, refused to alienate the Prussian aristocracy by enforcing higher taxes to reduce alcohol sales.

When Manteuffel proposed taxing every glass of liquor sold in restaurants and hotels, Bismarck objected on the grounds that a tax which most seriously affected the poorer people might encourage the socialists.[39] Supported by the Strasbourg beer breweries, the territorial committee endorsed a selective tax on the most harmful types of alcohol. Disregarding local sentiment, the government raised hotel and restaurant license rates, on the assumption that the higher fee would force some businesses to close, thereby making it more difficult to obtain liquor. While the new regulation damaged the hotel and restaurant business, it had little effect on the alcoholism rate. Although the territorial committee received over eighty petitions requesting repeal of the license fee increase, the government held firm. Victory on the liquor tax question, however, did not presage success for Bismarck's next financial adventure, his attempt to create an imperial tobacco monopoly. The fate of the Alsace-Lorraine tobacco industry depended on the outcome of the monopoly project, and when the Reichstag rejected it, the local tobacco industry suffered a damaging blow.

Bismarck wished to overhaul the imperial tax structure so as to free the imperial government from dependence on matricular contributions from the states composing the empire. By 1879, he had secured major tariff and excise reforms, but by adding to the original bill the so-called Franckenstein clause, the Reichstag limited the imperial share of new revenues. The government presented a new tax package in 1880, but the Federal Council rejected most of it. At this point, Bismarck decided to try for an imperial tobacco monopoly.

As early as 1872 Bismarck had sought to raise tobacco taxes; a Reichstag commission approved the proposed increase, but the Federal Council refused to take it up. In 1878 the government appointed a special commission to study tobacco taxes and the commission recommended a tobacco tax increase which the Reichstag passed in 1879.[40] Actually, the government already manufactured tobacco products. Manufacture and sale of tobacco products had been a state monopoly under the French regime. With the annexation of Alsace-Lorraine, the state-owned tobacco factory in Strasbourg fell into the hands of the German government. Third largest of the French imperial tobacco factories, the Strasbourg plant was a fine war prize. When most French officials in Alsace-Lorraine resigned rather than accept Germany's invitation to serve the new emperor, Bismarck abolished the tobacco monopoly in the Reichsland, since no experienced administrators were available to direct it. Although the government had technically abolished the monopoly, the Strasbourg tobacco factory remained a state-owned operation.[41]

State ownership of the factory aroused opposition from tobacco wholesalers in both Alsace-Lorraine and Germany, who objected to state interference with free enterprise.[42] The Saxon delegate to the Federal Council charged the factory administration with incompetence. Instead of proving to be a financial asset, the factory allegedly required large government subventions to keep it solvent. In 1882 a factory director was tried for misconduct in office, and a special commission examined the factory's account books.[43] Climaxing the drive to end government ownership of the factory, one hundred German tobacco manufacturers petitioned the Reich Chancellery to discontinue the Strasbourg operation. Reich Chancellery President Rudolf von Delbrück indicated the government was considering sale of the factory, but warned against pressure from private business. The government, he said, would decide for itself when to liquidate its tobacco interests.[44] Delbrück had to balance the pleas of the tobacco merchants against the demands of the tobacco growers who feared loss of an outlet for their crop, and of tobacco factory employees who feared loss of their jobs if the government sold the Strasbourg factory.[45]

In 1872 the Reichstag empowered Bismarck to sell the Strasbourg tobacco factory through competitive bidding. The German press cited the proposed sale as evidence that Bismarck had given up any idea of establishing an imperial tobacco monopoly. A syndicate made a reasonable offer for the factory, but for unexplained reasons this transaction was never completed. Negotiations for sale of the factory continued for several years, with a Reichstag commission urging in 1875 that the government sell the plant as quickly as possible. The factory was never sold.[46]

Bismarck, supported by Alsatian planters who feared they would be ruined by loss of the French market, had not given up the idea of an imperial tobacco monopoly. Although the French tobacco monopoly continued to purchase Alsatian tobacco until 1882, this sale was no longer guaranteed after 1871. In 1877 tobacco growers asked the German government to purchase the Alsatian crop, and in 1879 the territorial committee passed a motion supporting a German state tobacco monopoly.[47] The government had begun a propaganda campaign in Alsace-Lorraine to promote the monopoly project. Tobacco planters were promised the highest prices, and taxpayers were assured the income from a monopoly would enable the government to drop the federal matricular contribution from the Alsace-Lorraine budget. To smooth the way for an imperial tobacco monopoly, Bismarck sent the Bavarian Catholic Georg von Mayr to Strasbourg as undersecretary of state for finance.[48] The territorial committee cooperated in 1880 and again in 1881 by approving government requests for 500,000 marks to expand the sale of Strasbourg tobacco factory products throughout Germany. Anticipating a larger market once the monopoly went into effect, the government used part of the special appropriations to increase the stock of cigars in Strasbourg, and spent a considerable portion to purchase branch factories in neighboring Baden.

Establishment in Baden of branches of a state-owned tobacco factory alarmed German private tobacco interests. Selling tobacco products directly to consumers at factory prices constituted unfair government competition. The Augsburg chamber of commerce complained, and the Society of German Tobacco Manufacturers sent two delegations to hold discussions with Governor Manteuffel. Manteuffel, who supported Bismarck's monopoly plan, was unsympathetic. The governor's task was to promote the interests of the Reichsland, and he believed the development of the Strasbourg factory could only bring greater prosperity to the territory. In 1885, long after the Reichstag had rejected the tobacco monopoly bill, Manteuffel still supported the project and reported to Bismarck that local sentiment for the monopoly remained strong.[49] The governor may have overestimated local support, for when the purchase of the Baden factories became public knowledge, the initial enthusiasm for the monopoly declined considerably. Members of the territorial committee felt they had been duped by the government; Eduard Jaunez complained that, "I never would have voted for it [supplemental appropriations] if I had known that part of it would be capitalized in real estate in the Grand Duchy of Baden."[50] Although the huge stock of unsold cigars in the Strasbourg warehouses worried the territorial committee deputies, their anxiety temporarily subsided before assurances that the forthcoming imperial monopoly would dispose of the surplus. South German tobacco manufacturers, however, were not so easily placated, and controversy over the Strasbourg factory highlighted many Federal Council sessions.

Extension of Strasbourg factory operations to south Germany raised questions of jurisdiction in the affairs of Alsace-Lorraine. This was an imperial territory, legally subject to control by all of the German states acting together. Did not the other states have the right to protect themselves from competition from Strasbourg? Most German governments believed the Federal Council retained the right to intervene in the tobacco question. Delegates from Saxony, Württemberg, and Baden recommended that the Council examine the affairs of the Strasbourg tobacco factory. Defending the government, Georg von Mayr argued that the law of 1879 delegated the imperial chancellor's authority in the Reichsland to the governor, who thus became the final authority. The Federal Council, he claimed, could not meddle in Alsace-Lorraine's affairs. Only Prussia and Braunschweig supported Mayr.[51] While the Federal Council was willing to examine the affairs of the Strasbourg factory for signs of mismanagement, it adopted a hands-off policy on restricting competition. In January and again in June 1881, the Council refused to consider complaints of German tobacco manufacturing associations against the extension of the Strasbourg factory's activities into south Germany.[52]

The tobacco controversy still occupied the Federal Council in 1882 as the government introduced legislation for an imperial tobacco monopoly. Although the monopoly bill was part of Bismarck's new economic policy, the Federal Council debate on the

Strasbourg factory suggests that Bismarck might have waited for a more opportune moment to try for the monopoly. After discussing the monopoly on 24 April 1882, the Federal Council reluctantly gave its approval by a 36 to 22 vote. Württemberg gave the most spirited defense of the monopoly, which simply amounted to the admission that the empire needed money, and there seemed to be no other way to get it. Baden and Hesse objected to the monopoly on the grounds that it would damage important private tobacco works in their states, create unemployment, and incite either emigration or riots among the displaced workers. The representative from Bremen warned that his city's entire economy would be ruined by a tobacco monopoly.[53]

When the bill reached the Reichstag, Bismarck's conflict with the economic liberals came into full view. While the government contended that the monopoly would benefit consumers by eliminating the middle man, liberals such as Leopold Sonnemann, publisher of the *Frankfurter Zeitung,* argued against any curb on private enterprise. Sonnemann held that government competition would destroy private industry, since the government exercised extraordinary powers. Private enterprise, for example, could not simply annex capital as the state had done in the case of Alsace-Lorraine. A basic contradiction marred Bismarck's economic policy; while the government persecuted the working class with strong antisocialist laws, it promoted a socialistic tobacco monopoly. Persistence in the government monopoly project, warned Sonnemann, might alienate the middle class from the regime.[54]

Although France did maintain a successful tobacco monopoly, she had established it while the private tobacco industry was relatively undeveloped. Private tobacco interests in Germany, however, were quite substantial, and the cost to the government for buying out this private sector would have been enormous. With such stiff expropriation payments, the state's eventual profit from a tobacco monopoly would have been insignificant. The benefit to the consumer, cautioned Sonnemann, was equally questionable; once the private tobacco industry was destroyed, the state monopoly would be free to charge any price it desired.[55]

The Reichstag rejected the tobacco monopoly bill in June 1882 by a 277 to 43 vote. The bill's failure spelled disaster for the Strasbourg factory and the Alsatian tobacco planters. Anticipating the monopoly, the factory had been overstocked with what were now derisively termed "monopoly cigars." Just when the planters were beginning to feel pressure from imported tobacco, they lost the certain outlet for their crop which the monopoly would have provided.[56] Bismarck's defeat on the tobacco monopoly bill not only marked a severe setback to his general financial program, but also damaged government attempts to conciliate the Alsace-Lorrainers. Local condemnation of the government's tobacco policy was extremely bitter. The priest Landolin Winterer characterized the monopoly project as "a dangerous experiment in the satisfaction of imperial policy at the expense of the Alsace-Lorraine state treasury." "What has happened," he complained, "could not have happened in any other state of the German empire, because nowhere is the imperial interest so dominant as here."[57] Not even a friend of the government such as the tobacco planter Baron Hugo Zorn von Bulach could condone the government's tobacco policy. "I am a convinced monopolist," he admitted, "but improper direction of the Strasbourg tobacco factory ruined the monopoly plan we approved."[58]

A tobacco monopoly presented no real conflict of interest between the empire in general and Alsace-Lorraine in particular. The Alsatian economy would have benefited, and while the income from a monopoly would have strengthened the imperial finances, the expanded market would have favored the Alsatian tobacco industry. Despite objections from some south German states, Berlin exercised more influence and control in the Reichsland than in any other German state. The logical place for Bismarck to initiate new programs, Alsace-Lorraine served as a testing ground for imperial reform projects.

The clash of interests between Reichsland and empire arose only when the imperial government lost its gamble with Reichsland financial resources in a futile attempt to pave the way for an imperial tobacco monopoly. When the Reichstag rejected the monopoly bill, the government took no steps to protect the Alsatian tobacco industry. Bismarck soon lost interest in a tobacco monopoly, and ignored Manteuffel's suggestion in 1885 to revive the monopoly bill. A perceptive Alsatian wrote that, "we have always believed that Bismarck's enthusiasm for Alsace-Lorraine was lost in his great concern for the empire."[59] Bismarck showed interest in Alsace-Lorraine only when he felt the Reichsland might help him achieve larger goals in imperial financial and foreign policy.

CHAPTER 9 / POLITICAL ECONOMY IN THE REICHSLAND   185

Without the tobacco monopoly, the tobacco industry of Lower Alsace did not thrive. Acreage planted in tobacco steadily declined from a high of 3,859 hectares (one hectare equals 2.4710 acres) in 1875 to a low of 1,483 hectares in 1913. The number of tobacco planters likewise plunged from 12,562 in 1872 to 8,000 in 1913. Those who survived in 1910 formed a *Tabakbauverein*, and obtained an agreement from the Strasbourg factory to purchase about one-third of their crop. In general, however, the quality as well as quantity of Alsatian tobacco declined between 1871 and 1913, as planters refused to invest in improved methods of cultivation without the guarantee of a market for their crop.[60] Looking ahead past 1919, when Alsace-Lorraine was once again included in the French state monopoly system, one can see how Bismarck's monopoly proposal might have benefited the Reichsland. By 1928 tobacco accounted for 2,690 hectares, and the number of planters had risen to 10,800.[61]

German business associations had sought to prevent the annexation of Alsace-Lorraine in the first place. Having failed, they combined to defeat Bismarck's proposed imperial tobacco monopoly, which would have benefited Alsace-Lorraine at their expense, and later they blocked canal projects on the Moselle and Rhine rivers which would have enabled Lorraine iron ore and Strasbourg commercial firms to compete more favorably with German companies. The German government also refused to construct additional rail links with France through the Vosges mountains, a measure which the Alsatian textile interests very much desired.

The failure of the Moselle canal project forms part of the larger story of a conflict of interest between iron and steel interests in Lorraine and Rhineland-Westphalia. A canal from the Moselle to the Rhine would have enabled owners of Lorraine's iron ore to ship it cheaply to the steel processors in the coal-rich Rhineland-Westphalia area. Until about 1895, the coal and steel interests in the Rhineland, among them Krupp and Thyssen, favored a canal project, because there was no competition between the two regions at that time. There was an agreeable division of labor between Lorraine, which produced cast iron from local iron ore and coke from the Ruhr, and Rhineland-Westphalia, which manufactured steel products from cast iron purchased in Lorraine. So long as that division of labor persisted, nothing would have better suited the German steel interests than improved transportation along the Moselle.

By 1894 changes in the organization of the iron and steel industry in both Lorraine and the Ruhr produced a complete turnabout in attitudes toward the proposed Moselle canal. Cooperation gave way to competition as iron and steel firms in both Lorraine and the Ruhr integrated and consolidated themselves into units capable of performing all functions from the smelting of raw iron ore to the manufacture of finished steel products. No longer did Lorraine ship most of its iron ore to the Ruhr; the Lorraine plants now built their own blast furnaces and converted cast iron into steel and steel products, in direct competition with German firms in the Rhineland. Between 1898 and 1909, production of steel and steel products in Lorraine rose from 374,000 tons to 1,200,000 tons. In 1911 half of the iron ore produced in Lorraine was processed in local plants.[62] Simultaneously, Ruhr steel plants were importing an ever increasing proportion of their iron ore from Sweden, and no longer depended on a cheap supply of ore from Lorraine. At a time when the coal and steel giants of the Ruhr were expanding at breakneck speed, firms as large as Krupp and Thyssen had little capital to spare for investment in Lorraine; to fill the vacuum, the government permitted Belgian and Luxemburg capital to develop Lorraine's steel potential. Not content with bringing to bear their economic weight, the Westphalian metallurgists launched a vicious press attack against Governor Wedel, trying to unseat him with charges of failing to do his duty as a German. Under the guise of patriotism, the Westphalian industrialists hoped to rid themselves of dangerous competition from Lorraine.[63]

As a result of objective changes in the organization of the iron and steel industries, the Rhineland coal and steel interests vigorously opposed the Moselle canal project after 1895. Such a canal would have done much to tie Lorraine closer to the German empire. The Ruhr steel interests were determined to limit competition and thereby obstruct the economic integration of the Reichsland with the Reich. The imperial government recognized this as a hazardous policy, and tried unsuccessfully to secure construction of a Moselle-Saar canal. Under pressure from the industrialists, the Prussian government rejected a canal project on 7 April 1910. The imperial government then introduced in the Reichstag in 1911 a comprehensive plan to make all German waterways part of a national system subject to national regulation. As Germany entered the war in 1914, however, there was still no canal linking Lorraine's iron ore with the Ruhr industrial complex.[64]

Attempts to limit competition from Alsace-Lorraine—and thus to exclude the Reichsland from the phenomenal economic development of the empire on the eve of the Great War—were not limited to the case of Lorraine's iron and steel industry. The deepening and regulation of the Rhine river, and the development of the port of Strasbourg, produced a direct conflict of interest between commercial interests in Strasbourg and Baden. Except for a few months each summer, large vessels could travel up the Rhine only as far as Baden's port of Mannheim; thus it was Mannheim rather than Strasbourg which handled most of the river trade involving south Germany and Switzerland. Baden's government, supported by German railway interests, opposed any plan which might open the Rhine to Strasbourg. In 1885 the Alsace-Lorraine territorial administration proposed to the territorial committee a canal linking Strasbourg and Ludwigshafen, at a cost of thirty-eight million marks. The cost was considered too great, the canal project was dropped, and no further action was taken until 1893. In that year, Baden, Bavaria, and the Alsace-Lorraine territorial administration launched a cooperative study on how best to improve Rhine navigation. They reached no agreement, largely because Baden had little interest in a project which was certain to damage business in Mannheim. Meanwhile, Strasbourg, at her own expense, had been improving her port facilities since 1892, in the expectation that eventually the Rhine would be navigable.

Not until 1898 did Alsace-Lorraine, Baden, and Bavaria agree on a plan to regulate the Rhine, making navigation possible up to Strasbourg; but the parties failed to agree on how the costs would be shared. Alsace-Lorraine insisted that payment should be made in proportion to the length of shoreline each state possessed, while Baden and Bavaria favored a cost-sharing plan based on the economic advantage or disadvantage the project would have for each state. Under the Baden plan, Alsace-Lorraine would pay the largest share, since it stood to gain the most. The discussions over cost-sharing dragged on from 1898 to 1906, when agreement was finally reached. The total cost was set at thirteen and a half million marks. Bavaria agreed to put up 800,000 marks; Baden agreed to pay forty percent of the cost, with one million marks of her share being put up by the city of Strasbourg and a German coal syndicate; and Alsace-Lorraine was to finance fifty percent of the project, as well as any sum not covered by the contributions from Baden, Bavaria, and the city of Strasbourg. Work began on the project in 1907, with results clearly visible by 1913, when the tonnage handled at Strasbourg had risen to 1,988,310 against 627,020 in 1907. Strasbourg was on the way to becoming a major port, but at what cost! Alsace-Lorraine paid the greatest share of the cost of regulating the Rhine. The city of Strasbourg paid 700,000 marks of Baden's share; the city also had to pay the military treasury two and a half million marks for land needed to develop port facilities, and paid for the docks and warehouses as well. Moreover, while supposedly encouraging Strasbourg's development, the Germans began work on competing port facilities across the river at Kehl, which first opened for traffic in 1900. The Baden railways gave the Kehl facilities favorable rates, making it difficult for Strasbourg firms to compete for the south German and Swiss markets.[65] Strasbourg was clearly sacrificed to the economic interests of other German states. Had Strasbourg remained a German city after 1919, it probably would have lost out to Kehl in the long run. What prosperity Strasbourg did achieve between 1871 and 1919 came in spite of rather than because of the policies of German political and economic interests.[66]

The overall performance of Alsace-Lorraine's economy under the German regime is difficult to judge. Each sector of the economy demonstrated unique performance characteristics, and new industries controlled by Germans tended to perform better than old industries dominated by Alsace-Lorrainers. Industrial development was significant, but the manner in which it occurred probably benefited Germans more than Alsace-Lorrainers. The vast iron ore deposits in Lorraine, Lorraine metallurgy, the important Alsatian potash deposits whose exploitation began only in 1910, and the Alsatian oil fields at Pechelbronn—that is to say most of the new industry developed after 1871—were financed and managed mainly by German and foreign interests.[67] The textile industry, already well established in 1871, remained in the hands of Alsatian owners. But this segment of the territory's economy recorded one of the worst growth records, and barely managed to hold its own.[68]

A survey of Alsace-Lorraine's economy in 1914 indicates thriving new industries controlled by German and foreign interests, and a stagnating textile industry held by Alsatians. Regardless of any gains made toward the political integration of the Reichsland, the Alsace-Lorrainers could hardly have been pleased with their economic situation. Ever since the annexation, German manufacturing interests had done their best to thwart the economic integration of Alsace-Lorraine into the empire; integration meant competition.

Germany, of course, benefited from the development of Alsace-Lorraine's natural resources; the Reichsland might serve as a source of supply and supplement for German industries. In this limited sense, German industrialists favored some degree of economic integration of the Reichsland. Nevertheless, a basic assumption remained constant; economic integration would come not because the Alsace-Lorrainers either desired it or deserved it, but only when and if it suited the interests of German industrialists.

Cut off from their French markets, the Alsace-Lorrainers by 1914 wanted little more than access to the German market. They were willing to see themselves as Germans, insisting only that they be permitted to share in Germany's prosperity. Entrenched economic interests in Germany would have none of this; and so long as they resisted the economic integration of the Reichsland, the entire process of political integration and constitutional reform was jeopardized.

10
ZABERN AND ITS
AFTERMATH: BACK TO 1871

Created in the glory of Prussian military supremacy in 1871, the Reichsland Alsace-Lorraine dissolved under the shadow of Germany's military collapse in 1918. Lacking a thorough understanding of internal developments in the territory, it is easy for one to conclude that the Reichsland ended exactly as it had begun, no closer to integration in the German Empire than it had been in 1871. In the area of administration, this view which implies German "failure" in Alsace-Lorraine merits a respectful hearing. It is, however, equally possible to argue that by 1914, the people of Alsace-Lorraine would have been content with full German citizenship. The difficulty lay not with the people, but with a German government dominated by military interests, which insisted upon governing the territory in a dictatorial manner.

During the closing years of the Second German Empire, many of the weaknesses of the Bismarckian system began to emerge clearly, and it is questionable whether the system would have survived much longer even had military defeat not brought the entire structure down. Owing to its special status as an imperial territory, Alsace-Lorraine was the area most sensitive to the internal contradictions of the imperial system. The famous Zabern affair of 1913 is a case in point.

In a narrow sense, the Zabern affair indicated how official Germany regarded its "long-lost brothers" forty-two years after their return to the fatherland. A German lieutenant insulted Alsatian army recruits, a German officer struck Alsatian civilians, and a German colonel ordered the arrest of about thirty other civilians.

Although the military officers clearly exceeded their rightful author- ity over civilians, a military court exonerated them, and Chancellor Bethmann Hollweg defended their actions before the Reichstag. Not even the Reichstag's vote of censure against the chancellor could induce the government to upbraid the officers involved. Regarding Berlin's attitude as a vote of no confidence, Governor Wedel, Secre- tary of State Bulach, and all of the undersecretaries of state resigned early in 1914.[1]

That Wedel should have been so totally abandoned by the kaiser is one of the more disturbing elements in the Zabern affair. As a sign of confidence in his former adjutant, Wilhelm II had granted the new governor authority to appoint and dismiss his state secre- taries in November 1907.[2] It boded ill for the imperial constitutional structure that in 1913–14 the kaiser consented to the disgrace of a trusted general as a means of protecting the "honor" of the military establishment as a whole.

The outward appearance of unity behind the kaiser and the ultra- militarists was indeed deceptive, for there were military officers who felt the kaiser had not chosen the best method of protecting the army's reputation. Wedel, himself a general, would have avoided the entire controversy by furloughing and eventually dismissing Lieu- tenant Forstner; Colonel von Reuter could have been transfered to Pfalzburg, where the remainder of his regiment was garrisoned. As an old officer, Wedel neglected no opportunity to defend the military, but to try to cover up the army's misdeeds only served to further damage its reputation.[3] Because he had to defend his own position, Wedel cannot be considered an impartial witness, but testimony from less directly interested sources confirms Wedel's position. Count Bogdan Hutten-Czapski, Hohenlohe-Schillingsfürst's aide and adviser who had served as a brigade adjutant in Hanover and squad- ron commander in Kassel, recognized the Zabern affair as, "the first sign that a schism had developed in the structure of the army." "The real significance of the Zabern affair," explained the count, "was that the insubordination of a subordinate went unpunished." Czapski shared Wedel's opinion that an immediate transfer of Lieutenant Forstner and punishment of Colonel von Reuter would have fore- stalled the entire crisis.[4]

Czapski claimed to have the support of a number of high-ranking officers. Immediately following the Reichstag's 4 December 1913 vote of censure against the government's handling of the Zabern

affair, he wrote the chancellor that several senior officers had expressed to him the need to punish the Zabern officers; and the
stronger the punishment, the closer it would bind the army and the
people. General Walter Bronsart von Schellendorff, Prussian minister of war from 1893 to 1896, told Czapski that it would have been
preferable to announce publicly the government's intention to make
a legal investigation into the Zabern affair and punish any violation
of law. "My sense of smell may be deceiving me," wrote Bronsart,
"but it seems to me that for a long time the situation in Alsace has
been rotten."[5]

   That the thoughtless, stupid actions of a young German lieutenant
could lead to the censure of the imperial chancellor and the collapse
of the entire Strasbourg administration indicates that this was not a
simple local issue, not just one more "incident" to be added to the
long list of such occurrences since 1871. It may have been, as Hans-
Ulrich Wehler has argued, "the cause and expression of the last
great structural crisis of the late Wilhelmian empire before the war."[6]
This was a repeat performance of the Prussian constitutional conflict
of 1861–66 between a liberal parliament and militaristic monarchy.
During the closing years of the second empire, the middle and left
parties attempted to strengthen parliamentary control over the
imperial government and pull down the socially and politically
privileged classes in Prussia. The imperial political system had
lagged far behind Germany's social, industrial, and technological
development since Bismarck's miraculous act of creation in 1871.
The inherent dangers in a constitutional system which failed to
designate clearly the distinction between the emperor as a national
symbol and the emperor as an unlimited organ of power were now
compounded by the leadership of Wilhelm II, who gave little thought
to the legal basis of his powers and possibly had never read the
imperial constitution. In 1913 Wilhelm threatened to smash the
Alsace-Lorraine constitution to bits and transform the territory into
a Prussian province, as if he alone had the power to do that.[7] As the
liberals and socialists continued to press for constitutional clarification and reform, the Zabern affair sharply focused the broad debate
between liberals and conservative Junkers on the specific issue of the
relationship between civil and military authority.

   Even under Bismarck's iron hand, the army existed as a state
within the state, but Bismarck did manage with difficulty to keep
the direction of major domestic and foreign policies out of the

hands of the military. But the army's isolation from the rest of society led to increasing civil-military conflicts. The Prussian king and German emperor had always claimed a special *Kommandogewalt,* free from all restrictions of parliamentary control and ministerial countersignature. Although neither the Prussian nor the imperial constitution appeared to provide for such special command powers, the emperor nevertheless exercised these powers in practice. The real constitution of the empire thus lay in the power structure rather than in the written documents. Efforts to protect the army from political interference led the kaiser to transfer most responsibility from the Prussian war ministry to the Military Cabinet and General Staff. Having lost much of his authority, the war minister still had to defend the kaiser's *Kommandogewalt* before the Reichstag. The chancellor, too, was obliged to defend the emperor's command powers, and although Bethmann Hollweg had no desire to abdicate to the military over the Zabern incident, he had no choice but to back the army and risk the Reichstag's vote of censure.[8]

In Alsace-Lorraine, the civil-military conflict and the problem of the kaiser's command powers was particularly acute. Czapski summarized the problem with the observation that, "from the beginning the military believed they had the right to govern Alsace-Lorraine as a territory which they had conquered."[9] Tension increased as the military regarded the social boycott among the higher levels of Alsatian society as a sign of the most dangerous kind of animosity which demanded energetic punishment.[10] The Zabern affair "constituted an open power struggle between civil and military power, whose resolution made the deficiencies of the Bismarckian constitution even more alarming."[11] It was the task of the imperial leadership to find an acceptable solution which would have protected the population's civil rights without damaging the legitimate authority of the military. Gerhard Ritter believed it would not have been difficult to find such a solution; the problem was that no one in the government was responsible for doing it. In Bismarck's single-minded desire to relieve himself of the daily responsibility for the Reichsland's affairs, he had neglected to establish any institutional (as opposed to personal) control over the Alsace-Lorraine administration.[12] Only the kaiser could have saved the situation, but Wilhelm II never recognized any responsibility except to the military. It was this consideration which led Prince Alexander zu Hohenlohe-Schillingsfürst to conclude that a constitution which permitted a nation of seventy million to be ruled by such a man as Wilhelm II merely on the basis of his birth as a Hohenzollern was no longer workable in the modern age.[13]

The Zabern affair was a test of power, which the parliamentarizers and democratizers clearly lost. The outcome of the Zabern affair illuminated the powerlessness of parliament, and even the chancellor, over the military apparatus. The civil government watched in horror as the military wrecked its efforts to integrate the Alsace-Lorrainers into German political life. When the dust from the affair had settled, the ultimate fate of the empire was already largely determined; the idea of a constitutional state had been replaced by the absolutistic conception of irresponsible military authority. In the contest for power, the system based on the emperor's unrestricted command power had swept to victory. With this "triumph" under his belt, Wilhelm II entered a world-wide conflagration, encumbered by a socio-political system totally out of step with the aspirations of modern society.[14] Forty-six years later, Gerhard Ritter recognized the Zabern affair as, "the prelude to still more horrible experiences in World War I."[15] In the heat of the conflict, Wedel saw "a situation which is incompatible with the idea of a modern *Rechtsstaat*. How it will all end, God only knows."[16] But long after the German empire lay in ruins, there were still many Germans such as Czapski who failed to comprehend the significance of the Zabern affair. Czapski wrote in 1935 that the incident indeed clouded German politics, but it seemed to bind the monarch and the people in a closer union. Though the outward signs may have been lacking, the kaiser as he grew older was gaining a better understanding of the duties of a modern ruler. Had fate only granted him the time, dreamed Czapski, the kaiser would have made all of the necessary reforms.[17]

The consequences of the Zabern affair, so decisive for the future of the empire, were no less significant in the Reichsland itself. With the resignation of Governor Wedel and his staff, the way was opened for a return to the original administrative system of the high presidency, although in theory the 1911 constitution remained intact. In the heat of the Zabern affair, however, it has generally been forgotten that Wedel himself was not the most suitable personality to head the parliamentary system established in 1911. Although he had pushed for the 1911 constitutional reforms, Wedel dealt awkwardly with the parties represented in the new parliament. Seeking to construct a parliamentary majority for passage of tax reforms and improved salaries for lower and middle range state officials, Wedel invited representatives of the Alsace-Lorraine Center, the liberal party, and the Lorraine Bloc to a conference prior to the opening of the 1913 *Landtag* session. His intentional failure to invite the Social Democrats produced a good bit of hostility toward the government. While the *Strassburger Neue Zeitung* was technically correct in asserting that, "Count von Wedel can invite anyone he wishes to his home," it made little political sense to affront the second largest party in the territory. Wedel laid himself open to charges of taking advantage of political pluralism by adopting "divide and rule" tactics.[18]

Wedel's January 1914 resignation in the aftermath of the Zabern affair confronted the government with an unexpected crisis. Bethmann Hollweg and the emperor were unable to agree on Wedel's successor until March. During the interim, Count Siegfried von Roedern, the high president of Brandenburg, was transferred to Strasbourg as secretary of state. His appointment indicated a stiffening government attitude toward Alsace-Lorraine. Military circles meanwhile pressed for the appointment of a general to the governorship, while others suggested leading German princes for the post. There was even speculation that Bethmann Hollweg, his own position shaken by the Zabern affair, might assume the governorship were he forced to relinquish the chancellorship.[19] The appointment of Hans von Dallwitz, a bureaucrat who had risen through the ranks to become Prussian minister of the interior in 1910, came as a surprise. Compared to the princes, fieldmarshals, and diplomats previously assigned to the governorship, Dallwitz appeared a man of small stature; but his reputation as a conservative satisfied the demands of the military for stronger government in Alsace-Lorraine. Dallwitz's career included experience in suppressing a non-German population in the Polish provinces. He believed the repeal of the dictatorship paragraph, followed by the introduction of the German press and association laws in Alsace-Lorraine, had been a misguided policy encouraging nationalist agitation against which the government was now powerless. Dallwitz had also opposed Bethmann Hollweg's drive for the new Alsace-Lorraine constitution in 1911.

Dallwitz attributed the "failure" of German policy in the Reichsland to the fact that Germany continually underestimated the extent of anti-German sentiment in Alsace-Lorraine and refused to take it seriously.[20] Although Dallwitz did not include himself among those

misguided Germans, he seems to have misjudged the extent to which
the Alsace-Lorrainers objected to his nomination as governor in
1914. Dallwitz had no delusions concerning the liberal German
press, which "characterized me as a typical East Elbian Junker and
sinister reactionary sent to Alsace-Lorraine to institute draconic
measures." The new governor believed he had received a friendlier
reception from the territorial press in Alsace-Lorraine; they at least
adopted a wait-and-see attitude.[21] One wonders which newspapers
Dallwitz was reading. Noting that there was no real conservative
party in the territory, the clerical *Le Nouvelliste d' Alsace-Lorraine*
concluded that Dallwitz would have to change his ways if he wished
to avoid an unpleasant confrontation with the *Landtag*.[22] The *Courrier de Metz,* skeptical that "a convinced partisan of the retrograde
ideas in vogue with the circle of East Elbian *hobereaux"* could
reform himself, foresaw nothing but trouble for Alsace-Lorraine.[23]
Expressing disappointment with Dallwitz's appointment, the *Mülhauser Volkszeitung* consoled itself with the reassurance that the
constitution of 1911 was still intact. The *Strassburger Neue Zeitung,*
however, warned that, "we have lost a part of the constitutional
independence and political honor which we possessed after 1911."[24]

Dallwitz's appointment was an astute political move by Bethmann
Hollweg. While satisfying military demands for strong government
in Alsace-Lorraine, he opened the way for reform in Prussia. In the
chancellor's scheme, Dallwitz's nomination for the Strasbourg post
was a secondary consideration; it was more important that Dallwitz
was being removed from the Prussian *Staatsministerium*.[25] Although
Dallwitz ushered in a period of reaction in Alsace-Lorraine, his
appointment was part of Bethmann Hollweg's plan to obtain liberal
reforms in Prussia. For some years, the chancellor had sought a
modification of Prussia's three-class voting system. Although the
emperor had promised such a reform in 1908, the Prussian ministry,
led by Dallwitz, consistently withheld its approval. Dallwitz's "promotion" to the governorship conveniently removed him from Berlin
without causing him to lose face. Dallwitz realized why Bethmann
Hollweg had asked him to take the governorship. The chancellor, he
wrote, "wished to change the Ministry of Interior, and felt that giving
me the Alsace-Lorraine post was the only way to relieve me without
personal insult and alienating my political supporters. Since I could
no longer accomplish anything as Minister of Interior, due to my
conflicts with Bethmann Hollweg, I accepted the Alsace-Lorraine

position."[26] His successor as Prussian minister of the interior, Friedrich Wilhelm von Loebell, was a moderate conservative who understood the need for compromise between Right and Left. After serving as an undersecretary of state and chief of the Reich Chancellery during the Bülow regime, Loebell had been appointed high president of Brandenburg in 1909 but resigned in 1910 for "reasons of health." His recall to office by Bethmann Hollweg indicated the chancellor's determination to bring Prussian reform to a successful conclusion. Dallwitz was sent to Strasbourg to prepare the way for electoral reform in Prussia.[27] The chancellor apparently did not realize that the outcome of the Zabern affair had doomed Prussian constitutional reform.

Dallwitz's arrival in Strasbourg signaled a return to the system of the Möller high presidency of the 1870s. Dallwitz, like Möller, was a trained administrator. His program was about what one would expect from a professional administrator. The new governor was "determined to govern with strength against anti-German agitation, but also to treat the population with the greatest calm and objectivity. I regard it as my major function to iron out the administrative problems and promote the territory's economic development."[28] The administration of Alsace-Lorraine would end exactly as it had begun, under the direction of a Prussian bureaucrat. In view of the total transformation of the regional political and social structure since 1871, in view of the real progress toward integration, Dallwitz's appointment was wholly inappropriate.

What followed the Zabern affair and Dallwitz's appointment as governor was largely anticlimactic. Europe was soon at war, and the military finally had their opportunity to govern Alsace-Lorraine for a few brief years. Here at last was the chance to impose a "final solution" to the Alsace-Lorraine problem. Typical of the military's attitude toward the Reichsland while the war went well for Germany were remarks made to Secretary of State Count Siegfried von Roedern by Baron Ernst von Falkenhausen, the German troop commander in Alsace, and General Hans von Gaede, suggesting that the vicar general of Metz ought to be hung from the cathedral spire, and that troublemakers be hung or shot whether they be priests or *Landtag* deputies.[29] The military government managed to restrain itself from such wild acts of repression, but it did reduce the *Landtag's* functions to discussion of the budget, made arbitrary arrests, and established military tribunals to try citizens for alleged treason, aiding and abetting desertion, and other anti-German crimes. Military courts expelled and deprived of their German citizenship at least 5,600 persons.[30] Civilian officials gave way before the military onslaught, and in some cases the civilians even took the initiative in working out repressive measures. In 1917 General Erich von Ludendorff and the High Command demanded a military dictatorship in Alsace-Lorraine, including new measures to "Germanize" the clergy, expropriation of French interests, settlement of Germans in the border areas, and if all else failed, annexation of the Reichsland into Prussia; but as strong as Ludendorff's recommendations appeared, most of them had already been made in 1915 by Governor Hans von Dallwitz.[31]

As the war dragged on, military abuses increased and local support for the German regime declined. Seeking a total settlement of the empire's nationality problem, the kaiser, Chancellor Georg von Hertling, and Ludendorff agreed on 16 April 1918, that Kurland, Livland, and Estland would be joined with Prussia under a personal union, the Lithuanian duchy would go to a Saxon prince, and the Polish Kingdom to a Württemberg duke. As part of the general plan, Prussia would annex Lorraine, Bavaria was to take Lower Alsace, and Baden would receive Upper Alsace.[32] The war changed the outlook of even the most sympathetic Germans such as Karl von Wedel, who by 1915 had concluded that a change in Alsace-Lorraine's legal status was unavoidable in view of Germany's overriding national interest. While ruling out direct annexation by Prussia, Wedel could "see no other way" than to partition the Reichsland among several adjacent states.[33]

While the military steadfastly predicted victory, some Germans recognized the possibility that Germany might some day have to negotiate with the French. The strength of moderate sentiment in Germany became clear 19 July 1917, when the Reichstag passed Matthias Erzberger's resolution in favor of a peace of understanding without annexations. These realistic Germans argued that if the government granted Alsace-Lorraine her autonomy within the German Reich, the French would have no grounds for demanding the return of the territory. None of the German war-time chancellors supported such a move. Bethmann Hollweg in 1915 felt the risk of granting autonomy was too great; by the spring of 1917 he deferred to military pressure and supported partition of the Reichsland between Prussia and Bavaria. Bethmann Hollweg's successor, Georg

Michaelis, hinted at autonomy in order to avoid a direct confrontation with the "peace of understanding" faction in the Reichstag;
but he always maintained autonomy would have to wait until the
war was ended. In any event, Michaelis regarded the final disposition
of Alsace-Lorraine as an internal German matter, not to be discussed
with the Allies under any circumstances. Count Georg von Hertling,
who replaced Michaelis after the latter's brief term as chancellor,
wished to avoid any conflict with the military over Alsace-Lorraine;
as a former Bavarian minister-president, he sympathized somewhat
with the annexationist aims of the Bavarian king.[34]

The full impact of Germany's refusal to make Alsace-Lorraine a
true federal state has been debated since 1919. Gerhard Ritter has
argued that had Germany acted quickly in 1918 to grant the Reichsland real autonomy within the Reich, she might have been able to
save the territory. The Allied powers remained unconvinced of the
justice of France's demand for the return of the territory, the Left
in both Britain and France rejected the return of Alsace-Lorraine
as an indispensable war aim, and the socialists in both France and
the Reichsland were demanding a plebiscite rather than an arbitrary
solution imposed by the Great Powers. Woodrow Wilson did not
mention Alsace-Lorraine in the first draft of his Fourteen Points
speech of 8 January 1918; in the second draft, he merely demanded
that, "in the case Alsace-Lorraine is again incorporated in France,
Germany shall receive an equal compensation." Only at the last
moment did Wilson adopt his final formula demanding the return
of Alsace-Lorraine to France without mention of compensation.[35]

It is inconceivable that any French government would have consented to a peace which did not include the unconditional return of
Alsace-Lorraine; this was simply a nonnegotiable demand. The unfortunate territory had become a symbol of the power of both France
and Germany, and it is a rare nation which can summon the psychological strength to relinquish the symbols of power. To the Germans, however, Alsace-Lorraine may have meant even more than
it did to the French—the Reichsland was the cement that bound the
empire together. In 1875, responding to Thiers' apparent belief that
Germany might return Alsace-Lorraine in return for a large mone-
tary payment, State Secretary for Foreign Affairs Bülow wrote Ambassador Hohenlohe-Schillingsfürst in Paris that "possession of
Strasbourg and Metz is for Germany a matter of national necessity,
not simply a question of *amour propre*."[36] Twenty-seven years later,

Bülow the chancellor referred to Alsace-Lorraine as "the guarantee for the existence of the Reich," a territory which Germany could not relinquish without compromising national unity.[37]

As Germany's military position on the western front softened in 1918, the government recognized the possibility that Germany might indeed be forced to negotiate the Alsace-Lorraine question. In an apparent attempt to gain favor in the territory, the government called Strasbourg's Mayor Rudolf Schwander to Berlin to serve as state secretary in the imperial finance office (*Reichswirtschaftsamt*) from August to November 1917. As a final, futile gesture of good will in October 1918, Chancellor Prince Max named Schwander governor of Alsace-Lorraine, and appointed as his secretary of state Karl Hauss, leader of the pro-German wing of the Alsace-Lorraine Center. For the first time since 1871, Alsace-Lorrainers held the highest positions in the territorial administration.

Schwander's task was to establish an autonomous territorial government, but the hour for concessions had already passed. Wilhelm II abdicated 9 November 1918. The emperor's abdication posed serious legal problems for Alsace-Lorraine. The kaiser had exercised executive power in the Reichsland in the name of the Federal Council, had sanctioned all territorial legislation, and had appointed and instructed Alsace-Lorraine's three delegates to the Federal Council. The kaiser was no more. Did the Federal Council still retain control over the Reichsland? Indeed, without a kaiser, how could there be a Reichsland? German legal experts had no opportunity to offer their opinions. During the night of November 9–10, workers' and soldiers' committees formed in Strasbourg, declared a takeover of all public authority, assumed jurisdiction over the rationing of food, clothing, heat, and electricity, replaced the chief of police, and declared an end to restrictions imposed under the state of siege. As in Russia after the Bolshevik revolution, a sort of dual government emerged in Alsace-Lorraine. Challenging the actions of the soviets, the lower house of the *Landtag,* elected by universal suffrage, claimed legitimate jurisdiction over the territorial administration. On 11 November, Armistice Day, the lower chamber of the *Landtag* constituted itself as a "National Council," formed an Administrative Committee from among its own membership, distributed ministerial portfolios, and began to administer the territory in conjunction with the soviets. The Administrative Committee proposed to maintain order and carry on necessary business until a definitive regulation of the situation had been reached. The period of self-government lasted only until French occupation troops arrived in Strasbourg 22 November 1918. Once again, the Alsace-Lorrainers watched as the Great Powers decided their destiny.[38]

One is inevitably tempted to ask what might have happened in Alsace-Lorraine had the war not intervened. A clear answer to this question would tell us much about the "success" or "failure" of Germany's attempts to integrate the Reichsland into the Reich. The only honest answer is that no one will ever know what might have happened. The war disrupted normal political processes in the territory, and once again injected the problems of nationalism and patriotism into politics. The two major parties, the Alsace-Lorraine Center and the Social Democrats, had to reevaluate their positions, and in the process they began to split apart over the nationality issue. The Catholic leader Emile Wetterlé fled to France where he organized anti-German agitation. But the Center faction of the Alsace-Lorraine *Landtag* refused to support Wetterlé, and expelled him from the party.[39] The Alsace-Lorraine Center opposed plans to partition the Reichsland among adjacent German states, but might have approved annexation to Catholic Bavaria had the government decided on such a course. The Center leader Karl Hauss apparently accepted the post of secretary of state in October 1918 on the understanding that he was not committed to the continuation of the German regime.[40]

The territorial branch of the SPD found that its large membership of German immigrants created a wide chasm after 1914. Since 1871 the socialists had stood in the forefront among the protesters of the annexation, but as the immigrant population grew, this intransigent position softened. Even native Alsatian socialists such as Solomon Grumbach perceived certain advantages under the German regime; the authoritarian Berlin government had sanctioned far more social legislation than the petty bourgeoisie in France would tolerate. Only a month before the conflagration began, on 5 July 1914, the Alsace-Lorraine Social Democratic Party meeting in Strasbourg passed a peace resolution which proposed an autonomous Alsace-Lorraine republic within the German Reich as the basis for a Franco-German understanding and international peace. By 1916 socialists such as Grumbach were demanding the right of self-determination, a plebiscite to determine the fate of Alsace-Lorraine, regardless of which side won the war. They opposed the automatic return of the territory to France. Their cohorts in the German SPD went even farther; by 1916 they took the position that the "annexationist opponents" [the Allies] had no right to take the German territory of Alsace-Lorraine.[41] Although many of the socialist workers' and soldiers' councils favored a return to France, they were not unanimous on that point. In the course of the war, Social Democracy in the Reichsland suffered the same schism as it did in the rest of Germany and Europe. The Social Democrats had to decide whether they could be socialists and nationalists at the same time. In a borderland which had experienced both French and German rule, this problem was particularly difficult to resolve.[42]

How the Alsace-Lorrainers felt about the German Empire on the eve of World War I must remain uncertain. It is commonly assumed that the Germans failed to win over the people, who had only an overwhelming desire to become Frenchmen once again. Yet Gerhard Ritter tells us that "the German authorities were astounded by the loyal attitude of the people and the press" as the war began. Mobilization went smoothly in the Reichsland; most of the population, especially younger people and the rural population, had by 1914 accepted the fact that they were Germans.[43] The liberal Wilhelm Kapp claimed that by 1914 only a few pro-French agitators wished to see Alsace-Lorraine detached from the German cultural and national community.[44] But Prince Alexander zu Hohenlohe-Schillingsfürst, mindful of the increasing flood of French propaganda in the Reichsland during the years immediately preceding the war, estimated that French sympathy was on the increase in 1914.[45]

Estimates of public opinion at the close of the German regime are simply guesswork; no one ever took a scientific sampling. Had a poll been taken, the results would have proved only that there was no such animal as "the Alsace-Lorrainer." Prince Alexander admitted that differences between Alsatians and Lorrainers created difficulty in estimating public opinion in the Reichsland. "The 'Alsace-Lorrainer,'" he wrote, "was a creature which existed only on paper."[46] Robert Parisot, whose history of Lorraine remains the most satisfactory, cautiously concluded that, "we believe we can say that very few Lorrainers openly supported the German regime. But the number of irreconcilable protesters had greatly diminished. Despairing of becoming French again, most of the population had resigned themselves to the existing situation." Having offered this assessment, Parisot hastened to add that, "one would commit a great error if one were to imagine that there was a unanimity of views in 1914 among the inhabitants of Lorraine. Their sentiments varied according to their education, language, religious beliefs, and political opinions."[47] Prince Alexander zu Hohenlohe-Schillingsfürst made the same type of sociological distinctions between the upper bourgeoisie and the rural population. Even within those categories, there were differences of outlook between the two generations.[48]

No one could say with certainty that the German regime had "failed" in Alsace-Lorraine, but everyone raised objections to the manner in which Germany had governed the Reichsland. Hohenlohe's son Prince Alexander believed it would have been possible to reconcile the people with the German regime in one of three ways: by parceling the territory out to Prussia, Bavaria, Baden, and Württemberg, where the people would have participated in a true federal state; by promptly granting the territory autonomy within the Reich; or by governing the region with respect for Alsace-Lorraine's needs, desires, and individuality, culminating in the granting of self-administration. Everything was ruined in the very beginning when Bismarck gave way to Moltke's interpretation that the Reichsland was to be nothing more than Germany's first line of defense.[49] Indeed, the overwhelming evidence points to the incompatible aims of military security and "Germanization" as the cause of many of Germany's problems in the Reichsland. The Germans generally failed to recognize their irreconcilable goals, and most often attributed their "failures" to personality defects in the highest territorial administrators. Personal attacks upon governors, secretaries of state, and other cabinet ministers continually disrupted territorial political life and made impossible the implementation of any continuous policy. According to most critics, it was the administrators, not the system itself, which was at fault.

Although governors and state secretaries bore the brunt of the criticism, it was the kaiser, acting as the agent of the Federal Council, who bore the ultimate responsibility for German policy in the Reichsland. To Wilhelm I, Alsace-Lorraine represented little more than the scene of famous battlefields such as Wissembourg and Wörth, and the "magnificent" fortifications around Metz. He generally visited the Reichsland annually to observe military maneuvers, and seems to have judged the success of German policy by the ovations he received rather than by the official reports from the territorial government.[50] Friedrich III's brief reign in 1888 brought no

basic change in policy, though it was believed he might be more
liberal than either of the two Wilhelms. As a Prussian prince, Friedrich had serious reservations about the extent of the annexation in
1871, but as kaiser he never for a moment doubted Germany's right
to govern the entire territory. In an address to the people of the
Reichsland delivered 15 March 1888, Kaiser Friedrich referred to
Alsace-Lorraine as a German territory which had been reunited with
the fatherland in 1871. While promising to treat the population as
Germans should be treated, with care for their welfare and prosperity, he demanded of the people their trust, cooperation, and
obedience to the law. Through an impartial, sympathetic, but nevertheless firm administration, Friedrich expected to bind the Reichsland to the Reich once again.[51]

Wilhelm II found the Reichsland so pleasant that he established
a hunting lodge there, but his view of Alsace-Lorraine as a bastion
of German military power differed little from that of Wilhelm I.
He considered "Metz and my army corps as the keystone of Germany's military might," the surest guarantee of European peace. The
Alsace-Lorrainers were Germans and would forever remain Germans, "so help us God and our German sword."[52] Aside from his
concern for Germany's military security, Wilhelm II cared little
about what happened in the Reichsland. Recalling the kaiser's visits
to Alsace-Lorraine between 1898 and 1906, when he [Prince Alex-
ander] served as district president of Upper Alsace at Colmar,
Prince Alexander zu Hohenlohe-Schillingsfürst complained of the
emperor's apparent disinterest. Although the kaiser saw Prince Alexander fairly often, he never asked the prince about the situation in
either Upper Alsace or the electoral district he represented in the
Reichstag from 1893 to 1903.[53] Internal and external security was
all that mattered to Wilhelm II, and in that respect the Hohenlohe-
Schillingsfürst clan, devoid of military rank as they were, had little
to offer the kaiser. It was considerations of security which dictated
to Wilhelm II the timing of the repeal of the dictatorship paragraph.
Why did he wait fourteen years to repeal the hated law? When he
became kaiser, Wilhelm explained, he had first to win the confidence
of his subjects and the trust of his princely colleagues in Germany;
then he had to convince the foreign powers that he was not an irresponsible war-monger. Having established his own position firmly
by 1902, he was prepared to extend a sign of trust and consideration
to the people of the Reichsland.[54]

Given the single-minded concern for security which characterized the outlook of Wilhelm I and Wilhelm II, it is not surprising that territorial administrators making concessions in the interest of reconciling the population felt the wrath of the kaiser's military following. The greatest outpouring of venom was reserved for those accused of attempting to make deals with the territorial religious and economic "notables" or pillars of the community. The list of those scorned for following the notable policy included Governors Manteuffel, Hohenlohe-Schillingsfürst, and Wedel, and Secretary of State Köller. Well before the Zabern affair, Wedel's position had become nearly untenable in the face of vicious attacks in the German press. A Rhenish-Westphalian newspaper which accused the governor of "failing to perform his national duty" was let off with a mere 200-mark fine by a civil tribunal in Essen.[55] Hohenlohe-Schillingsfürst's critics pointed to his weakness and willingness to accede to policies he found distasteful, while Hohenlohe-Langenburg has been described as a "nullity."[56] Evaluations of the highest authorities by their contemporaries often reflect personal loyalties and prejudices. Prince Alexander zu Hohenlohe-Schillingsfürst was convinced that his father was the only man who could have reconciled the Alsace-Lorrainers with his sympathetic and understanding attitude. But Manteuffel, too, had come to the Reichsland pledged to conciliate the population. Prince Alexander conceded that Manteuffel meant well and tried to understand regional needs, and his policy of dealing with the territorial leadership was basically correct. Manteuffel differed from Hohenlohe in that he sometimes went too far with his conciliation program, trying to win support at any price, placing his own reputation in jeopardy. In a remarkable intellectual gyration, Prince Alexander concluded that High President Eduard von Möller had been the most expert administrator during the entire regime. If only Möller's "less original and glittering but more solid, practical, intelligent, and considerate administration" had lasted until 1885, wrote Alexander, Hohenlohe-Schillingsfürst would have found a much better situation on which to build. Aside from Möller, Max von Puttkamer was the best administrator after 1871; a follower of the Bismarckian school, he carried out his orders and never tried to win a popularity contest.[57] No contrast could be greater than that between Hohenlohe-Schillingsfürst and Möller, the *grand seigneur* and the efficient Prussian bureaucrat. That Prince Alexander could regard them both as examples of the best in territorial administration

illustrates with remarkable clarity Germany's schizophrenia in dealing with Alsace-Lorraine. Lurking behind every act of conciliation
was the veiled threat of coercion.

Admitting the validity of some of the criticism leveled against
particular governors and subordinate officials in the Reichsland, one
must nevertheless conclude that the real basis of the "Alsace-
Lorraine problem" lay in fundamental political and structural deficiencies affecting the German Empire as a whole. Granting of the
1911 constitution, with a *Landtag* elected by universal suffrage, accelerated the process of politicization. But having granted the constitution, the government refused to accept the decisions of the
popularly elected parliament. By 1914 Alsace-Lorraine possessed
all of the institutions needed for true parliamentary government.
There was a wide range of political parties, and a *Landtag* in which
they could play the game of politics. The chancellor and emperor
abused the spirit of the 1911 constitution in appointing Dallwitz
governor. The process of political integration with the empire suffered from the government's decision to govern as if no democratic
institutions existed in Alsace-Lorraine.

The process of politicization had done its work in preparing
Alsace-Lorraine for integration into the German empire; ultimate
success or failure now rested with the German government. The
only logical development from the 1911 constitution was toward
real parliamentary government. If integration failed, it was because
the German government refused to accept the logic of political
developments which it had set in motion in 1911.

In the "Alsace-Lorraine problem," Bismarck's genius encountered
its limit; deficiencies in the Bismarckian system which might otherwise have passed unnoticed came into sharp focus in the Reichsland.
The hastily contrived imperial structure, full of compromises needed
to secure the approval of the German princes, was fraught with ambiguity. The lack of any adequate distinction between civil and
military authority stood forth in the Zabern affair. Was the emperor
merely a symbol of national unity, or had Bismarck intended him
to be a real organ of power? How, if at all, did Alsace-Lorraine fit
into the imperial structure? The very existence of a Reichsland, an
imperial territory, cast the shadow of ambiguity over the basic
structure of the empire itself. Despite the apparent hegemony of
Prussia, the empire was supposed to be a federal state; but through

its possession of Alsace-Lorraine as a Reichsland, the empire took on a much more unitary appearance.

The presence of foreign nationality groups further complicated the imperial structure. Although the *kleindeutsche* solution to the problem of German unification had triumphed as early as 1848, Bismarck's wars of unification ended with the inclusion of groups in the Prussian eastern provinces, north Schleswig, and Alsace-Lorraine which were foreign by ethnic-linguistic or political standards. Alsace-Lorraine was itself an ambiguous territory, a "mixed" region culturally, which had already changed hands politically several times. Was it French or was it German? No one could say, and perhaps it was not a valid question to raise in the first place. The Germans themselves had mixed emotions, sometimes hoping to integrate their Alsatian "brothers," sometimes ruling the "foreigners" with an iron hand. As the final result of this cultural and political ambiguity, Alsace-Lorraine became a pawn in the larger game of international power politics. The fact that the Reichsland held international significance tended to strengthen the hand of the military against civil authorities.[58]

Some Germans recognized the weaknesses and ambiguities in the imperial structure and the administration of Alsace-Lorraine. There was, however, hardly a chance for reform. The reform movement in Alsace-Lorraine was doomed to failure, for even if the necessary good will on the part of the government had existed, the Bismarckian constitution was inflexible. To raise Alsace-Lorraine to full *Bundesstaat* status, with full voting rights in the Federal Council, would destroy the delicate balance of power established in 1871. Viewed in the context of the imperial constitution, the reform movement in Alsace-Lorraine made about as much headway between 1871 and 1914 as one might reasonably expect. The "failure" of German policy in Alsace-Lorraine portended nothing less than the ultimate collapse of the empire itself.

Notes

CHAPTER 1

1. The ten towns forming the Alsatian union were Colmar, Hagenau, Kayserberg, Landau, Münster, Obernai, Rosheim, Sélestat, Turckheim, and Wissembourg.
2. Gaston Haehling, "Le Rhin sous la Révolution et l'Empire," *Deux Siècles d'Alsace Française:1648, 1798, 1848* (Strasbourg, Paris, 1948), p. 289.
3. Fernand L'Huillier, "Les grands courants de l'opinion publique en Alsace sous la Révolution, le Consulat et l'Empire," *Deux Siècles d'Alsace Française*, p. 235 ff.
4. Ibid., pp. 257–69.
5. Robert Parisot, *Histoire de Lorraine* (Paris, 1924), 3: 256–63.
6. Friedrich Koenig, "Der Elsass-Lothringische Partikularismus," *Elsässische Kulturfragen*, 2nd ser., no. 3 (November 1911), pp. 111–12.
7. Félix Ponteil, *L' Opposition politique à Strasbourg sous la monarchie de Juillet* (Paris, 1932), pp. 1–2; Paul Leuilliot, "L'Opposition libérale en Alsace à la fin de la Restauration," *Deux Siècles d'Alsace Française*, p. 307. The best account of Alsace during the Restoration is Leuilliot's *L'Alsace au debut du XIXe siècle*, 3 vols. (Paris, 1959–1960).
8. Parisot, *Histoire de Lorraine*, 3: 266, 271–72.
9. Ibid., pp. 270, 273.
10. Leuilliot, in *Deux Siècles d'Alsace Française*, p. 307; André Brandt, "Mulhouse, ville française," *Deux Siècles d'Alsace Française*, p. 425; Ponteil, *L'Opposition politique*, pp. 16–25.
11. Leuilliot, in *Deux Siècles d'Alsace Française*, pp. 298, 308–310; Ponteil, *L'Opposition politique*, p. 9.
12. Ponteil, *L'Opposition politique*, p. 45; Brandt, in *Deux Siècles d'Alsace Française*, p. 426.
13. Parisot, *Histoire de Lorraine*, 3: 279.
14. Ibid., p. 283; Paul Muller, *La Révolution de 1848 en Alsace* (Paris, Mulhouse, 1912), p. 18.
15. Strasbourg received about 400 refugees between December 1831 and March 1832. See Ponteil, *L'Opposition politique*, pp. 229–30, 248, and Parisot, *Histoire de Lorraine*, 3: 280.
16. Ponteil, *L'Opposition politique*, 761–69.
17. Ibid., pp. 770–73.
18. Ibid., pp. 796–803, 812–13.
19. Ibid., pp. 867–81.
20. Muller, *La Révolution en Alsace*, pp. 111–12.
21. Ibid., p. 33; Brandt, in *Deux Siècles d' Alsace Française*, p. 426.
22. Muller, *La Révolution en Alsace*, pp. 52–53.

23. Parisot, *Histoire de Lorraine*, 3: 290.
24. Eduard Stadtler, "Die Judenkrawalle von 1848 im Elsass," *Elsässische Monatsschrift für Geschichte und Volkskunde* 2 (1911): 673–86; Félix Ponteil, "En manière de conclusion: L'Alsace en 1848," *Deux Siècles d'Alsace Française*, p. 503; Ponteil, *L'Opposition politique*, p. 898; Muller, *La Révolution en Alsace*, pp. 28, 31.
25. Parisot, *Histoire de Lorraine*, 3: 293–95.
26. Ibid., pp. 298–99.
27. Karl Marx, *The Eighteenth Brumaire of Louis Bonaparte* (New York, 1963), p. 113.
28. The Bonapartist fear of strong republican opposition in Alsace and Lorraine turned out to be unjustified. See John B. Wolf, *France: 1814–1919* (New York, 1963), pp. 231–32.
29. Muller, *La Révolution en Alsace*, pp. 34–35, 40.
30. The results were as follows: Haut-Rhin: Louis Napoléon, 65,026, Cavaignac, 19,735, Ledru-Rollin, 3,867; Bas-Rhin: Louis Napoléon, 60,255, Cavaignac, 46,505, Ledru-Rollin, 4,375. See Muller, *La Révolution en Alsace*, pp. 58, 131.
31. Believing Strasbourg would rally to the call of a Bonaparte, Louis Napoléon chose that city as the focal point of his attempted *coup* in 1836. See Haehling, in *Deux Siècles d'Alsace Française*, p. 290.
32. For the attitude of the business community toward Louis Napoléon, see the Haut-Rhin prefect's report of 20 March 1852 in Muller, *La Révolution en Alsace*, p. 150. Raess' views are also recorded in Muller, p. 88.

CHAPTER 2

1. For further discussion of the free-trade and protectionist controversy, see Chapter 9, below.
2. Muller, *La Révolution de 1848 en Alsace*, pp. 107, 171.
3. Ibid., pp. 96, 105–6, 152, 171; *Bulletin des lois*, 35 (1870), p. 677; Parisot, *Histoire de Lorraine*, 3: 304–7. Thus, of 274,613 registered voters in Alsace, over 40,000 voted "no," and another 51,000 abstained.
4. Henry Laufenburger, *Cours d'Economie alsacienne*, vol. 1: *Les Bases matérielles, morales et juridiques* (Paris, 1930), pp. 101–13.
5. Henry Laufenburger and Pierre Pflimlin, *Cours d'Economie alsacienne*, vol. 2: *L'Industrie de Mulhouse* (Paris, 1932), pp. 120, 372.
6. *Courrier du Bas-Rhin*, 9–12 July 1870; Fernand L'Huillier, La Lutte *ouvrière à la fin du second empire* (Paris, 1957), pp. 64–70; Fréderic Eccard, *L'Alsace sous la domination allemande* (Paris, 1919), p. 17.
7. Sensing the danger to Alsace and Lorraine, three Haut-Rhin deputies voted against the declaration of war.
8. *Courrier du Bas-Rhin*, 25, 26 July 1870.
9. Ibid., 21 July 1870.
10. Georg Wolfram, ed., *Das Reichsland Elsass-Lothringen*, vol. 2, pt. 2: *Verfassung und Verwaltung von Elsass-Lothringen, 1871–1918* (Berlin, 1937), p. 3.
11. This is confirmed by archival records cited in L'Huillier, *La Lutte ouvrière*, p. 71.
12. Paul Galien, *Ephémerides alsaciennes de l'année terrible 14 juillet 1870–1 mars 1871* (Colmar, 1910), pp. 24–25.
13. Ibid., p. 114; *Bulletin de la Société Industrielle de Mulhouse* (hereafter cited as *Bulletin*) 41 (1871): 5.

14. Gustave Fishback, *Le Siège et bombardement de Strasbourg* (Paris, 1871), p. 216.
15. Galien, *Ephémerides alsaciennes*, p. 46.
16. August Schneegans, *Memoiren. Ein Beitrag zur Geschichte des Elsasses in der Übergangzeit* (Berlin, 1904), pp. 52–53.
17. Ferdinand Graf Eckbrecht von Dürckheim, *Erinnerungen alter und neuer Zeit* (Stuttgart, 1888), 2: 260–61. Kablé, a member of the Strasbourg municipal council, proposed that Strasbourg declare itself a free city, and then negotiate with Germany to establish a neutral autonomy for the entire region.
18. Edmond About, *L'Alsace, 1871–1872* (Paris, 1873), pp. 207–8.
19. Compare M. Kärnbach, "Die staatsrechtliche Entwicklung Elsass-Lothringens 1871–1879 im Spiegel der deutschen Reichspolitik," *Jahrbuch der Elsass-Lothringischen Wissenschaftlichen Gesellschaft zu Strassburg* 6 (1933): 146–48, with the account in Auguste Lalance, *Mes Souvenirs, 1830–1914* (Paris, 1914), p. 50.
20. League of Alsace, *La Ligue d'Alsace, 1871–1872*, Bulletin No. 5 (Paris, 1873), pp. 41–43; No. 1-A, p. 1; No. 3, p. 21.
21. Ibid., No. 3, pp. 26–31.
22. Bismarck to the general government in Strasbourg, 1 February 1871, *Archives départmentales du Bas-Rhin* (hereafter cited as *A.D.B.R.*), AL 87, paquet 447, no. 1849.
23. Of 145,000 registered voters in Bas-Rhin, about 100,000 cast ballots, while in Haut-Rhin, 74,000 of the 123,000 registered voters went to the polls.
24. For the story of the Strasbourg municipal council election list, see *Histoire des élections à l'Assemblée Nationale dans le département du Bas-Rhin* (1871), pp. 2–4. On the problem of Gambetta and Favre, see Johann Schneider, *Die elsässische Autonomistenpartei, 1871–1881*, Schriften des Wissenschaftlichen Instituts der Elsass-Lothringer im Reich an der Universität Frankfurt, N.F. No. 9 (Frankfurt a.M., 1933), p. 10.
25. *Histoire des élections*, p. 18.
26. For an analysis of the results of the elections for the Bordeaux Assembly, see *Histoire des élections*, and *Auguste Scheurer-Kestner, Les Représentants de l'Alsace et de la Lorraine à l'Assemblée Nationale de Bordeaux* (Paris, 1887), pp. 25–35. A Catholic priest, Alois Spitz, argued that the election proved that Catholics were practically without influence in Alsace-Lorraine politics in 1871. See Alois Spitz, *Der Sozialismus im Reichslande* (Trier, 1891), p. 23. Eight of the candidates elected in Bas-Rhin, however, did appear on the clerical list.
27. Hartmann's election to the National Assembly illustrates the confusion which marked Alsatian politics between 1869 and 1871. An industrialist from Münster, where he served as mayor and was elected to the Haut-Rhin *conseil general* during the Second French Empire, Hartmann hardly seemed to deserve the abuse to which he was subjected in 1871. His uncle, a parliamentary deputy, had been named a peer of France by Louis Philippe. As the liberal opposition to Napoléon III gained momentum in 1869, Hartmann's connection with the government in the *conseil general* cost him a seat in the French parliament, as he lost the election to Léon Lefebvre. After his defeat, Hartmann turned against the administration, presumably because he felt the government had failed to support him adequately in the 1869 campaign. Hartmann organized the anti-plebiscitary movement in Colmar in 1870. So well did he succeed in

rehabilitating his image that he won a seat in the National Assembly in February 1871. Shortly thereafter, the League of Alsace labeled him a traitor for his attempts to negotiate a tariff accommodation with Bismarck. See Muller, *La Révolution en Alsace*, p. 171.

28. An account of the preparation of the first protest is given in Scheurer-Kestner, *Représentants à l'Assemblée*, pp. 3–8. Keller was chosen to read the protest over the objections of a group led by Scheurer-Kestner, who felt Keller was not sufficiently committed to the republican point of view, and resented Keller's clerical connections. The clerical-protester alliance reappeared in the 1874 Reichstag election.

29. Guy Chapman, *The Third Republic of France: The First Phase, 1871–1894* (New York, 1962), p. 378.

30. Schneegans, *Memoiren*, pp. 104, 119; Karl Stählin, *Geschichte Elsass-Lothringens* (Munich, 1920), p. 217. Despite Schneegans' claim that he did not favor the protest, he has nevertheless been listed as a member of the committee charged with drawing up the declaration. See Scheurer-Kestner, *Représentants à l'Assemblée*, p. 7.

31. Schneegans, *Memoiren*, pp. 99–100.

32. Scheurer-Kestner, *Représentants à l'Assemblée*, pp. 16–19.

33. Maximilian Freiherr du Prel, *Elsass-Lothringen, seine Vergangenheit, seine Zukunft* (Strasbourg, 1877), p. 25.

34. Wilhelm Fischer, *Manteuffel in Elsass-Lothringen und seine Verdeutschungspolitik* (Basel, 1885), p. 8.

35. Karl Jacob, *Bismarck und die Erwerbung Elsass-Lothringens 1870–1871* (Strasbourg, 1905), p. 24; Walter Platzhoff, "Die elsass-lothringische Frage im Weltkrieg und im Versailler Frieden," *Elsass-Lothringisches Jahrbuch* 13 (1934): 284.

36. Reichstag, *Stenogr. Ber.*, 1st Leg. Per., 1st Sess., 1871, I: 518; Gustav Anrich, "Eine Denkschrift Julius Weizsäckers über Elsass-Lothringen vom August, 1870," *Elsass-Lothringisches Jahrbuch* 8 (1929): 285–96.

37. The question of German public opinion on the demand for the annexation of Alsace-Lorraine has become a matter of extreme controversy among German historians. Until 1963, it had been widely assumed that Bismarck agreed to the annexation only under massive pressure from the general public and the military. Otto Pflanze, in his *Bismarck and the Development of Germany: The Period of Unification, 1815–1871* (Princeton, N. J., 1963), pp. 475–76, was among the first to suggest that evidence for an overwhelming public demand for annexation was sparse during the first weeks of the war. Bismarck helped to create the proper climate for public opinion by encouraging the press and nationalistic leaders to demand annexation. Taking a similar approach, Walter Lipgens, "Bismarck, die öffentliche Meinung und die Annexion von Elsass und Lothringen 1870," *Historische Zeitschrift* 199 (1964): 31–112, argued that there was no storm of demands for annexation until Bismarck had manipulated the press and liberal politicians. Four years later, Lothar Gall savagely attacked the Lipgens thesis in "Zur Frage der Annexion von Elsass und Lothringen 1870," *Historische Zeitschrift* 206 (1968): 265–326, and received support in another article in the same issue of that journal, Rudolf Buchner, "Die deutsche patriotische Dichtung vom Kriegsbeginn 1870 über Frankreich und die Elsässische Frage," pp. 327–36. Gall claimed Lipgens had failed to consult the newspaper press, failed to cite sources which detracted from his own argument, and misinterpreted other sources. Lipgens attempted a reply, without complete success, in "Bismarck und die Frage der Annexion

1870. Eine Erwiderung," *Historische Zeitschrift* 206 (1968): 586–617. Lipgens claimed that Gall had misrepresented some of his arguments, and that in the end, Gall had accepted his basic point, that Bismarck had planned to annex the territory before the war began, and made his decision independent of public opinion. Eberhard Kolb, "Bismarck und das Aufkommen der Annexionsforderung 1870," *Historische Zeitschrift* 209 (1969): 318–56, vigorously disputes Lipgens.

38. Gabriel Monod, *Allemands et Français: Souvenirs de campagne. Metz, Sedan, la Loire* (Paris, n.d.), p. 151. This is a report of a conversation between Monod and Treitschke in 1872.

39. Walter Platzhoff argues that Britain and France did not regard the proposed annexation as an injustice to France; it was the natural penalty against a defeated aggressor. See Platzhoff, in *Elsass-Lothringisches Jahrbuch* 13 (1934): 285.

40. Otto von Bismarck, *Die gesammelten Werke*, vol. 6c (Berlin, 1935), p. 104. Platzhoff, however, claims that, "the recovery of Alsace . . . was Bismarck's war aim from the beginning, and an integral part of his policy." See Walter Platzhoff, "Bismarck und die Annexion Elsass-Lothringens," *Elsass-Lothringisches Jahrbuch* 3 (1924): 2.

41. Platzhoff in *Elsass-Lothringishes Jahrbuch* 3 (1924): 4; Jacob, *Bismarck und die Erwerbung*, p. 33.

42. Friedrich III, *Briefe, Reden und Erlasse des Kaisers und Königs Friedrich III* (Berlin, 1907), pp. 199–203.

43. Elsass-Lothringen, Oberpräsidial-Bureau, *Verordnung und amtliche Nachrichten für Elsass-Lothringen aus der Zeit vom Beginn der deutschen Occupation bis Ende März 1872* (Strasbourg, 1872), p. 2.

44. Edgar Löning, "L'Administration du Government-General de l'Alsace durant la guerre de 1870–1871," *Revue de droit international et de legislation comparée* 4 (1872): 629–30. This was originally published as, *Die Verwaltung des General-Gouvernments in Elsass* (Strasbourg, 1872). For a study of the entire four-year occupation period in French Lorraine, see Emile Chantriot, *La Lorraine sous l'occupation allemande, mars 1871–septembre 1873* (Nancy–Paris–Strasbourg, 1922).

45. Gerhard Ritter, *Staatskunst und Kriegshandwerk*, (Munich, 1954), 1: 322.

46. *Kaiser Wilhelms des Grossen Briefe, Reden und Schriften*, ed. Ernst Berner (Berlin, 1906), 2: 234, 238, letters of 29 August, 7 September 1870; Platzhoff, in *Elsass-Lothringisches Jahrbuch* 3 (1924): 6.

47. Heinrich von Poschinger, *Conversations With Prince Bismarck*, ed. Sidney Whitman (New York, 1900), p. 98.

48. On Bismarck's conflicts with the generals, see Pflanze, *Bismarck and the Development of Germany*, p. 458 ff., and Ritter, *Staatskunst und Kriegshandwerk*, 1: 287–88, 322, 328. Ritter emphasizes Bismarck's moderating influence.

49. Parisot, *Histoire de Lorraine*, 3: 323.

50. Richard Hartshorne, "The Franco-German Boundary of 1871," *World Politics* 2 (1950): 209–50; Parisot, *Histoire de Lorraine*, 3: 323–24; Fernand Engerand, *L'Allemagne et le fer: Les Frontières Lorraines et la force allemande* (Paris, 1916), pp. 170–96; H. Germain, "Die natürlichen Grundlagen der lothringischen Eisenindustrie und die Verfassung vor 1870," *Jahrbuch der Gesellschaft für lothringische Geschichte und Altertumskunde* 24 (1912): 422–26; F. Sauvaire-Jourdan, "Un Conflit dans la métallurgie allemande," *Revue politique et parlementaire*, 69 (1911): 250–51. Bismarck at times displayed an almost nonchalant

attitude in the matter of iron ore resources during boundary negotiations with the French. When the French minister of finance Pouyer-Quertier indicated the personal hardship inflicted by the loss of the forges at Villerupt, of which the minister was a principal shareholder, Bismarck agreeably dropped his demand for that commune. See Hartshorne, p. 242; Germain, p. 426; Engerand, p. 196.

51. Paul Wentzke, "Zur Entstehungsgeschichte des Reichslands Elsass-Lothringen," *Süddeutsche Monatshefte* 8 (1911): 613; Heinrich von Treitschke, "What We Demand from France," *Germany, France, Russia, and Islam* (New York, 1915), pp. 158 ff.

52. Wentzke, in *Süddeutsche Monatshefte* 8: 616.

53. Moritz Busch, *Bismarck: Some Secret Pages of His History* (New York, 1898), 1: 80. Conversation of 24 August 1871. See also, Reichstag, *Stenogr. Ber.*, 1st Leg. Per., 1st Sess., 1871, I: 519.

54. Wentzke, in *Süddeutsche Monatshefte*, 8: 621; Wentzke, *Der deutschen Einheit Schicksalsland* (Munich, 1921), pp. 100–1. Gall, in *Historische Zeitschrift* 206: 322–24, discounts the importance of Alsace-Lorraine in Bismarck's attempt to win support for the idea of establishing an empire. Instead, Gall argues that Bismarck hoped to promote European peace by weakening France and thereby creating a stable European balance of power. The annexation of Alsace-Lorraine was to serve this end. Lipgens, in *Historische Zeitschrift* 206: 615, disputes Gall. Why, asks Lipgens, did Bismarck not mention his concern for peace and a European balance of power in his circulars to the neutral powers in the fall of 1870?

55. Wentzke, in *Süddeutsche Monatshefte* 8: 618, 626; idem in *Der deutschen Einheit*, pp. 83–84.

56. Wentzke, *Der deutschen Einheit*, p. 85; idem in *Süddeutsche Monatshefte*, 8: 620.

CHAPTER 3

1. Prince Chlodwig zu Hohenlohe-Schillingsfürst, *Denkwürdigkeiten* (Stuttgart and Leipzig, 1907), 2: 381. Speech of 30 January 1886.

2. Reichstag, *Stenogr. Ber.*, 1st Leg. Per., 1st Sess., 1871, p. 856.

3. Ibid., p. 922.

4. Kärnbach, in *Jahrbuch der Elsass-Lothringischen Wissenschaftlichen Gesellschaft* 5 (1932): 38; Ernst von Ernsthausen, *Erinnerungen eines preussischen Beamten* (Bielefeld and Leipzig, 1894), p. 363.

5. Georg Karl Wolfram, *Oberpräsident Eduard von Möller und die Elsass-Lothringische Verfassungsfrage* (Berlin, 1925), pp. 6–7; *Gesetzblatt für Elsass-Lothringen* (Strasbourg, 1872), pp. 51–52; microfilmed documents from the German Foreign Office, University of California, Series I, reel 66, frame 707, 28 August 1871. See Bibliography for original file.

6. Reichstag, *Stenogr. Ber.*, 1st Leg. Per., 3rd Sess., 1872, III (*Anlagen*): 622.

7. Möller to Bismarck, 27 April 1872 in *A.D.B.R.*, AL 32, no. 3.

8. Rudolf Morsey, *Die oberste Reichsverwaltung unter Bismarck, 1867–1890* (Münster, 1957), p. 173.

9. Möller to Bismarck, 4 February 1874, *A.D.B.R.*, AL 32, no. 3.

10. *Gesetzblatt* (1874), pp. 37–38; *Frankfurter Zeitung*, 18 May 1876. The creation of the territorial committee was a simple administrative act; this method was probably chosen to avoid discussion of the Alsace-

Lorraine constitutional question in the Reichstag. See the *Augsburger Allegemeine Zeitung,* 11 November 1874.
11. Schneegans, *Memoiren,* pp. 274, 279, 281.
12. Reichstag, *Stenogr. Ber.,* 2nd Leg., Per., 2nd Sess., 1874–75, I, 393.
13. Möller still apparently had the confidence of the kaiser. In a conflict with the district president of Lower Alsace, Ernst von Ernsthausen, Möller succeeded in having Ernsthausen transferred to Colmar. Further evidence of royal support came 13 March 1875, when the kaiser appointed Möller as one of the Prussian representatives in the Federal Council. Although Alsace-Lorraine was not formally granted a Federal Council seat, Möller now represented the territory's interests. See Wolfram, *Oberpräsident,* p. 45.
14. Kärnbach, in *Jahrbuch der Elsass-Lothringischen Wissenschaftlichen Gesellschaft* 6: 157; Herbert Hachenberger, *Bismarck und Elsass-Lothringen* (Jena, 1932), pp. 42–43; Albert Stollsteimer, *Die Stellungnahme der Frankfurter Zeitung zur Elsass-Lothringische Verfassungsfrage, 1870–79* (Pforzheim, 1929), pp. 91–92.
15. This was a promotion for Herzog. On 8 June 1876, Bismarck ordered Möller to give up his Federal Council seat to Herzog. Möller refused to comply with this demand on three separate occasions and apparently had the support of the kaiser.
16. Morsey, *Die oberste Reichsverwaltung,* pp. 177, 180; Wolfram, *Das Reichsland,* 2, pt. 1, *Verfassung und Verwaltung,* p. 26.
17. Quoted in Schneegans, *Memoiren,* p. 60.
18. Prior to the assassination attempts on the kaiser, Prince Friedrich had expressed willingness to assume the governorship if asked to do so. See Friedrich III, *Briefe, Reden und Erlasse,* pp. 269–70; William I, *The Correspondence of William I and Bismarck,* trans. J. A. Ford (London, 1903), 2: 197. Friedrich to Bismarck, 14 May 1878.
19. Bismarck, *Ges. Werke,* 8: 299; Schneegans, *Memoiren,* pp. 382–83.
20. Reichstag, *Stenogr. Ber.,* 4th Leg. Per., 2nd Sess., 1879, I: 565.
21. Ibid.
22. See the letter from Klein to Schneegans, 6 April 1878, quoted in Schneegans, *Memoiren,* p. 353. Klein was the only Alsatian to receive an offer of one of the undersecretaryships in the new ministry. He at first refused the post, but Schneegans convinced him to change his mind and accept it. His initial refusal, which seems to have been hoped for by the Germans, had already been telegraphed to Berlin, and the position went to Georg von Mayr, a Bavarian Catholic. Schneegans hoped to be appointed Alsace-Lorraine's representative in the Federal Council, but instead received a post as advisor in the interior department. Treated coldly by the Germans, he soon left the Reichsland to become German consul at Messina in May 1880. By that time, Julius Klein had forced Schneegans to relinquish leadership of the autonomist party. See Schneegans, *Memoiren,* pp. 411–19.
23. Reichstag, *Stenogr. Ber.,* 4th Leg. Per., 2nd Sess., 1879, 1: 565.
24. In a conversation with Ernsthausen, 27 March 1879, the kaiser indicated he would like to name Möller governor, but indicated there were "difficulties" which prevented this. See Ernsthausen, *Erinnerungen,* p. 397.
25. Gordon A. Craig, *The Politics of the Prussian Army, 1640–1945* (Oxford, 1955), pp. 148–59.
26. Chantriot, *La Lorraine sous l'occupation allemande,* pp. 55–60, 451–64, 610–11; Parisot, *Histoire de Lorraine,* 3: 327–28.
27. Chantriot, *Lorraine sous l'occupation,* p. 611.

28. *Frankfurter Zeitung*, 16 July 1877, evening edition; Bismarck to kaiser, 23 February 1875, *A.D.B.R., AL* 87, paquet 646, no. 3058.

29. Kaiser to Manteuffel, 1 February 1880, in Hans Goldschmidt, "Aus den Papieren des Grafen Wilhelm Bismarck. Bismarck und Edwin von Manteuffel," *Elsass-Lothringisches Jahrbuch* 15 (1936): 172.

30. Bogdan Graf von Hutten-Czapski, *Sechzig Jahre Politik und Gesellschaft* (Berlin, 1936), 1: 116.

31. Ibid., p. 129. For a discussion of Manteuffel's relations with the military see pp. 116–24.

32. Morsey, *Die oberste Reichsverwaltung,* p. 182.

33. Prior to 1880, the transfer from Prussian to imperial service entailed giving up one's position in the Prussian service, including seniority and pension rights. After Boetticher refused to transfer, Bismarck had the regulations changed, so that time spent in imperial service counted toward Prussian service benefits. Although the governorship carried no pension rights, the governor of Alsace-Lorraine was the highest paid official in the imperial bureaucracy. See Morsey, *Die oberste Reichsverwaltung,* pp. 189, 193.

34. Herbert von Bismarck wrote to Friedrich von Holstein that Manteuffel felt "Hofmann had become quite useless and that he [Manteuffel] wished to have him replaced by Maximilian von Puttkamer, head of the Judicial Department in the Alsace-Lorraine ministry." Hofmann outlasted Manteuffel, but later resigned as a sacrifice to military demands for "reform" after the 1887 election. Puttkamer eventually became Alsace-Lorraine's secretary of state, 1889–1901. See Rich, ed., *Holstein Papers,* 3: 91. Letter of 30 September 1883.

35. Morsey, *Die oberste Reichsverwaltung,* pp. 186, 269, 270. Mayr, a Bavarian Catholic, was the only non-Prussian undersecretary at this time. For a full discussion of Bismarck's financial program in 1878–79, see Helmut Böhme, *Deutschlands Weg zur Grossmacht: Studien zum Verhältnis von Wirtschaft und Staat während der Reichsgründungszeit 1848–1881* (Köln, Berlin, 1966).

36. Hutten-Czapski, *Sechzig Jahre Politik,* 1: 113–14.

37. *Holstein Papers,* 2: 49–50. 7 January 1884.

38. Ibid., 2: 49–50 and 3: 90, 124–25; Hutten-Czapski, *Sechzig Jahre Politik,* 1: 122–25.

39 *Holstein Papers,* 3: 146–147.

40. The kaiser seems to have made some effort to reserve the governorship for his more impecunious friends.

41. *Holstein Papers,* 2: 221. 13 July 1885. Holstein also quotes Bismarck as telling Count Paul von Hatzfeldt, state secretary in the foreign ministry, that Hohenlohe was, "a quiet man who never makes a mess of things. In any case, his task consists of tactfully waiting upon events." See ibid., p. 220. 7 July 1885.

42. Helmuth Rogge, *Holstein und Hohenlohe* (Stuttgart, 1957), p. 239.

43. Prince Alexander von Hohenlohe-Schillingsfürst, *Aus meinem Leben* (Frankfurt a.M., 1925), p. 32.

44. *Holstein Papers,* 2: 208–9, diary entry 28 June 1885; and 3: 146, Hatzfeldt to Holstein, 26 June 1885.

45. Chlodwig zu Hohenlohe-Schillingsfürst, *Denkwürdigkeiten,* 2: 371–72.

46. Alexander zu Hohenlohe-Schillingsfürst, *Aus meinem Leben,* pp. 38–39.

47. Generalfeldmarschall Alfred Graf von Waldersee, *Aus dem Briefwechsel des Generalfeldmarschalls Alfred Grafen von Waldersee,* ed. H. O. Meisner (Berlin and Leipzig, 1928), I: 15–16.

48. Wilhelm Seydler, *Fürst Chlodwig zu Hohenlohe-Schillingsfürst als Statthalter im Reichslande Elsass-Lothringen, 1885–1894* (Frankfurt a.M., 1929), pp. 34–35.
49. Alexander zu Hohenlohe-Schillingsfürst, *Aus meinem Leben*, p. 39.
50. Waldersee, *Aus dem Briefwechsel*, pp. 1–5.
51. Chlodwig zu Hohenlohe-Schillingsfürst, *Denkwürdigkeiten*, 2: 388.
52. Ibid., p. 371. Hohenlohe to Bismarck, 8 November 1885. See also Rogge, *Holstein und Hohenlohe*, pp. 247–48, 291.
53. Hohenlohe, *Denkwürdigkeiten*, 2: 406–7. Hohenlohe to Bismarck, 11 February 1887.
54. Ibid., 2: 408–9. Bismarck to Hohenlohe, 18 February 1887. Hohenlohe's son, Prince Alexander, experienced similar problems in his relations with the military. As district president of Upper Alsace from 1898 to 1906, he felt ill at ease with the military officers since he, like his father, held no military rank. On the kaiser's birthday, regulations required Prince Alexander to wear his district president's uniform and deliver the kaiser's birthday speech. When the Colmar garrison was upgraded to a division headquarters, the division general, whose rank took precedence over that of the district president, assumed responsibility for delivering the kaiser's address. See Alexander von Hohenlohe-Schillingsfürst, *Aus meinem Leben*, pp. 195–96.
55. Hohenlohe, *Denkwürdigkeiten*, 2: 410–14. Hohenlohe to Holstein, 22 February 1887 and diary entries of 22 February, 19 March 1887.
56. Rogge, *Holstein und Hohenlohe*, pp. 269, 282; Generalfeldmarschall Alfred Graf von Waldersee, *Denkwürdigkeiten des Generalfeldmarschalls Alfred Grafen von Waldersee*, ed. H. O. Meisner (Stuttgart and Berlin, 1922–1923), I: 316, 318.
57. Waldersee, *Aus dem Briefwechsel*, 1: 69, Loë to Waldersee, 25 March 1887. Hohenlohe had discussed the possibility of war with a number of generals prior to the 1887 election. Heuduck felt optimistic about the outcome, but another high-ranking officer told the governor that Germany's officers were too old to provide vigorous leadership in wartime. See *Holstein Papers*, 3: 196–97; Rogge, *Holstein und Hohenlohe*, pp. 264–65. Hohenlohe to Holstein, 16, 17 December 1886.
58. Hohenlohe, *Denkwürdigkeiten*, 2: 411–14; Rogge, pp. 274–77.
59. Hohenlohe, *Denkwürdigkeiten*, 2: 405–6.
60. Ibid., p. 407. Hohenlohe to Bismarck, 11 February 1887.
61. Waldersee, *Aus dem Briefwechsel*, pp. 62–63. Bock to Waldersee, 20 February 1887.
62. Rogge, *Holstein und Hohenlohe*, p. 266.
63. The relatively moderate Grand Duke Friedrich of Baden congratulated Hohenlohe on his war-scare speech. See ibid., p. 266. Friedrich to Hohenlohe, 20 February 1887.
64. Ibid., pp. 277–78. Hohenlohe to Ratibor, 5 March 1887.
65. Hohenlohe, *Denkwürdigkeiten*, 2: 414. Diary entry 19 March 1887.
66. Ibid., pp. 425–26; Rogge, *Holstein und Hohenlohe*, pp. 286–87.
67. Hohenlohe, *Denkwürdigkeiten*, 2: 414. Hohenlohe encountered some difficulty with Back's replacement, Schraut. Bismarck first told the governor he needed Schraut in Berlin, but later relented. Bismarck's banker, Gerson Bleichröder, recommended Puttkamer's immediate appointment as secretary of state, "to satisfy the National Liberals," but could not convince Bismarck. With the appointment of Back and Studt, Hohenlohe had a ministry composed entirely of Prussians. See ibid., p. 416. Diary entry 27 March 1887.

68. Ibid., p. 416.
69. Ibid.; Rogge, *Holstein und Hohenlohe*, p. 284.
70. Hohenlohe, *Denkwürdigkeiten*, 2: 414. 19 March 1887.
71. Ibid., pp. 416–19. 29 March 1887.
72. Rogge, *Holstein und Hohenlohe*, pp. 261–62; Hohenlohe, *Denkwürdigkeiten*, 2: 402–3. Hohenlohe to Holstein, 21 November 1886.
73. Hohenlohe, *Denkwürdigkeiten*, 2: 414; Anon., "Die Statthalterschaft des Hohenlohe," *Die Heimat*, 1929, p. 341, and 1930, no. 1, pp. 21–24; no. 2, pp. 48–49.
74. Hohenlohe, *Denkwürdigkeiten*, 2: 421–22. 1 July 1887.
75. Ibid., p. 432. 8 May 1888.
76. Ibid.
77. Ibid., p. 433. 10 May 1888.
78. Rogge, *Holstein und Hohenlohe*, pp. 307–8. Holstein to Hohenlohe, 22 January 1888, and Hohenlohe to Holstein, 2 February 1888.
79. Ibid., p. 297. Puttkamer to Hohenlohe, 18 May 1887.
80. Schnaebele, an Alsatian who had emigrated to France and become a French police officer, was indicted before the Imperial Court at Leipzig for high treason against the German empire. He was captured by a ruse, in which he was invited across the frontier by a German police official presumably to discuss certain local police matters. For a full discussion of the incident and its impact on Bismarck's diplomacy, see J. V. Fuller, *Bismarck's Diplomacy at its Zenith*, Harvard Historical Studies, vol. 26 (Cambridge, Mass., 1922), pp. 173–84.
81. Hohenlohe, *Denkwürdigkeiten*, 2: 404; Rogge, *Holstein und Hohenlohe*, pp. 296–97.
82. Hohenlohe, *Denkwürdigkeiten*, 2: 436. Audience of 25 May 1888.
83. *Holstein Papers*, 2: 375–76.
84. Rogge, *Holstein und Hohenlohe*, pp. 318–19, 322. Hohenlohe to Bismarck, 9 May 1888 and Bismarck to Hohenlohe, 14 May 1888.
85. Hohenlohe, *Denkwürdigkeiten*, 2: 434–35. Hohenlohe to Wilmowski, 17 May 1888 and 17 May diary entry. See also Rogge, *Holstein und Hohenlohe*, pp. 321–22, and *Holstein Papers*, 2:376 on the possibility of sending Caprivi to replace Hohenlohe.
86. Rogge, *Holstein und Hohenlohe*, pp. 315–16. Ratibor to Hohenlohe, 5 May 1888.
87. For a general discussion of passports, including the Alsace-Lorraine situation, see Werner Bertelsmann, *Das Passwesen; eine völkerrechtliche Studie* (Strasbourg, 1914), pp. 29–43.
88. Hohenlohe, *Denkwürdigkeiten*, 2: 462. 15 December 1889. While Hohenlohe pressed for a more liberal passport policy, he could be quite repressive in other matters. In the 14 December conversation with Bismarck, for example, the governor noted that, "With my opinion that protesters who openly made protests in their electioneering program should not be tolerated, he [Bismarck] declared himself agreed, and considered their removal as decided on." Ibid.
89. Ibid., p. 448. 21 January 1889.
90. Ibid., p. 463. 22 March 1890. He wrote his son Alexander that, "I stand very well with Caprivi." See Rogge, *Holstein und Hohenlohe*, p. 337. Letter of 27 March 1890.
91. Rogge, *Holstein und Hohenlohe*, pp. 338–40.
92. Ibid., p. 349; Hohenlohe, *Denkwürdigkeiten*, 2: 475; *Holstein Papers*, 3: 368; *Grosse Politik*, 7: 271–85.
93. *Holstein Papers*, 3: 368. Münster to Holstein, 5 March 1891; Rogge,

Holstein und Hohenlohe, p. 352. Münster to Hohenlohe, 7 March 1891. Hohenlohe and the Grand Duke of Baden added their complaints, in Rogge, pp. 354–55.
94. Hohenlohe, *Denkwürdigkeiten*, 2: 475–76.
95. On Marschall, see Hohenlohe's 18 March 1891 diary entry in ibid., p. 475. For Miquel's position, see Rogge, *Holstein und Hohenlohe*, p. 348, entry of 25 January 1891. Miquel refused to commit the National Liberals in support of Hohenlohe. See Alexander zu Hohenlohe-Schillingsfürst, *Aus meinem Leben*, pp. 62–63.
96. Hohenlohe, *Denkwürdigkeiten*, 2: 478. 22 May 1891.
97. Rogge, *Holstein und Hohenlohe*, p. 370. Caprivi to Hohenlohe, 22 July 1891.
98. Ibid.
99. Hohenlohe, *Denkwürdigkeiten*, 2: p. 481. 20, 21 September 1891. See also Rogge, *Holstein and Hohenlohe*, p. 373; Bertelsmann, *Das Passwesen*, pp. 36–37.
100. Alexander zu Hohenlohe-Schillingsfürst, *Aus meinem Leben*, pp. 226–32; Waldersee, *Denkwürdigkeiten*, 2: 329–30, entries of 29, 30, 31 October 1894; Wolfram, *Das Reichsland*, vol. 2, pt. 1, *Verfassung und Verwaltung*, pp. 50–52.
101. *Holstein Papers*, 3: 601. Holstein to Prince Hugo von Radolin.
102. For the kaiser's struggle for power after Bismarck, see J. C. G. Röhl, *Germany Without Bismarck: The Crisis of Government in the Second Reich, 1890–1900* (Berkeley, Calif., 1967).
103. Bismarck, *Ges. Werke*, 6: 166–69.
104. Hohenlohe, *Denkwürdigkeiten*, 2: 441. 27 June 1887. Bleichröder told Hohenlohe that Bismarck introduced the passport system only to show the kaiser he could take strong action against the French, and thereby take the wind out of the sails of the military party.

CHAPTER 4

1. Hohenlohe, *Denkwürdigkeiten*, 2: 419–20.
2. Stollsteimer, *Die Stellungnahme der Frankfurter Zeitung*, p. 78; Gustav Rasch, *Die Preussen in Elsass und Lothringen* (Braunschweig, 1874), p. 31.
3. Ernst R. Lepsius, *Nationalitätswechsel und Optionsrecht der Elsass-Lothringer nach den deutsch-französischen Friedensverträgen des Jahres 1871* (Halle, 1912), pp. 10–11.
4. Ibid., p. 38; *Augsburger Allgemeine Zeitung*, 16 March 1872.
5. J. and F. Régamey, *L'Alsace au lendemain de la conquête* (Paris, 1911), 321–22.
6. Lepsius, *Nationalitätswechsel und Optionsrecht*, p. 66.
7. Eugene Hepp, *Du Droit d'option des Alsaciens-Lorrains pour la nationalité française* (Paris, 1872), pp. 35–36.
8. *Augsburger Allgemeine Zeitung*, 31 August, 9 April 1872; Abbé Griser, *Programme des Catholiques de l'Alsace-Lorraine devant l'annexion* (Strasbourg, 1871), p. 5.
9. Lepsius, *Nationalitätswechsel und Optionsrecht*, p. 13. A court decision of December 1876 stated that just as minors did not have the right to opt without their parents, parents did not have the right to opt without their children. The peace treaty, argued the judge, had no intention of

separating children from their parents. See *Juristische Zeitschrift für das Reichsland Elsass-Lothringen* 2 (1877): 56.
10. League of Alsace, Bulletin No. 7, p. 55; Griser, *Programme des Catholiques*, pp. 4–7.
11. Edouard Heim, "La Question des optants en Alsace-Lorraine," *Revue alsacienne*, 4 (1880–81):65; Société de Protection des Alsaciens et des Lorrains demeurés Français, *De l'Option pour la nationalité française* (Paris, 1872), pp. 4–6; *Revue alsacienne*, 1 (1877–78): 292–95; Georges Delahache, *L'Exode* (Paris, 1914), pp. 145–46. Founded by Count Joseph Othenin Bernard Cleron d'Haussonville in Paris, the Société de Protection des Alsaciens et des Lorrains spent nearly five million francs between 1872 and 1894 to aid Alsace-Lorrainers who opted and left the Reichsland. The French National Assembly voted on 21 June 1871 to grant 100,000 hectares (about 250,000 acres) to emigrants from Alsace-Lorraine, free of charge. Each man was to receive an urban plot for a home, and a rural plot for cultivation. Transportation, centers for food and water, communications facilities, schools, churches, and a town hall, were to be provided by the government. Haussonville's society spent nearly 800,000 francs to establish three villages in Algeria. It has been estimated that between 1871 and 1874, various aid societies spent over twenty million francs to aid refugees from Alsace-Lorraine.
12. According to official figures, 378,777 natives of the territory who were residing in France at the time of the annexation also opted for French citizenship. Another 2,485 persons who were born in French departments not included in the annexed region, but who were living in Alsace-Lorraine at the time of the annexation, departed for France before the option deadline. Thus, approximately 541,053 persons elected French citizenship before the deadline.
13. Kaiserliches Statistisches Amt, *Statistik des deutschen Reichs*, 44 (1892): 7.
14. *Augsburger Allgemeine Zeitung*, 8 November 1872. Quoted from the *Strassburger Zeitung*, 3 November 1872.
15. Despite the emigration, an official report dated 28 December 1888 showed that of 1,101 properties of over 50 hectares (one hectare = 2.47 acres), nearly two-thirds were owned by French proprietors or by Alsace-Lorrainers whose sons had emigrated to France. See Paul Matter, "Les Tentatives de colonisation allemande en Alsace-Lorraine," *Revue des sciences politiques* 43 (1920): 188.
16. H. Baulig, "La Population de l'Alsace et de la Lorraine en 1921," *Annales de géographie* 32 (1923): 14–18; W. Gley, "Zur Bevölkerungsentwicklung in Elsass-Lothringen," *Elsass-Lothringisches Jahrbuch* 12 (1933): 318–19; Statistisches Bureau des Ministeriums für Elsass-Lothringen, *Das Reichsland Elsass-Lothringen: Landes-und Ortsbeschreibung* (Strasbourg, 1898–1901), vol. 1, pt. 2, pp. 163–65.
17. The final paragraph of the option declaration had originally read, "Following the official verification of this declaration, Mr. ————, as well as the members of his family, lose their citizenship in the German empire, effective the same date." After Möller's edict of 7 March 1872, this was changed to read, "It is recognized by me that this option of nationality will not be valid unless I fix my domicile in France before 1 October 1872." See Un Patriot alsacien, *Les Preussiens en Alsace* (Paris, 1874), pp. 79–82.
18. *Gesetzblatt* (1873), pp. 17–18.
19. Bismarck, *Ges. Werke*, 6c: 23. 24 October 1872.

20. Landesausschuss, *Verhandlungen*, 7th Sess., 1879–80, II: 311, 692.
21. Paul Vidal de la Blache, "Exode et immigration en Alsace-Lorraine," *Revue des sciences politiques* 35 (1916): 308–9.
22. Busch, *Bismarck*, 1: 80.
23. G. Barthelmé, "Les Alsaciens et les Lorrains à la Legion Etrangère," *L' Alsace Française* 19 (1930): 125.
24. Bismarck, *Ges. Werke*, 8: 31–32.
25. *Augsburger Allgemeine Zeitung*, 6, 17 January 1872.
26. Ibid., 9 November, 3 December 1873; Rodolph Reuss, *Histoire d'Alsace* (Paris, 1920), p. 392; Georg Mitscher, *Elsass-Lothringen unter deutscher Verwaltung* (Berlin, 1874), p. 60.
27. Landesausschuss, *Verhandlungen*, 7th Sess., 1879–80, II, 692; Charles Grad, *Delegation d' Alsace-Lorraine. Discours prononcées pendant la session de 1879* (Strasbourg, 1880), pp. 232–33.
28. Elsass-Lothringen, Oberpräsidial-Bureau, *Verordnungen und amtliche Nachrichten* (1871), 372–73. See also G. d'Elstein, *L'Alsace-Lorraine sous la domination allemande* (Paris, 1877), p. 105.
29. *Frankfurter Zeitung*, 12 February 1878.
30. Anton Nystrom, *Elsass-Lothringen und die Möglichkeit einer deutsch-französischen Allianz* (Berlin, 1904), p. 51; Otto Michaelis, *Grenzland-kirche: Eine Evangelische Kirchengeschichte Elsass-Lothringens, 1870–1918* (Essen, 1934), pp. 85–86.
31. It is not clear what these figures on fitness prove; they may indicate that the population of Alsace-Lorraine was healthier and better educated than most Germans, or they may simply indicate that induction officials lowered their standards in the Reichsland as a means of imposing a heavier military service obligation on the territorial population.
32. Dr. E. N., "Elsass-Lothringen und das deutsche Heer," *Elsässische Kulturfragen*, ser. 2, 12 (December, 1912): 478–80; Vidal de la Blache, in *Revue des sciences politiques* 35 (1910): 312; H. Baulig, in *Annales de géographie* 32 (1923): 18.
33. Henry Contamine, "La Place forte de Metz de 1866 à 1914," *Annales de l'Est*, ser. 4, 2 (1934): 344–47.
34. Ibid., pp. 348–54.
35. Hartshorne, in *World Politics* 2 (1950): 212, 216–17; Paul Levy, *Histoire linguistique d'Alsace et de Lorraine* (Paris, 1929), the second volume of which treats the period 1789–1918.
36. Maximilian Freiherr du Prel, *Die deutsche Verwaltung in Elsass-Lothringen, 1870–1879* (Strasbourg, 1879), p. 95.
37. The exceptions were significant. In 1881, for example, special exemptions permitted the teaching of French in such key cities and towns as Mulhouse, Colmar, Thann, Altkirch, and Gebweiler. There were other means of circumventing the language restrictions. In 1875 an estimated 2,000 children age nine to eighteen were attending schools in France; between 1902 and 1910, an estimated average of 995 schoolchildren still attended foreign schools. Where French instruction was prohibited, many communes established "special classes" for this purpose. Recognizing that the law was being abused, the government issued a regulation in 1897 empowering towns desiring to teach French to either establish a middle school, or add middle-school grades to their elementary schools. Many communes took advantage of this relaxation of the rules, and provided subsidies to enable poor students to attend the middle school beyond the age of fourteen. See B. Baier, *Die Sprachenfrage im Volksschulwesen Elsass-Lothringens* (Frankfurt a.M., 1928), pp. 56–59.

38. Wolfram, *Das Reichsland*, Vol. 2, pt. 2, p. 70; Griser, *Programme des Catholiques*, pp. 25–26; Paul Levy, "La Luttle pour l' allemand en Alsace et en Lorraine de 1870 à 1918, d'aprés des documents officiels," *Mercure de France* 154 (1922): 110.

39. Baier, *Sprachenfrage*, p. 96; Seydler, *Hohenlohe-Schillingsfürst*, p. 132. The 1888 repression also affected Alsatian industrial schools, where German was required beginning in February 1888.

40. The reliability of German figures has been questioned by Maurice Toussaint, *La Frontière linguistique en Lorraine: Les Fluctuations et la délimitation actuelle des langues française et germanique dans la Moselle* (Paris, 1955), pp. 43–48.

41. Baier, *Sprachenfrage*, pp. 105–6.

42. Ibid., p. 61.

43. Michaelis, *Grenzlandkirche*, p. 27; Baier, *Sprachenfrage*, pp. 15–17.

44. Baier, *Sprachenfrage*, pp. 84–87.

45. Ibid., pp. 86–89.

46. Ibid., p. 110; Wolfram, *Das Reichsland*, vol. 2, pt. 2, p. 76.

47. Michaelis, *Grenzlandkirche*, pp. 35–36.

48. Hohenlohe, *Denkwürdigkeiten*, 2: 427. Ministerial conference of 27 October 1887.

49. Levy, in *Mercure de France* 154 (1922): 102–4.

50. Ibid., pp. 113–15; Toussaint, *Frontière linguistique*, p. 43.

51. For a brief survey of the university's history, see Christian Pfister, *Pages alsaciennes* (Paris, 1927), pp. 229–56.

52. Faculty recruitment posed no problem; the roster of outstanding scholars included Lujo Brentano and Paul Laband in law and political science, and Georg Dehio and Wilhelm Windelband in philosophy.

53. Rogge, *Holstein und Hohenlohe*, pp. 305–6.

54. Wolfram, *Das Reichsland*, 3: *Wissenschaft, Kunst und Literatur in Elsass-Lothringen, 1871–1918* (Berlin, 1934), pp. 18, 27; Pfister, *Pages alsaciennes*, p. 251; Heinrich von Poschinger, *Fürst Bismarck und der Bundesrat* (Stuttgart and Leipzig, 1897–1901), 3: 255.

55. Paul Wentzke et al., *Elsass-Lothringen, 1871–1918* (Frankfurt a.M., 1938), p. 83.

56. Alexander zu Hohenlohe-Schillingsfürst, *Aus meinem Leben*, pp. 128, 136.

57. Hohenlohe, *Denkwürdigkeiten*, 2: 397. 18 October 1886.

58. Clericus, "Bischof Zorn von Bulach," *Elsass-Lothringen. Heimatstimmen* 3 (1925): 75–82.

59. Alexander zu Hohenlohe-Schillingsfürst, *Aus meinem Leben*, pp. 140–41.

60. Ernst Theodor, "Die Ausnahmegesetze für Elsass-Lothringen," *Cahiers alsaciens* 2 (1913): 192.

61. Wolfram, *Das Reichsland*, vol. 2, pt. 1, p. 227. In a publication of the Ministerium für Elsass-Lothringen, *Handbuch für Elsass-Lothringen, 1880* (Strasbourg, 1880), 192 towns are listed as having mayors appointed by the kaiser.

62. Ernsthausen, *Erinnerungen*, pp. 325–31; Rasch, *Die Preussen in Elsass-Lothringen*, pp. 84–85, 325–27; August Schneegans, *Aus dem Elsass* (Leipzig, 1875), p. 120. Rasch claimed that Lauth never told Möller he only awaited the return of the French. This story, said Rasch, was merely an excuse fabricated to cover up the real reasons for removing Lauth.

63. Ernsthausen, *Erinnerungen*, p. 376; G. d'Elstein, *L'Alsace-Lorraine sous la domination allemande*, p. 297.

64. As population migration infused German blood into the cities, the government dared to hold municipal elections again in Strasbourg and Metz in 1886, with results very satisfactory to the administration. See Hohenlohe, *Denkwürdigkeiten*, 2: 381; Rogge, *Holstein und Hohenlohe*, p. 249; Parisot, *Histoire de Lorraine*, 3: 355.

65. Eugene Hepp, *L'Alsace-Lorraine et l'empire germanique* (Paris, 1881), p. 117.

66. *Frankfurter Zeitung*, 5 March 1874; Ernst Hochschild, "Der Diktaturparagraph in Elsass-Lothringen," *Elsass-Lothringisches Jahrbuch* 4 (1925): 157.

67. Wolfram, *Oberpräsident von Möller*, p. 12; Parisot, *Histoire de Lorraine*, 3: 359–60.

68. Alexander zu Hohenlohe-Schillingsfürst, *Aus meinem Leben*, pp. 208–10.

69. Chancellor Caprivi opposed the introduction of the imperial press law into Alsace-Lorraine. See Hohenlohe, *Denkwürdigkeiten*, 2: 503.

70. Parisot, *Histoire de Lorraine*, 3: 359. Secretary of state for Alsace-Lorraine, Matthias von Köller, generally considered a hard-line Prussian bureaucrat, pushed hard for repeal of the dictatorship paragraph. See Alexander zu Hohenlohe-Schillingsfürst, *Aus meinem Leben*, p. 210.

71. Albert von Mutius, ed., "Aus dem Nachlass des ehemaligen kaiserlichen Statthalters von Elsass-Lothringen, früheren preussischen Ministers des Innern von Dallwitz," *Preussische Jahrbücher* 214 (1928): 164; Alexander zu Hohenlohe-Schillingsfürst, *Aus meinem Leben*, p. 210.

72. Governor Wedel opposed exceptional laws, maintaining that if the Germans wished to govern in a dictatorial manner, they should never have repealed the dictatorship paragraph. See Graf Karl von Wedel, "Statthalter-Briefe aus Elsass-Lothringen: Unveröffentlichte Briefe des Grafen von Wedel an einen deutschen Professor," *Der Türmer: Monatschrift für Gemüt und Geist* 26 (1924): 304.

73. Mutius, in *Preussische Jahrbücher* 214 (1928): 164.

74. Ibid., pp. 151–56; Matter, in *Revue des sciences politiques* 43 (1920): 185–187; Joachim Mai, *Die preussisch-deutsche Polenpolitik, 1885 bis 1887* (Berlin, 1962).

75. Matter, in *Revue des sciences politiques* 43 (1920): 187–89.

76. Ibid., pp. 194–95.

CHAPTER 5

1. In 1871 the territorial population included 1,200,000 Catholics, 250,000 members of the Reformed and Lutheran churches, 40,000 Jews, and 3,000 Methodists, Baptists, and Mennonites. Only 13,000 Protestants resided in Lorraine. By 1910 Protestant population had risen to 360,000 (from sixteen to twenty percent of the total), 60,000 in Lorraine (from three to ten percent of the Lorraine total). See Statistisches Bureau des Ministeriums für Elsass-Lothringen, *Das Reichsland*, vol. 1, pt. 2, p. 171; Michaelis, *Grenzlandkirche*, p. 2.

2. Wentzke et al., *Elsass-Lothringen*, pp. 106–7.

3. Joseph Brauner, "Briefe von Joseph Guerber an den jungen Carl Marbach, den späteren Weihbischof von Strassburg, aus den Jahren 1859 bis 1871," *Archiv für Elsässische Kirchen-Geschichte*, 8 (1933): 441.

4. Charles Downer Hazen, *Alsace-Lorraine Under German Rule* (New York, 1917), p. 223.
5. Franz Schnabel, *Deutsche Geschichte im neunzehnten Jahrhundert*, 4: *Die religiösen Kräfte* (Freiburg im Breisgau, 1951), pp. 76–94.
6. Brauner, in *Archiv für Elsässische Kirchengeschichte* p. 437; Griser, *Programme des catholiques*, p. 30.
7. *Frankfurter Zeitung*, 9 June 1877.
8. Abbé Felix Klein, *L'Evêque de Metz. Vie de Mgr. Dupont des Loges, 1804–1886* (Paris, 1899), pp. 321–22.
9. *Archiv für Katholisches Kirchenrecht*, N.F. 27 (1872): 117.
10. Lujo Brentano, *Elsässer Erinnerungen* (Berlin, 1918), p. 17.
11. *Archiv für Katholisches Kirchenrecht*, N.F. 43 (1880): 410; Wentzke et al., *Elsass-Lothringen*, p. 107; Rodolph Reuss, *Histoire d'Alsace* (Paris, 1920), p. 378.
12. Bismarck, *Ges. Werke*, 11: 322, 328.
13. Article Six also provided that Reformed, Lutheran, and Jewish congregations in Alsace-Lorraine would cease to recognize French ecclesiastical authority, and that the Lutheran Consistory and Directory in Strasbourg would relinquish control over Lutherans in France. See *Grosse Politik*, 1: 39–40.
14. Microfilmed documents from the German Foreign Office, University of California, Series II, reel 32, frame 248. In abbreviated form, U.C., II, 32/248. Negotiating the final peace treaty with France in April 1871, Count Harry von Arnim had assured Bismarck that agreement on the adjustment of diocese boundaries was just a matter of language; at any rate, Arnim regarded the diocese boundary problem as a matter of slight importance, simply a question of detail. See *Grosse Politik*, 1: 17. Arnim to Bismarck, 21 April 1871.
15. U.C., I, 67/19. 4 March 1872.
16. U. C., I. 67/7. 31 August 1871.
17. Bishop Foulon of Nancy deplored the annexation in a 26 July 1873 pastoral leter. Priests in the districts of Sarrebourg and Château-Salins read the letter from their pulpits 3 August, and were arraigned before a tribunal at Zabern. Tried *in absentia* along with the priests, Bishop Foulon received a two-month prison sentence. See Parisot, *Histoire de Lorraine*, 3: 457–58.
18. U.C., I, 67/97, 103. 14, 26 February 1874.
19. *Augsburger Allgemeine Zeitung*, 5 August 1874.
20. Griser, *Programme des catholiques*, p. 15. See Henri Didio, *L'Eglise catholique en Alsace depuis l'annexion, 1871–1889* (Lille, 1889), pp. 11–14, regarding a decrease in the Catholic population after 1871.
21. Ernst Thiele, "Die deutsche Regierung und das Konkordat im Elsass nach 1870," *Archiv für Elsässische Kirchengeschichte* 2 (1927): 350–53; Didio, *L'Eglise catholique en Alsace*, p. 4.
22. Löning, in *Revue de droit international et de legislation comparée* 5 (1873): 119–20; U.C., II, 32/252.
23. *Archiv für Katholisches Kirchenrecht*, N.F. 45 (1881): 303, and 43 (1880): 415; Bismarck, *Ges. Werke*, 6; 15–16. Antonelli's letter dated 3 January 1872.
24. *Archiv für Katholisches Kirchenrecht*, N.F. 43 (1880): 415; U.C., II, 32/319.
25. Thiele, in *Archiv für Elsässisches Kirchengeschichte* 2 (1927): 362; U.C., I, 67/8. 18 February 1872.
26. U.C., II, 34/205. 7 April 1875; August Schricker, *Elsass-Lothringen im*

Reichstag vom Beginn der ersten Legislatur-Periode bis zur Einführung der Reichsverfassung (Strasbourg, 1873), pp. 181, 192.

27. *Augsburger Allgemeine Zeitung*, 29 October 1873; Klein, *L'Evêque de Metz*, pp. 364–65; Alois Spitz, *Zur Lage und Stimmung in Elsass-Lothringen* (Strasbourg, 1894), p. 15.

28. Klein, *L'Evêque de Metz*, p. 420. 4 November 1880.

29. *Gesetzblatt* (1881), pp. 3, 87.

30. The kaiser may have referred to a French decree of 7 January 1808 when approving the coadjutor. See *Archiv für Katholische Kirchenrecht*, N.F. 45 (1881): 311, and U.C., I 66/660, a memorandum issued by Bismarck, 30 January 1881.

31. For these contradictory accounts, see Hutten-Czapski, *Sechzig Jahre Politik*, 1: 113; Rogge, *Holstein und Hohenlohe*, pp. 341–42.

32. U.C., I, 67/19. 4 March 1872.

33. Hohenlohe, *Denkwürdigkeiten*, 2: 472; Rogge, *Holstein und Hohenlohe*, pp. 341–42.

34. Hutten-Czapski, *Sechzig Jahre Politik*, 1: 199–200.

35. Ibid., 1: 71–72, for a discussion of the 1879 negotiations.

36. Hohenlohe, *Denkwürdigkeiten*, 2: 472.

37. Hutten-Czapski, *Sechzig Jahre Politik*, 1: 201–2, 215.

38. Ibid. By his own admission, Hutten-Czapski seems to have been rather unpopular. He claimed to have opponents in the German Center party, in the Polish Reichstag faction, among palace and government officials, and in the royal family.

39. By Helmuth Rogge's account, Kraus, an unwilling candidate, was both "enticed and terrified" by his nomination. By the time his candidacy collapsed, Kraus had apparently overcome his fears, and allegedly participated in the intrigue leading to Hutten-Czapski's removal from the negotiations. See Rogge, *Holstein und Hohenlohe*, p. 342, and Hutten-Czapski, *Sechzig Jahre Politik*, 1: 220.

40. J. G. Röhl has claimed that the kaiser made the final decision to accept Fritzen without so much as informing Caprivi, Prussian Minister of Ecclesiastical Affairs Gustav von Gossler, or Foreign Secretary Baron Adolf Marschall von Bieberstein. See Röhl, *Germany Without Bismarck*, p. 60. For Hutten-Czapski's account of the negotiations, see his *Sechzig Jahre Politik*, 1: 198–220.

41. Mgr. Hammant, "Les petits Séminaires d'Alsace-Lorraine sous le régime allemand," *Revue ecclésiastique de Metz* 37 (1930): 352 ff., 418.

42. Clericus, in *Elsass-Lothringen. Heimatstimmen* 3 (1925): 75–82.

43. *Gesetzblatt* (1873), pp. 37–38.

44. Elsass-Lothringen, Oberpräsidial Bureau, *Verordnungen und amtliche Nachrichten*, pp. 162–63, 178.

45. Bismarck, *Ges. Werke*, 6c: 20. 12 June 1872. In the margin of Bismarck's order to close the institutions, Möller wrote. "I have long sought a law which would give me this power, but to the best of my recollection, I never received a reply."

46. G. d'Elstein, *L'Alsace-Lorraine sous la domination allemande*, p. 202.

47. Bismarck, *Ges. Werke*, 6c: 20, 12 June 1872; 11: 322 16 May 1873.

48. Landesausschuss, *Verhandlungen*, 7th Sess., 1879–80, II: 458.

49. Klein, *L'Evêque de Metz*, pp. 403–4, 411.

50. Arnold Sachse, "Erinnerungen aus der elsass-lothringischen Schulverwaltung, *Elsass-Lothringisches Jahrbuch* 5 (1927): 234–35; Wolfram, *Das Reichsland*, vol. 2, pt. 2, pp. 27–28.

51. Hohenlohe, *Denkwürdigkeiten*, 2: 382, 394, 399.

52. Seydler, *Hohenlohe-Schillingsfürst*, pp. 138–39.
53. Ibid., p. 135.
54. For the negotiations for the Catholic theological faculty, see Conrad Bornhack, "Die Begründung der katholischtheologischen Fakultät in Strassburg," *Elsass-Lothringisches Jahrbuch* 12 (1933): 249–69.
55. Wedel, "Statthalter-Briefe," in *Der Türmer* 25 (1924): 305. Letter of 27 May 1912. For Wedel's conflict with Bishop Benzler, see Clericus, in *Elsass-Lothringen. Heimatstimmen* 3 (1925): 80–81; Sachse, in *Elsass-Lothringisches Jahrbuch* 6 (1927): 234–35; Parisot, *Histoire de Lorraine*, 3: 363, 467.
56. Michaelis, *Grenzlandkirche*; Landesausschuss, *Verhandlungen*, 6th Sess., 1879, II: 200; *Revue alsacienne* 6 (1883): 334–35; Karl Heinrich Keck, *Das Leben des General-Feldmarschalls Edwin von Manteuffel* (Bielefeld and Leipzig, 1890), pp. 316–18.
57. Alexander zu Hohenlohe-Schillingsfürst, *Aus meinem Leben*, p. 124.
58. Reichstag, *Stenogr. Ber.*, 4th Leg. Per., 2nd Sess., 1879, II: 1627.

CHAPTER 6

1. Modern political parties developed slowly in the Reichsland. This and succeeding chapters will trace the politicization of the territory.
2. *A.D.B.R.*, AL 29, paquet 6, no. 10. Letter from the president of the Committee to all priests, 8 November 1872, and report of the Strasbourg police director, Otto Back, 22 February 1873.
3. Since the radical opposition tended to emigrate from Alsace-Lorraine after 1871, it is difficult to trace their role in Alsatian politics under the German regime.
4. *Elsässisches Volksblatt für Stadt und Land* (Mulhouse), 30 January 1874.
5. Ibid., 25 June 1875; 9 January 1874; 30 January 1874.
6. Georges Delahache (pseud. Lucien Aaron), *L'Exode* (Paris, 1914), p. 127.
7. *Augsburger Allgemeine Zeitung*, 21 January 1874.
8. Eccard, *L'Alsace sous la domination allemande*, p. 81.
9. Lalance, *Souvenirs*, p. 48.
10. *L'Industriel Alsacien* (Mulhouse), 30 Januray 1874.
11. *Strassburger Zeitung und Amtliche Nachrichten*, 22 January 1874.
12. Heinrich Brück, *Die Kulturkampfbewegung in Deutschland* (Münster, 1905), 2: 299.
13. *Revue alsacienne* 8 (1884–85): 30–31.
14. Alberta von Puttkamer, *Die Aera Manteuffel. Federzeichnungen aus Elsass-Lothringen* (Stuttgart and Leipzig, n.d.), pp. 93–94; Arnold Sachse, "Die Kirchenpolitik des Statthalters Freiherr von Manteuffel," *Elsass-Lothringisches Jahrbuch* 5 (1926): 149; Goldschmidt, in *Elsass-Lothringishes Jahrbuch* 15 (1936): 149–51.
15. Brentano, *Elsässer Erinnerungen*, p. 40.
16. *A.D.B.R.*, AL 47, paquet 127. Manteuffel to kaiser, 30 October 1881.
17. Keck, *Manteuffel*, pp. 312–13. Reports circulated at the time that Manteuffel threatened to resign if the protester candidates were returned to the Reichstag. See articles from *Le Voltaire* and *Le Figaro* (Paris), in *A.D.B.R.*, AL 47, paquet 127.
18. *Le Messin*, 8 February 1887; *Elsass-Lothringische Volkszeitung* (Mulhouse), 2 June 1893.

19. *Le Messin*, 17 February 1887.
20. *Elsass-Lothringische Volkszeitung*, 26 May 1893; J. Wagner, "Le Journal politique intime de Mgr. Winterer," *Revue catholique d'Alsace* (1931): 580. On the day before the election, Hohenlohe wrote that the clergy paid no attention to the pope, and worked against the military bill. The seat of the trouble, in the governor's opinion, lay in the fact that the government made no attempt to Germanize the seminaries immediately after the 1870 war. See Hohenlohe, *Denkwürdigkeiten*, 2: 409. Letter of 20 February 1887.
21. *A.D.B.R.*, AL 47, paquet 129. 15 February 1887.
22. Rogge, *Holstein und Hohenlohe*, p. 400. Holstein to Hohenlohe, 9 May 1893.
23. Ibid., p. 399. Hohenlohe to Kayser, 5 May 1893.
24. Ibid., p. 400; Hohenlohe, *Denkwürdigkeiten*, 2: 500–1. Diary entries of 19, 21, 26 May 1893.
25. J. Alden Nichols, *Germany After Bismarck* (New York, 1968), pp. 204–64. Nichols has portrayed the general situation Caprivi faced on the army bill; the implications for Alsace-Lorraine are the responsibility of the present author.
26. Prince Alexander's margin of victory declined in 1898, when he received 11,437 votes against 8,521 for the clerical and 1,596 for the Social Democratic candidate. Despite his 12,060 votes in 1903, Alexander failed to defeat the clerical Heinrich Wiltberger, who polled 11,-686 on the first ballot, and a socialist with 1,787 votes. On the second ballot, Wiltberger won, 13,382 to 12,935. Alexander claimed Wiltberger had government support with Chancellor Bülow's blessing. But among the majority Alsatian Catholics, Alexander was known as "der Combess," the Alsatian dialect's rendering of Emile Combes, the French anticlerical leader. See Alexander zu Hohenlohe-Schillingsfürst, *Aus meinem Leben*, pp. 185–93.
27. *St. Odilienblatt*, 5 November 1881.
28. Landolin Winterer, *Le Socialisme contemporain* (Paris, 1901), pp. 45, 48; Spitz, *Der Sozialismus im Reichslande*, pp. 7, 17.
29. *L'Industriel Alsacien*, 30 January 1874. In 1903 the Catholic press still portrayed local socialists as tools of the German SPD. See the *Mülhauser Arbeiterfreund*, 23 May, 20 June 1903.
30. *Frankfurter Zeitung*, 25 August 1876. For a general account of the SPD's attitude toward Alsace-Lorraine, see Hans-Ulrich Wehler, *Sozialdemokratie und Nationalstaat* (Würzburg, 1962), pp. 44–75.
31. *A.D.B.R.*, D 68, paquet 3. Poster circulated by the *Alsacien-Lorrain* (Paris) for the 1893 election.
32. Winterer, *Le Socialisme contemporain*, p. 401; idem, *Arbeit und Religion: Ein kleiner sozialer Katechismus* (Rixheim, 1897).
33. There is a clear anti-Semitic tone in much of the Catholic antisocialist literature in Alsace-Lorraine.
34. Victor Guerber, *Sozialismus der Erzfeind steht vor der Thüre* (Strasbourg, 1891), pp. 20, 40–56; Heinrich Cetty, *La Famille ouvrière en Alsace* (Rixheim, 1883), pp. 238, 248–57.
35. Guerber, *Sozialismus der Erzfeind*, pp. 16–17. There are some striking parallels between this Catholic social and economic analysis, and the orthodox Marxist interpretation.
36. Heinrich Meyer, *Wiederaufbau des Mittelstandes in Elsass-Lothringen* (Strasbourg, 1918). The difficulties in using the term *Mittelstand*, which does not appear to represent any well-defined class, have been exposed

most recently in Harold J. Gordon's review of Herman Lebovics, *Social Conservatism and the Middle Classes in Germany, 1914–1933* (Princeton, 1969), in the *American Historical Review* 75 (1970): 1147–48.

37. Cetty, *La Famille ouvrière*, pp. 8–29, 235–36. For alcoholism statistics, see pages 43–46; stillbirth figures are given on page 182. Michaelis, *Grenzlandkirche*, pp. 80–83, provides more statistics on alcoholism and stillbirths. According to Cetty, the Mulhouse municipal hospital admitted four patients for alcoholism in 1871, two of whom died. In 1877 alcoholism admissions had risen to thirty-seven, five of whom died. Besides those admitted specifically for treatment of alcoholism in 1877, most cases admitted had some alcohol complications. See Cetty, pp. 46–47.

38. *Journal de Colmar*, 5 June 1898.

39. *Strassburger Post*, 22 October 1884; *Revue catholique d'Alsace* 8 (1889): 261.

40. Guerber, *Sozialismus der Erzfeind*, passim, and Cetty, *La Famille ouvrière*, pp. 26–29. Cetty expressed alarm at the growing number of libraries in Mulhouse. In 1867 there were thirty-three libraries holding 13,170 volumes; by 1876 Mulhouse libraries held 55,638 volumes, about 25,000 of them in German.

41. *Mülhauser Arbeiterfreund*, 10 June 1893.

42. *A.D.B.R.*, AL 27, paquet 53. Report of the district president at Colmar to the governor, 28 April 1897, and an announcement of the *Christlicher Textilarbeiterverband*, included in a report by the Mulhouse police commissioner.

43. Anton Krieger, *Die Textilindustrie von Mülhausen i. E. in den letzten 20 Jahren, sowie die soziale Lage ihrer Arbeiter* (Kreuznach, 1911), pp. 73–74, 79.

44. Laufenburger and Pflimlin, *Cours d'Economie alsacienne*, 2: *L'Industrie de Mulhouse*, pp. 373–74. The free textile unions in Alsace-Lorraine boasted 1,270 members in 1905; 5,399 in 1908; 2,675 in 1911; and 3,673 in 1914. In 1914 the Alsace-Lorraine branch of the Christian Federation of German Textile Workers encompassed 2,231 members, against the 3,673 for the free textile unions.

45. Of the Christian Federation's 2,231 members in 1914, 972 were women.

46. Krieger, *Textilindustrie von Mülhausen*, pp. 72–73.

47. See Michaelis, *Grenzlandkirche*, pp. 80–88.

48. Ibid., pp. 80–84.

49. Ibid., p. 44.

50. *Elsass-Lothringische Volkszeitung*, 21 May 1893.

51. *A.D.B.R.*, AL 29, paquet 6, no. 10. Altkirch county director to Möller, 7 June 1878.

52. Emile Wetterlé, *Les Coulisses du Reichstag; Seize années de vie parlementaire en Allemagne* (Paris, 1918), pp. 10–11.

53. Alexander zu Hohenlohe-Schillingsfürst, *Aus meinem Leben*, pp. 127–28.

54 Jean and Fréderic Régamey, "La Vote de l'Alsace-Lorraine," *L'Europe Nouvelle* (March 1907), p. 4.

55. H. Reumont, "Die parteipolitische Entwicklung in Lothringen," in *Lothringen und seine Hauptstadt: Festschrift zur 60. Generalversammlung der Katholiken Deutschlands in Metz, 1913*, ed. A. Kuppel (Metz, 1913), pp. 114–16; W. Kapp, "Parteiprobleme in Elsass-Lothringen," *Elsässische Kulturfragen* 2 (1911–12): 310–12.

56. For details of the establishment of a Catholic party in Alsace-Lorraine

between 1890 and 1906, see J. Rossé, M. Sturmel et al., *Das Elsass von 1870–1932* (Colmar, 1936), 2: 143–65.

57. Karl Bachem, *Vorgeschichte, Geschichte und Politik der deutschen Zentrumspartei* (Cologne, 1927–1932), 6: 200.

58. *Elsass-Lothringische Volkspartei*, 14 June 1911.

59. Charles Brocard, "Le Parti socialiste en Alsace-Lorraine," *Revue politique et parlementaire* 64 (1910): 58–59.

60. Ibid., pp. 60–61.

CHAPTER 7

1. See the *Elsass-Lothringische Volkspartei*, 8 June and 23 June 1903, for the democratic-socialist alliance, and the *Mülhauser Arbeiterfreund*, 3 May, 30 May 1903, for the liberal-Catholic alliance.

2. *Mülhauser Arbeiterfreund*, 12 January 1907. Letter of 30 December 1906.

3. The Alsace-Lorraine Center received 41.9 percent, the Social Democrats 23.7 percent, and the liberal-democrats 17.2 percent. In 1912, the Center won 34 percent, the Social Democrats 31.7 percent, and the liberal-democrats 19.5 percent.

4. Wilhelm Fischer, *Manteuffel in Elsass-Lothringen und seine Verdeutschungspolitik* (Basel, 1885), p. 26. For a description of the government pressure, see *Revue alsacienne* 6 (1882–83): 35.

5. Theobald von Bethmann Hollweg, *Betrachtungen zum Weltkrieg* (Berlin, 1919), 1: 15, 19.

6. Hohenlohe, *Denkwürdigkeiten*, 2: 498. Diary entry of 20 February 1893.

7. Fritz Bronner, *Die Verfassungsbestrebungen des Landesausschusses für Elsass-Lothringen, 1875–1911* (Heidelberg, 1926), p. 187.

8. Cited in ibid., p. 189.

9. Nichols, *Germany After Bismarck*, pp. 118–19.

10. Michael Balfour, *The Kaiser and His Times* (London, 1964), p. 300.

11. *Holstein Papers*, 4: 496–97.

12. Ibid., p. 495.

13. Ibid. Holstein to Bülow, 26 September 1907.

14. Ibid., pp. 496–97. Bülow to Holstein, 29 September 1907.

15. Mutius, "Aus dem Nachlass Dallwitz," *Preussische Jahrbücher* 214 (1928): 292.

16. Wedel, "Statthalter-Briefe," *Der Türmer* 26 (1924): 303. Letter of 18 August 1911.

17. Hans-Günter Zmarzlik, *Bethmann Hollweg als Reichskanzler, 1909–1914* (Düsseldorf, 1957), p. 93.

18. Rudolf Schwander and Fritz Jaffe, *Verfassung und Verwaltung von Elsass-Lothringen, 1871–1918* (Berlin, 1936), pp. 73–74.

19. Schwander and Jaffe maintain that Bülow was able to secure the assent of the other ministers to Wedel's proposals, while Zmarzlik asserts that this conclusion is not supported by the evidence. Zmarzlik is probably correct, for if the Prussian ministry had approved Wedel's plans, constitutional reform probably would have been put through the Reichstag in 1909 rather than in 1911.

20. This was not simply a liberal movement; Bethmann Hollweg himself, certainly no liberal, promoted Prussian electoral reform. On Dallwitz, see Mutius, in *Preussische Jahrbücher* 214 (1928): 159.

21. *Holstein Papers*, 4: 497.
22. Zmarzlik, *Bethmann Hollweg*, pp. 92, 94. Bethmann Hollweg to Bülow, December 1908; Prussian ministry session of 11 October 1909.
23. For texts of these motions see Reichstag, *Stenogr. Ber.*, 12th Leg. Per., 2nd Sess., CCLXV: 1812.
24. Ibid., CCLX: 2090.
25. Zmarzlik, *Bethmann Hollweg*, p. 95. Bethmann Hollweg to Wedel, 19 April 1910.
26. For texts of the 1911 constitution and the *Landtag* electoral law see Edwin H. Zeydel, *Constitutions of the German Empire and the German States* (Washington, 1919), pp. 479–86.
27. Reichstag, *Stenogr. Ber.*, 12th Leg. Per., 2nd Sess., CCLXIII: 4162–63. Speech of Clemens von Delbrück.
28. For Kapp's analysis see Wilhelm Kapp, "Die 'Aera Mandel'," *Elsass-Lothringen. Heimatstimmen* 3 (1925): 18–23.
29. *Strassburger Neue Zeitung*, 27 January 1911; *Freie Presse*, 4 February 1911; *A.D.B.R.*, AL 69, no. 438, vol. 3. Report of Strasbourg police director Petri, 8 January 1911.
30. Landesausschuss, *Verhandlungen*, 38th Sess., 1911, II: 42–43, 463.
31. Ibid., pp. 48–49.
32. During the commission's second reading of the bill, this amendment was discarded, and the original government text was reinstated.
33. *Strassburger Neue Zeitung*, 27 June 1911.
34. Landesausschuss, *Verhandlungen*, 38th Sess., 1911, II: 44, 479.
35. Ibid., p. 465.
36. Ibid., pp. 46, 464–65.
37. *Freie Presse*, 30 January 1911.
38. Although only 634,735 people voted, a total of 1,273,998 votes was cast under the plural vote system. Of those who voted, 53.79 percent voted for Social Democratic candidates, while only 46.21 percent voted for candidates of the middle-class parties. As the result of plural voting, however, the Social Democrats received only 38.66 percent of the votes cast, while the middle-class parties received 61.43 percent of the votes cast. Of the voters who possessed two votes, 54.12 percent voted for Social Democrats; 26.45 percent of those with three votes cast ballots for socialists, while only 8.26 percent of those with four votes voted for Social Democratic candidates. See the *Frankfurter Zeitung*, 6 February 1910.
39. Mutius, in *Preussische Jahrbücher* 214 (1928): p. 295.
40. Reichstag, *Stenogr. Ber.*, 12th Leg. Per., 2nd Sess., CCLXXXI: 5321. Delbrück made an important distinction. Alsace-Lorraine could be considered as a Federal State, without actually being one.
41. Ibid., CCLXXXIII: 7040.
42. Wehler, *Sozialdemokratie und Nationalstaat*, pp. 57–75. As the German Social Democrats came to play a larger role in German politics after the repeal of the antisocialist laws in 1890, they sought to increase their parliamentary strength further by democratizing the Prussian electoral laws. The new electoral law for Alsace-Lorraine seemed to be a precedent which might be used to force concessions elsewhere; but to obtain the new electoral law in the Reichsland, the SPD felt it necessary to compromise with the government on the issue of the upper chamber of the *Landtag*. In the *Freie Presse* of 23 May 1911, the Alsatian Social Democrats assumed an uncompromising position, and asked the German Social Democrats to vote against the government bills.

43. Landesausschuss, *Verhandlungen*, 38th Sess., 1911, II: 39.
44. William L. Langer, ed., *An Encyclopedia of World History* (Cambridge, Mass., 1952), p. 693.
45. Koppel S. Pinson, *Modern Germany: Its History and Civilization* (New York, 1955), p. 290.
46. William Harbutt Dawson, *The German Empire and the Unity Movement* (New York, 1919), 2: 362.
47. A few of the many relevant works by German legal scholars are, Alfred Döring, *Die staatsrechtliche Stellung des Statthalters von Elsass-Lothringen* (Mulhouse, 1912); Wilhelm Lepsius, *Die Verantwortlichkeit des Statthalters von Elsass-Lothringen* (Borna-Leipzig, 1915); Ernst Marten, *Der Statthalter in Elsass-Lothringen* (Greifswald, 1914); Otto Nelte, "Die staatsrechtliche Stellung des Statthalters von Elsass-Lothringen," *Archiv des öffentlichen Rechts*, 27 (1911): 1–42, 133–74; Otto Nelte, "Das neue Verfassungsgesetz für Elsass-Lothringen," *Archiv des öffentlichen Rechts*, 28 (1912): 45–96; James Rosenberg, *Die Rechtsnatur Elsass-Lothringens* (Hamburg, 1913); Eduard Schalfejew, *Die staatsrechtliche Stellung Elsass-Lothringens nach dem neuen Verfassungsgesetz* (Berlin, 1913); Willi Supf, *Elsass-Lothringen und die staatsrechtliche Natur des deutschen Reichs* (Greifswald, 1912); Rudolf Weyrich, *Die staatsrechtliche Stellung des Statthalters in Elsass-Lothringen* (Strasbourg, 1911).
48. Friedrich Koenig, "Der Elsass-Lothringische Partikularismus," *Elsässische Kulturfragen*, ser. 2, vol. 3 (1911), p. 111.
49. Otto-Günther von Wesendonk, *Darstellung und rechtspolitische Würdigung der durch das Reichsgesetz vom 31. Mai 1911 in dem verfassungsrechtlichen Verhältnis zwischen Elsass-Lothringen und dem Reich eingetretenen Veränderung* (Borna-Leipzig, 1913), pp. 99–100.
50. Lepsius, *Verantwortlichkeit des Statthalters*, pp. 30–32.
51. Döring, *Stellung des Statthalters*, p. 28.
52. Landesausschuss, *Verhandlungen*, 38th Sess., 1911, II: 477.
53. *Freie Presse*, 6 February, 3 April 1911; the Catholic *Le Nouvelliste d'Alsace-Lorraine* (Colmar), 17 May 1911.
54. Landesausschuss, *Verhandlungen*, 38th Sess., 1911, II: 52.
55. Ibid., p. 72.
56. *Le Nouvelliste d'Alsace-Lorraine*, 18 February 1911.

CHAPTER 8

1. Landesausschuss, *Verhandlungen*, 38th Sess., 1911, II: 26.
2. Wilhelm Kapp, "Der Nationalistenbund," *Mitteilungen der Elsass-Lothringischen Vereinigung*, ser. 2, vol. 1 (July 1911), pp. 3–4; *A.D.B.R.*, AL 27, paquet 57, no. 246.
3. Vonderscheer's name was omitted from a list of clerical Reichstag deputies from Alsace-Lorraine who were praised for their conduct during the constitutional debate. See the *Elsass-Lothringische Volkspartei*, 14 June 1911.
4. Ibid.
5. Wilhelm Kapp, "Die Wahlen," *Mitteilungen der Elsass-Lothringischen Vereinigung*, ser. 2, vol. 2 (October 1911), pp. 59–60.
6. *Freie Presse*, 7 October 1911.
7. Ibid., 23 September 1911; *Strassburger Neue Zeitung*, 10 October 1911; *A.D.B.R.*, AL27, paquet 57, no. 246.

8. Ibid.
9. Ibid., for electoral manifestos of the Alsace-Lorraine Center and the Strasbourg committee of the Center.
10. Salomon Grumbach, *Das Schicksal Elsass-Lothringens* (Neuchâtel, 1915), pp. 29–45.
11. Kapp, "Parteiprobleme," in *Elsässische Kulturfragen* 2 (1911–12): 306–11.
12. *A.D.B.R.*, AL 27, paquet 57, no. 246.
13. Wilhelm Kapp, "Elsass-Lothringen und die Aera Hohenlohe-Schillingsfürst," *Elsass-Lothringen. Heimatstimmen*, 3 (1925): 116; idem, "Karl Hauss," ibid., p. 72.
14. See the article by André Morizet in *L'Humanité*, 19 May 1914. For an explanation of liberal opposition to the *Nationalbund*, see the *Elsass-Lothringische Volkspartei*, 10 October 1911.
15. *Elsass-Lothringische Volkspartei*, 16 September 1911.
16. *A.D.B.R.*, AL 27, paquet 57, no. 246, for manifesto of the Strasbourg committee of the *Nationalbund*, and a speech by Karl Burger.
17. Ibid. The manifesto of the Alsace-Lorraine Center, and the *Freie Presse*, 14 October 1911, should be consulted for criticism of the Center position on the progressive income tax. The Strasbourg Center electoral committee denied that Laugel's views represented those of the party.
18. Ibid., for the positions of the liberal, Karl Burger, and the Alsace-Lorraine Center.
19. *Elsass-Lothringische Volkspartei*, 19 August 1911; *Le Nouvelliste d'Alsace-Lorraine*, 9 January 1912; *A.D.B.R.*, AL 32, no. 39, vols. 1–3; AL 32, no. 40.
20. The Alsace-Lorraine Center received 93,101 votes (31 percent); the Social Democrats, 71,476 (15.9 percent); the Lorraine Bloc, 39,374 (13.1 percent). See Rossé, Sturmel et al., *Das Elsass*, 4: 73, and *A.D.B.R.*, AL 27, paquet 57, no. 246.
21. *A.D.B.R.*, AL 27, paquet 57, no. 246; *Strassburger Neue Zeitung*, 25 October 1911.
22. *Elsass-Lothringische Volkspartei*, 9 September 1911.
23. Ibid., 25, 29 October 1911.
24. F. E., "Le Bilan des élections à la seconde chambre," *Cahiers alsaciens* 1 (1912): 18.
25. Paul Harelle, "Réflexions sur les élections Lorraines," ibid., p. 26; Parisot, *Histoire de Lorraine*, 3: 365.
26. F. E., in *Cahiers alsaciens* 1 (1912): 16–17.
27. *Le Nouvelliste d'Alsace-Lorraine*, 8 January 1912; *Freie Presse*, 11 January 1912. In view of the possibility of a run-off ballot, no one wished to make irreconcilable enemies whose aid might be needed later.
28. *Strassburger Neue Zeitung*, 5 January 1912; *Freie Presse*, 3 January 1912.
29. *Freie Presse*, 3, 4 January 1912; *Strassburger Neue Zeitung*, 5 January 1912; *Elsass-Lothringische Volkspartei*, 6 January 1912.
30. For Alsace-Lorraine election statistics, see Rossé, Sturmel et al., *Das Elsass*, 4: 81–82. The Social Democrats failed to register gains in traditional Catholic strongholds. See article from *Vorwärts* (n.d.) in *A.D.B.R,.* AL47, paquet 133.
31. *Freie Presse*, 17 January 1912.
32. In the 1911 *Landtag* election, the Lorraine Bloc had won only 57 per-

cent of the vote in Metz II district, compared with a high of 97 percent in Bolchen-Falkenberg. See Friedrich Koenig, "Die parteipolitischen Verhältnisse Lothringens," *Elsässische Kulturfragen*, ser. 2, 12 (December, 1912): 491, for the percentages in each Lorraine district.

33. *A.D.B.R.*, AL 132, paquet 5, no. 9. Article from *Berliner Tageblatt*, 6 January 1912.

34. Ibid. Reports appeared in the *Rheinische-Westphälische Zeitung*, 7 July 1914, and the *Neue Stuttgarter Tageblatt*. They were denied in the *Strassburger Bürger-Zeitung*, 8 July 1914, and the *Strassburger Neue Zeitung*, 10 July 1914.

35. *A.D.B.R.*, AL 27, no. 219.

36. *A.D.B.R.*, 132, paquet 5, no. 10. Pamphlet No. 2 of the *Elsass-Lothringen Mittelpartei*, March 1913.

37. *A.D.B.R.*, 132, paquet 5, no. 10. Article from *Frankfurter Zeitung*, 25 1914.

38. Even the German-based *Bund der Landwirte* elected one *Landtag* delegate in 1911. See ibid., *Freie Presse* article of 8 February 1913.

39. Charles Brocard, "Le Parti socialiste en Alsace-Lorraine," *Revue politique et parlementaire* 64 (1910): 56.

40. Kapp, "Aera Hohenlohe-Schillingsfürst," in *Elsass-Lothringen. Heimatstimmen* 3 (1925): 116.

41. Wedel, "Statthalter-Briefe," in *Der Türmer* 26 (1924): 306. Letter of 8 June 1912. For Wedel's views on Alsatian particularism, see ibid., p. 459, letter of 7 July 1912, and p. 304, letter of 16 December 1912, where Wedel speaks not only of Alsace-Lorraine particularism, but of a special Lorraine particularism. In Lorraine, contended Wedel, the population liked the monarchical system and tended toward authoritarianism.

CHAPTER 9

1. Laufenburger and Pflimlin, *Cours d'Economie alsacienne*, 2: 197–98; Alphonse Barthelmé, *Le Développement des courants commerciaux d'Alsace depuis la guerre* (Strasbourg, 1931), p. 9.

2. Barthelmé, *Courants commerciaux*, pp. 13–14; Laufenburger, *Cours d'Economie alsacienne*, 1: 199; Laufenburger, "Die weltwirtschaftliche Stellung des Elsass," *Weltwirtschaftliches Archiv* 35 (1932): 235.

3. Chambre de Commerce de Mulhouse, *Admissions temporaires des tissus écrus. Rapport de M. Edouard Koechlin* (Mulhouse, 1867), pp. 3–5.

4. André Brandt and Paul Leuilliot, "Les Elections à Mulhouse en 1869," *Revue d'Alsace* 99 (1960): 109.

5. Sanford H. Elwitt, "Politics and Social Classes in the Loire: The Triumph of Republican Order, 1869–1873," *French Historical Studies* 6 (1969): 109.

6. Société Industrielle de Mulhouse, *Histoire documentaire de l'industrie de Mulhouse et de ses environs au XIXe siécle* (Mulhouse, 1902), 2: 935–37.

7. André Brandt, "Le Sort de Mulhouse en 1871," *Bulletin de la Société Industrielle de Mulhouse* (hereafter *B.S.I.M.*), (1951): 26–30; A. Staub, *Die Baumwollen-Industrie und die Annexion von Elsass-Lothringen* (Berlin, 1870), p. 9.

8. Brandt, in *B.S.I.M.* (1951): 31–35.

9. Staub, *Die Baumwollen-Industrie*, pp. 2–11.

10. Numerous sources indicate the importance of the temporary admission issue after 1871. See Lalance, *La Crise*, pp. 24–27; Charles Grad, *Lettres d'un bourgeois sur la politique en Alsace-Lorraine* (Mulhouse, 1881), pp. 63–69; Chambre de Commerce de Colmar, *Rapport de M. Kiener sur le tissage et les importations temporaires* (Colmar, 1884), pp. 1–4; Ferdinand Dieffenbach, *Elsass-Lothringen und der Freihandel* (Strasbourg, 1877), passim; Gustav Bergmann, *Zur industriellen Enquête* (Strasbourg, 1877), passim; *Die Zollfreie Admission temporaire von Baumwollengarnen vor dem Reichstag* (Berlin, 1885), pp. 25–29; *Reichs-Enquête für die Baumwollen-und Leinen Industrie* (Berlin, 1879), pp. 198 ff.

11. Eccard, *L'Alsace sous la domination allemande*, p. 42. Negotiations for the peace treaty were begun in Brussels, and were transferred to Frankfurt 6 May 1871, only four days prior to the signing of the agreement.

12. Brandt, in *B.S.I.M.* (1951): 31; Dürckheim, *Erinnerungen*, 2: 264; *Process-verbal de la séance tenue à la mairie de Colmar le 24 mars 1871 pour délibérer sur les mesures à prendre en vue de sauvegarder les intérêts alsaciens au point de vue des conséquences de l'annexion* (Strasbourg, 1871), pp. 4–17.

13. J. Wagner, "Le Journal politique intime de Mgr. Winterer," *Revue Catholique d'Alsace* (1930): 129–31; Brauner, in *Archiv für Elsässische Kirchen-Geschichte*, 8 (1933): 439. Letter of 7 March 1871. Dürckheim and Dollfus did give accounts of their missions.

14. Albert Dumont, *L'Administration et la propagande prussiennes en Alsace* (Paris, 1871), pp. 206–7; Bismarck, *Ges. Werke*, 8: 31–32; Un Patriot alsacien, *Les Prussiens en Alsace* (Paris, 1874), pp. 8–9, which quotes Dollfus' letter of 25 April 1871.

15. Société Industrielle de Mulhouse, *Histoire documentaire*, 2: 937. German currency was not required in Alsace-Lorraine until 1876. Had they been required to use German currency, the Alsatian industrialists would have lost about one and one-half percent on all foreign transactions, because of the lower value of the German mark on the international money market. See the *Frankfurter Zeitung*, 23 August 1874.

16. *Die grosse Politik der europäischen Kabinette, 1871–1914* (Berlin, 1922–27), 1: 76.

17. Ibid., pp. 79, 91–95.

18. Laufenburger and Pflimlin, *Cours d'Economie alsacienne*, 2: 14–15, 68.

19. Barthelmé, *Courants commerciaux*, pp. 36–37.

20. Laufenburger and Pflimlin, *Cours d'Economie alsacienne*, 1: 131–34; 2: 271–72.

21. Ibid., 1: 142; 2: 33. The higher number represents finer thread.

22. Laufenburger and Pfllimlin, *Cours d'Economie alsacienne*, 2: 36; J.H. Clapham, *The Economic Development of France and Germany, 1815–1914* (Cambridge, England, 1921), p. 246. For lists of factories which shifted operations to France see Marie-Joseph Bopp, "L'Oeuvre sociale de la haute bourgeoisie haut-rhinoise au XIXe siècle," *La Bourgeoisie alsacienne* (Strasbourg and Paris, 1954), p. 402; André Brandt, "Apports alsaciens à l'industrie textile de la Lorraine et de la Franche-Comté au XVIIIe et XIXe siècles," *Trois Provinces de l'Est: Lorraine, Alsace, Franche-Comté* (Strasbourg, 1957), pp. 133–38.

23. Dieffenbach, *Elsass-Lothringen und der Freihandel*, p. 42.

24. Laufenburger and Pflimlin, *Cours d'Economie alsacienne*, 2: 37–38, 69.

25. Ibid., p. 145.

26. Laufenburger and Pflimlin, *Cours d'Economie alsacienne*, 2: 104; *Reichs-Enquête*, 1: 307.
27. Laufenburger and Pflimlin, *Cours d'Economie alsacienne*, 2: 81–82.
28. Wolfram, ed., *Das Reichsland Elsass-Lothringen*, vol. 3: Max Schlenker, *Die wirtschaftliche Entwicklung Elsass-Lothringens 1871 bis 1918* (Frankfurt a.M., 1931), p. 179; Parisot, *Histoire de Lorraine*, 3: 406; Dieffenbach, *Elsass-Lothringen und der Freihandel*, p. 43.
29. Friedrich Engel-Dollfus, "L'Industrie de Mulhouse et son évolution économique de 1870 à 1881 au point de vue special de l'avenir de ses institutions de prévoyance," *B.S.I.M.* 52 (1882): 227–43; Auguste Dollfus, "Rapport statistique du comité du commerce," ibid., 48 (1878): 906–8; Société Industrielle de Mulhouse, *Histoire documentaire*, 1: 58–63.
30. *B.S.I.M.* 43 (1873): 5; *Reichs-Enquête*, 1: 289.
31. Barthelmé, *Courants commerciaux*, pp. 37–38.
32. For Caprivi's trade agreements, see Nichols, *Germany After Bismarck*, pp. 113–153.
33. Leo Berkholz, *Die Wirkung der Handelsverträge auf Landwirtschaft, Weinbau und Gewerbe in Elsass-Lothringen* (Tübingen and Leipzig, 1902), pp. 54, 71 ff.
34. Ibid., pp. 150–53.
35. Ibid., pp. 95–96, 100–1.
36. Ibid., p. 88.
37. Hans Goldschmidt, in *Elsass-Lothringisches Jahrbuch* 15 (1936): 146. Bismarck's plan for an imperial railway system may have been developed with special reference to Alsace-Lorraine. See Paul Dehn, *Die kaiserliche Tabaksmanufaktur in Strassburg als Vorläuferin eines deutschen Tabaks-monopols* (Berlin, 1880), p. 7.
38. Edouard Heim, "L' Alcoolisme en Alsace-Lorraine," *Revue alsacienne* 3 (1879–80): 151–57.
39. Goldschmidt, in *Elsass-Lothringisches Jahrbuch* 15 (1936): 147.
40. Dawson, *The German Empire and the Unity Movement*, 2: 70–71.
41. Dehn, *Die kaiserliche Tabaksmanufaktur*, pp. 4–5.
42. L. H. Marx, *Denkschrift über die Nothwendigkeit der Einstellung des Betriebs der kaiserlichen Tabaksmanufaktur zu Strassburg*, which appeared as a special edition of the *Neuen Strassburg*, 9 October 1875, p. 3.
43. Ibid., pp. 3–5. See also *A.D.B.R.*, AL 27, paquet 191, Hauschild to Manteuffel, 20 May 1881; *A.D.B.R.*, AL 27, paquet 186.
44. Dehn, *Die kaiserliche Tabaksmanufaktur*, p. 6. The request was submitted 7 January 1872. On 12 March 1872 the Strasbourg Chamber of Commerce also petitioned the government to end the unfair competition by selling the factory. See Marx, *Denkschrift*, p. 3 ff.
45. *Mémoire concernant le maintien de la manufacture des tabacs de Strasbourg* (Strasbourg, 1871), p. 6. Others claimed, however, that the Strasbourg factory purchased only about twelve percent of the annual Alsatian tobacco crop. See Marx, *Denkschrift*, p. 4.
46. Dehn, *Die kaiserliche Tabaksmanufaktur*, p. 6; *Frankfurter Zeitung*, 11 December 1875.
47. Landesausschuss, *Verhandlungen*, 3rd Sess., 1877, 2: 20–21; 7th Sess., 1879, 191.
48. Dehn, *Die kaiserliche Tabaksmanufaktur*, pp. 7, 16–17; Leopold Sonnemann, *Die Strassburger Tabaksmanufaktur und das Tabaksmonopol* (Mannheim, 1880), p. 3; Landesausschuss, *Verhandlungen*, 10th Sess., 1883, II, 668, speech by Baron Hugo Zorn von Bulach.

49. *Augsburger Allgemeine Zeitung*, 7 January 1881, 19 March 1881; *A.D.B.R.*, AL 27, paquet 180. Manteuffel to Bismarck, 30 March 1881 and 13 February 1885.
50. Laudesausschuss, *Verhandlungen*, 9th Sess., 1881–82, II: 407.
51. *A.D.B.R.*, AL 27, paquet 191. Hauschild to Manteuffel, 20, 28 May 1881.
52. Ibid.; Heinrich von Poschinger, *Fürst Bismarck und der Bundesrat* (Stuttgart and Leipzig, 1898), 4: 400–1.
53. Ibid., 5: 94–102. The number of workers employed in Alsatian cigar factories was small compared to some other German states, but they were concentrated in a few large factories, as the following table indicates:

German Cigar Factories, 1875

	Factories	Workers	Workers per Factory
Alsace-Lorraine	19	1,277	67.21
Prussia	6,621	59,648	9.00
Baden	491	13,496	27.48
Saxony	1,208	12,341	10.21
Hesse	261	7,140	27.36
Lübeck	32	305	9.53

Source: Hans Uhlmann, *Die Entwicklung von Unternehmung und Betrieb in der deutschen Zigarren-Industrie unter besonderer Berücksichtigung der Tabakbesteurung* (Halle, 1934), p. 39.
54. Sonnemann, *Strassburger Tabaksmanufaktur*, pp. 5–8.
55. Ibid., pp. 9–10, 16. Sonnemann estimated it would require 700,000,000 marks to buy out the German tobacco industry. The government monopoly bill provided for compensation to the private interests involved, but the total planned compensation amounted to less than one year's estimated revenue from the proposed monopoly. See Dawson, *The German Empire and the Unity Movement*, 2: 71.
56. Landesausschuss, *Verhandlungen*, 11th Sess., 1883–84, II: 449. In 1912 the imperial government adopted a tobacco price support plan. Planters could acquire seed from the imperial factory at Strasbourg. The Strasbourg factory agreed to purchase all tobacco grown from its seed, according to specifications set by the factory, at a price higher than it paid for other tobacco. See the article from the *Strassburger Korrespondenz*, 4 November 1912, *A.D.B.R.*, AL27, paquet 44.
57. Landesausschuss, *Verhandlungen*, 10th Sess., 1883, II: 679.
58. Ibid., p. 688.
59. These are the thoughts of Catholic priest Landolin Winterer. See J. Wagner, in *Revue catholique d'Alsace* (1931), p. 15.
60. Laufenburger and Pflimlin, *Cours d'Economie alsacienne*, 1: 34–36; Emil Thisse, *Die Entwicklung der elsässischen Landwirtschaft in der zweiten Hälfte des 19. Jahrhunderts* (Berlin, 1911), pp. 57–60.
61. Laufenburger and Pflimlin, *Cours d'Economie alsacienne*, 2: 36.
62. Parisot, *Histoire de Lorraine*, 3: 408; F. Sauvaire-Jourdan, "Un Conflit dans la métallurgie allemande," *Revue politique et parlementaire* 49 (1911): 253.
63. "La Leçon de Graffenstaden," *Cahiers alsaciens*, 1 (1912): 174–75; "L'Intérêt de l'Alsace-Lorraine et l'incident Wetterlé," ibid., 2 (1913): 68.
64. Sauvaire-Jourdan, in *Revue politique et parlementaire*, 49 (1911): 252–61; Schlenker, *Die wirtschaftliche Entwicklung Elsass-Lothringens*, pp.

192–98; Hermann Schumacher, *Die westdeutsche Eisenindustrie und die Moselkanalisierung* (Leipzig, 1910), pp. 22 ff., 113 ff., 146–53.
65. August Schneider, "Geschichte der Rheinregulierung Strassburg-Sonderheim," *Elsass-Lothringisches Jahrbuch* 2 (1923): 72–107; André E. Sayous, "L'Évolution de Strasbourg entre les deux guerres, 1871–1914," *Annales d'histoire économique et sociale* 6 (1934): 130–31.
66. Ibid., pp. 124–31.
67. Laufenburger and Pflimlin, *Cours d'Economie alsacienne*, 1: 48–52 for the potash industry, and pp. 44–45 for the oil industry.
68. Ibid., 1: 144 and 2: 36; Barthelmé, *Courants commerciaux*, p. 35; Laufenburger, in *Weltwirtschaftliches Archiv*, 35 (1932): 237. The following table indicates the sluggish growth rate of the Alsatian cotton industry under the German regime:

Increase in Cotton Spindles, 1887–1914:

Alsace	28%	Hannover	346%
Baden	39%	Bavaria	153%
Württemberg	148%	Germany (minus Alsace)	170%
Saxony	187%	Germany (with Alsace)	131%
Rhineland-Westphalia	364%		

Source: Schlenker, *Die wirtschaftliche Entwicklung Elsass-Lothringens*, p. 264.

CHAPTER 10

1. For a detailed account of the Zabern affair, see Martin Kitchen, *The German Officer Corps, 1890–1914* (Oxford, 1968), pp. 187–221.
2. Parisot, *Histoire de Lorraine*, 3: 362.
3. Wedel, "Statthalter-Briefe," *Der Türmer*, 25 (1924): 461–62.
4. Hutten-Czapski, *Sechzig Jahre Politik*, 2: 127–29.
5. Ibid.
6. See two works by Hans-Ulrich Wehler, "Der Fall Zabern: Rückblick auf eine Verfassungskrise des wilhelminischen Kaiserreichs," *Die Welt als Geschichte*, 23 (1963): 29 and "Elsass-Lothringen von 1870 bis 1918: Das 'Reichsland' als politisch-staatsrechtliches Problem des zweiten deutschen Kaiserreichs," *Zeitschrift für die Geschichte des Oberrheins*, N.F. 60 (1961): 179–80.
7. Theodore Schieder, *Das deutsche Kaiserreich von 1871 als Nationalstaat* (Köln, 1961), pp. 83–84; Kitchen, *German Officer Corps*, p. 197.
8. For Gerhard Ritter's discussion of the *Kommandogewalt* problem, see his *Staatskunst und Kriegshandwerk: Das Problem des "Militarismus" in Deutschland*, vol. 2: *Die Hauptmächte Europas und das wilhelminische Reich, 1890–1914* (Munich, 1960), pp. 148–67.
9. Hutten-Czapski, *Sechzig Jahre Politik* 1: 121.
10. Friedrich Curtius, "Ein Wort zu Alexander von Hohenlohe's Memoiren," *Hochland* 23 (1925–26): 612.
11. Gerhard Ritter, *Staatskunst und Kriegshandwerk*, 2: 168.
12. Ibid., p. 169.
13. Alexander zu Hohenlohe-Schillingsfürst, *Aus meinem Leben*, p. xii.
14. Wehler, in *Die Welt als Geschichte*, 23 (1963): 42–46.
15. Gerhard Ritter, *Staatskunst und Kriegshandwerk*, 2: 170.
16. Wedel, "Statthalter-Briefe," in *Der Türmer* 26 (1924): 462. Letter of 29 December 1913.

17. Hutten-Czapski, *Sechzig Jahre Politik*, 2: 130–31.
18. *A.D.B.R.*, AL 132, paquet 6, no. 11. Article from the *Journal d'Alsace-Lorraine*, 17 February 1914.
19. Ibid. Article from the *Hamburger Nachrichten*, 21 April 1914.
20. Mutius, ed., "Nachlass Dallwitz," *Preussische Jahrbücher*, 214 (1928): 291.
21. Ibid., p. 297.
22. *A.D.B.R.*, AL 132, paquet 6, no. 12. Article from *Le Nouvelliste d'Alsace-Lorraine*, 20 April 1914.
23. Ibid. Article from the *Courrier de Metz*, 20 April 1914.
24. Ibid. Articles from the *Mülhauser Volkszeitung*, 6 May 1914, and the *Strassburger Neue Zeitung*, 29 April 1914.
25. Ibid. Article from the *Frankfurter Zeitung*, 20 April 1914.
26. Mutius, ed., "Nachlass Dallwitz," *Preussische Jahrbücher*, 214 (1928): 160–61.
27. *A.D.B.R.*, AL 132, paquet 6, no. 12. Article from the *Swäbischer Merkur*, 20 April 1914. The reform failed to materialize. On 14 March 1917, Bethmann Hollweg promised the Prussian Diet that electoral reforms would be instituted at the conclusion of the war.
28. Mutius, ed., in *Preussische Jahrbücher* 214 (1928): 297.
29. Gerhard Ritter, *Staatskunst und Kriegshandwerk*, vol. 3: *Die Tragödie der Staatskunst. Bethmann Hollweg als Reichskanzler, 1914–1917* (Munich, 1964), pp. 23–24.
30. Ibid., vol. 4: *Die Herrschaft des deutschen Militarismus und die Katastrophe von 1918* (Munich, 1968), p. 164. For lists of citizens condemned by military tribunals and deprived of their citizenship, see Eugène Florent-Matter, *L'Alsace-Lorraine pendant la guerre* (Paris, Nancy, 1918), pp. 113–239; Alfred Stephany, *Germanisation, Willkürregierung und Polizeiwirtschaft in Elsass-Lothringen* (Zurich, 1906), p. 16.
31. Gerhard Ritter, *Staatskunst und Kriegshandwerk*, 4: 171–72.
32. Ibid., p. 181.
33. Wedel, "Statthalter-Briefe," in *Der Türmer* 26 (1924): 535.
34. Gerhard Ritter, *Staatskunst und Kriegshandwerk*, 4: 166 for Bethmann Hollweg's attitude, pp. 175–76 for Michaelis, and p. 181 for Hertling.
35. Ibid., pp. 173–74 on Wilson; Grumbach, *Das Schicksal Elsass-Lothringens*, pp. 13–14 for socialist opinion.
36. *Grosse Politik*, 1: 304–5. 28 December 1875.
37. Anton Nystrom, *Elsass-Lothringen und die Möglichkeit einer deutsch-französischen Allianz* (Berlin, 1904), p. 76.
38. The politics and administration of the Reichsland in its final hours is discussed in, Robert Redslob, "Le Changement de régime en Alsace-Lorraine après la défaite allemande," *Revue politique et parlementaire* 104 (1920): 389–91.
39. Rossé et al., *Das Elsass*, 2: 191.
40. Ibid., pp. 192–94.
41. Grumbach, *Das Schicksal Elsass-Lothringens*, pp. 13–14, 77; E. Lothar, "Die deutsche Sozialdemokratie und Elsass-Lothringen," *Questions d'Alsace-Lorraine*, (July 1918), pp. 5–20. Lothar draws heavily on Hermann Wendel, *Elsass-Lothringen und die Sozialdemokratie* (Berlin, 1916).
42. Although the Social Democratic *Kreisverein* at Mulhouse voted on 22 July 1917, in favor of German retention of Alsace-Lorraine, the members of the *Verein* who did not share this view had already walked out.

See *A.D.B.R.*, AL 69, no. 438. Report of the Colmar *Bezirkspräsident* to the ministry in Strasbourg, 24 July 1917.

43. Gerhard Ritter, *Staatskunst und Kriegshandwerk*, 4: 164.
44. Wilhelm Kapp, in *Elsass-Lothringen. Heimatstimmen* 3 (1925) 116.
45. Alexander zu Hohenlohe-Schillingsfürst, *Aus meinem Leben*, p. 212.
46. Ibid., p. 203.
47. Parisot, *Histoire de Lorraine*, 3: 366–67.
48. Alexander zu Hohenlohe-Schillingsfürst, *Aus meinem Leben*, pp. 205–8.
49. Ibid., pp. 216–20.
50. Ernst Berner, ed., *Kaiser Wilhelms des Grossen Briefe, Reden und Schriften* (Berlin, 1906), 2: 323. Letter to General Fieldmarshal Count von Roon, 17 August 1877; Wilhelm I, *Politische Correspondenz Kaiser Wilhelms I* (Berlin, 1890), p. 352. Letter to Möller, 26 September 1879.
51. Friedrich III, *Briefe, Reden und Erlasse des Kaisers und Königs Friedrich III* (Berlin, 1907), pp. 344–45.
52. Wilhelm II, *Die Reden Kaiser Wilhelms II* (Leipzig, 1897–1913), 1: 242–44. Metz speeches of 3, 4 September 1893.
53. Alexander zu Hohenlohe-Schillingsfürst, *Aus meinem Leben*, p. 147.
54. Wilhelm II, *Reden*, 3: 83–84. 21 May 1902.
55. Anon., "La Leçon de Graffenstaden," *Cahiers alsaciens* 1 (1912): pp. 174–75; "L'Intérêt de l'Alsace-Lorraine et l'Incident Wetterlé," ibid., 2: (1913): 68.
56. Kapp, in *Elsass-Lothringen. Heimatstimmen*, 3 (1925): 119.
57. Alexander zu Hohenlohe-Schillingsfürst, *Aus meinem Leben*, pp. 46–51 for his opinion of Manteuffel; pp. 50–51 on Möller; pp. 128–29 on Puttkamer.
58. Wehler, in *Zeitschrift für die Geschichte des Oberrheins* N.F. 70 (1961): 133–36; Schieder, *Das deutsche Kaiserreich*, pp. 17, 84–85.

Bibliography

UNPUBLISHED SOURCES

Archives départmentales du Bas-Rhin (A.D.B.R., Strasbourg). This archive contains an inexhaustible collection of official government documents of the period 1871–1919, relating to all phases of political, economic, and religious activity in the Reichsland.

Documents from the German Foreign Office. Microfilmed by the University of California. The following files were used:

Series I, reel 66, frames 639–698: Deutschland. Elsass-Lothringen. I.A.A.b. Secret. Acta secr. betreffend die Verhältnisse Elsass-Lothringens, October 1880–March 1882.

Series I, reel 66, frames 699–762: Auswärtiges Amt, Abt. A. Deutschland. 96 adh. Krieg 1870–71. Akten betr. die Verhältnisse Elsass-Lothringens. (Gasteiner Reise-Akten des Fürsten Bismarck).

Series I, reel 67, frames 1–710: Deutschland. Elsass-Lothringen. I.A.A.b. 96. Acta betr. die Verhältnisse Elsass-Lothringens. (Four volumes covering the years 1871–86.)

Series II, reel 32, frames 229 ff.: Italien. I.A.Be. 56. Vol. I. Acta betr. die Reglung der Kirchlichen Verhältnisse in Elsass-Lothringen und die Staatlichen Beziehungen zur Katholischen Kirche.

Series II, reel 34, frames 151–209: Italien. I.A.Be. 56. Vol. XII. Acta betr. das Verhältnis des Staats zur Kirche, 1 January 1875–15 April 1875.

PUBLISHED SOURCES

Gesetzblatt für Elsass-Lothringen. Strasbourg, 1879–1881.

Die grosse Politik der europäischen Kabinette, 1871–1914. 40 vols. Berlin, 1922–1927.

Jahrbuch für Elsass-Lothringen. Strasbourg, 1872–1873.

Kaiserliches Oberpräsidial-Bureau, *Verordnungen und amtliche Nachrichten für Elsass-Lothringen aus der Zeit vom Beginn der deutschen Occupation bis Ende März 1872.* Strasbourg, 1872.

———. *Mittheilungen aus der Verwaltung von Elsass-Lothringen während der Jahre 1871–1878.* Strasbourg, 1879.

Kaiserliches Statistisches Amt. *Statistik des deutschen Reichs.* Berlin, 1871–1918.

————. *Statistisches Jahrbuch für das deutsche Reich.* Berlin, 1871–1918.

————. *Vierteljahresheft zur Statistik des deutschen Reichs.* Berlin, 1871–1918.

Ligue d'Alsace. *Bulletin de la Ligue d'Alsace.* Nos. 1–27. Paris, 1873.

Ministerium für Elsass-Lothringen. *Amtsblatt des Ministeriums für Elsass-Lothringen* (October 1879–December 1882). Strasbourg, 1873.

————. *Handbuch für Elsass-Lothringen.* Strasbourg, 1880.

————. *Das Reichsland Elsass-Lothringen*: *Landes-und Ortsbeschreibung.* 3 vols. Strasbourg, 1898–1901.

Poschinger, Heinrich von. *Fürst Bismarck und der Bundesrat.* 5 vols. Stuttgart and Leipzig, 1897–1901.

Reichs-Enquête für die Baumwollen-und Leinen-Industrie. 2 vols. Berlin, 1879.

Société de Protection des Alsaciens et Lorrains Demeurés Français. *Rapports.* Paris, 1891–1903.

Verhandlungen der IV. Vertreterversammlung der Liberalen Landespartei in Elsass-Lothringen. Strasbourg, 1907.

Verhandlungen des deutschen Reichstags.

Verhandlungen des Landesausschusses für Elsass-Lothringen.

MEMOIRS, LETTERS, DIARIES, SPEECHES

Anrich, Gustav. "Eine Denkschrift Julius Weizsäckers über Elsass-Lothringen vom August 1870." *Elsass-Lothringisches Jahrbuch,* 8 (1929): 285–96.

Bamberger, Ludwig. *Bismarcks grosses Spiel*: *Die geheimen Tagebücher Ludwig Bambergers.* Edited by Ernest Feder. Frankfurt a.M., 1932.

Brauner, Joseph. "Briefe von Joseph Guerber an den jungen Carl Marbach, den späteren Weihbischof von Strassburg, aus den Jahren 1859 bis 1871." *Archiv für elsässische Kirchen-Geschichte,* 8 (1933): 371–448.

Brentano, Lujo. *Elsässer Erinnerungen.* Berlin, 1918.

Busch, Moritz. *Bismarck*: *Some Secret Pages of his History.* 2 vols. New York, 1898.

Curtius, Friedrich. *Deutsche Briefe und elsässische Erinnerungen.* Frauenfeld, 1920.

Dallwitz, Hans von. "Aus dem Nachlass des ehemaligen kaiserlichen Statthalters von Elsass-Lothringen, früheren Preussischen Ministers des Innern von Dallwitz," ed. Albert von Mutius. *Preussische Jahrbücher,* 214 (1928): 1–22, 147–66, 290–303.

Eckbrecht-Dürckheim, Ferdinand Graf von. *Erinnerungen alter und neuer Zeit.* 2 vols. Stuttgart, 1888.

Ernsthausen, A. Ernst von. *Erinnerungen eines preussischen Beamten.* Bielefeld and Leipzig, 1894.

Friedrich Wilhelm. *Briefe, Reden und Erlasse des Kaisers und Königs Friedrich III.* Edited by G. Schuster. Berlin, 1907.

Goldschmidt, Hans. "Aus den Papieren des Grafen Wilhelm Bismarck. Bismarck und Edwin von Manteuffel." *Elsass-Lothringisches Jahrbuch*, 15 (1936): 133–82.

Grad, Charles. *Délégation d'Alsace-Lorraine. Discours prononcés pendant la session de 1879.* Strasbourg, 1880.

———. *Lettres d'un bourgeois sur la politique en Alsace-Lorraine.* Mulhouse, 1881.

Griser, Abbé. *Programme des catholiques de l'Alsace-Lorraine devant l'annexion.* Strasbourg, 1871.

Hauviller, Ernest. "Correspondance inédite relative à la coadjutorerie et à l'épiscopat de Mgr. Raess." *Revue d'Alsace* 81 (1934): 583–605.

Hohenlohe-Schillingsfürst, Alexander, prinz zu. *Aus meinem Leben.* Frankfurt a.M., 1925.

Hohenlohe-Schillingsfürst, Chlodwig fürst zu. *Denkwürdigkeiten des Fürsten Chlodwig zu Hohenlohe-Schillingsfürst.* Edited by Friedrich Curtius. 2 vols. Stuttgart and Leipzig, 1907.

Hutten-Czapski, Bogdan Graf von. *Sechzig Jahre Politik und Gesellschaft.* 2 vols. Berlin, 1936.

Lalance, Auguste. *Mes Souvenirs, 1830–1914.* Paris, 1914.

Moltke, Generalfeldmarschall Helmuth von. *Gesammelte Schriften und Denkwürdigkeiten.* 7 vols. Berlin, 1892.

Monod, Gabriel. *Allemands et français; Souvenirs de Campagne. Metz, Sedan, la Loire.* Paris, n.d.

Rich, Norman, and M. H. Fisher, eds. *The Holstein Papers.* 4 vols. Cambridge, England, 1955–1963.

Rittner, Karl Heinrich. *Erinnerungen eines höheren Reichsbeamten aus Elsass-Lothringen, 1871–1873.* Saarbrücken, 1894.

Rogge, Helmuth. *Holstein und Hohenlohe.* Stuttgart, 1957.

Schneegans, August. *Aus dem Elsass: Zustände, Stimmungen und Erwartungen im neuen Reichsland.* Leipzig, 1875.

———. *Memoiren. Ein Beitrag zur Geschichte des Elsasses in der Uebergangszeit.* Berlin, 1904.

Steinheil, G. *Ma Participation au mouvement électoral en février, 1890.* Nancy, 1890.

Valentin, Veit. "Das Reichsland unter Manteuffel. Materialien zur Kenntnis der ersten Statthalterschaft in Elsass-Lothringen." *Deutsche Revue* 36 (1911): 1–11, 129–39.

Vogt, Karl. *Karl Vogts politische Briefe an Friedrich Kolb.* Biel, 1870.

Waldersee, Generalfeldmarschall Alfred Graf von. *Denkwürdigkeiten.* Edited by H. O. Meisner. 3 vols. Stuttgart and Berlin, 1922–1923.

———. *Aus dem Briefwechsel.* Edited by H. O. Meisner. Berlin, 1928.

Wedel, Karl Graf von. "Statthalter-Briefe aus Elsass-Lothringen: Unveröffentlichte Briefe des Grafen von Wedel an einen deutschen Professor." *Der Türmer*, 26 (1924): 302–6, 458–613, 533–540.

Wilhelm I. *Kaiser Wilhelms des Grossen Briefe, Reden und Schriften.* Edited by Ernst Berner. 2 vols. Berlin, 1906.

———. *Politische Correspondenz Kaiser Wilhelms I.* Berlin, 1890.

————. *The Correspondence of William I and Bismarck*. Trans. J. A. Ford. 2 vols. London, 1903.

Wilhelm II. *Die Reden Kaiser Wilhelms II*. Edited by Johannes Penzler. 4 vols. Leipzig, 1897–1913.

NEWSPAPERS AND PERIODICALS

L'Alsacien-Lorrain (Paris)
Augsburger Allgemeine Zeitung
Bulletin de la Société Industrielle de Mulhouse
Courrier du Bas-Rhin (Strasbourg)
Echo de Schiltigheim
Elsässer Journal (Strasbourg)
Elsässisches Volksblatt für Stadt und Land (Mulhouse)
Elsass-Lothringische Volkspartei (Colmar)
Elsass-Lothringische Volkszeitung (Mulhouse)
Frankfurter Zeitung und Handelsblatt
Freie Presse (Strasbourg)
L'Industriel Alsacien (Mulhouse)
Metzer Katholisches Volksblatt
Metzer Zeitung
Le Messin
Mulhauser Arbeiterfreund
Le Nouvelliste d'Alsace-Lorraine (Colmar)
St. Odilienblatt
Presse von Elsass und Lothringen (Strasbourg)
Strassburger Neue Zeitung
Strassburger Post
Strassburger Zeitung und amtliche Nachrichten
Union von Elsass-Lothringens (Strasbourg)
Der Volksfreund (Strasbourg)

SECONDARY SOURCES

About, Edmond Francois. *L'Alsace, 1871–1872*. Paris, 1873.

Ackermann, Eugène. *L'Industrie minière et métallurgique en Alsace 40 ans après l'annexion*. Rixheim, 1911.

Adam, Juliette. "Les élections en Alsace-Lorraine pour le Reichstag." *L'Europe nouvelle* (Paris), March 1907, pp. 3–4.

Aimond, Charles. *Histoire des Lorrains: Essai sur leur vie politique, sociale, économique et culturelle*. Bar-le-Duc, 1960.

Anrich, Gustav. "Zwei typische Elsässer." *Süddeutsche Monatshefte* 29 (1931): 167–71.

Antony, Alfred. "Le Budget d'Alsace-Lorraine." *Revue des sciences politiques* 27 (1912): 41–56, 239–57; 28 (1912): 23–41.

Bachem, Karl. *Vorgeschichte, Geschichte und Politik der deutschen Zentrumspartei.* 9 vols. Cologne, 1927–1932.

Baier, B. *Die Sprachenfrage im Volksschulwesen Elsass-Lothringens.* Frankfurt a.M., 1928.

Baldy, Robert. *L'Alsace-Lorraine et l'empire allemand, 1871–1911.* Montpellier, 1912.

Barthelmé, Alphonse. *Le Développement des courants commerciaux de l'Alsace depuis la guerre.* Strasbourg, 1931.

Barthelmé, G. "Les Alsaciens et les Lorrains à la Légion Étrangère." *L'Alsace française* 19 (1930): 125–26.

Baulig, H. "La Population de l'Alsace et de la Lorraine en 1921." *Annales de géographie* 32 (1923): 12–25.

Die Baumwollen-Industrie diesseits und jenseits der Vogesen. Ulm, n.d.

Becker, Josef. "Baden, Bismarck, und die Annexion von Elsass-Lothringen." *Zeitschrift für die Geschichte des Oberrheins* 115 (1967): 167–204.

Berger, Martin. *Pascal David und die politische Entwicklung Elsass-Lothringens, 1882–1907.* Munich, 1910.

Bergmann, Gustav. *Zur Industriellen Enquête.* Strasbourg, 1877.

Berkholz, Leo. *Die Wirkung der Handelsverträge auf Landwirtschaft, Weinbau und Gewerbe in Elsass-Lothringen.* Tübingen and Leipzig, 1902.

Bertelsmann, Werner. *Das Passwesen: Eine völkerrechtliche Studie.* Strasbourg, 1914.

Bismarck, Otto, fürst von. *Die gesammelten Werke.* 15 vols. Berlin, 1924–1932.

Blumenthal, Daniel. *Alsace-Lorraine.* New York, 1917.

Bornhack, Conrad. "Die Begründung der katholischen-theologischen Fakultät in Strassburg." *Elsass-Lothringisches Jahrbuch,* 12 (1933): 249–69.

La Bourgeoisie alsacienne. Strasbourg, 1954.

Brabant, Frank Herbert. *The Beginning of the Third Republic in France: The National Assembly.* London, 1940.

Brandt, André. "Apports alsaciens à l'industrie textile de la Lorraine et de la Franche-Comté aux XVIIIᵉ et XIXᵉ siècles." In *Trois Provinces de l'Est: Lorraine, Alsace, Franche-Comté.* Strasbourg, Paris, 1957, pp. 129–140.

———. "Mulhouse, ville française." In *Deux Siècles d'Alsace française: 1648, 1789, 1848.* Strasbourg, Paris, 1948, pp. 417–427.

———. "Le Sort de Mulhouse en 1871." *B.S.I.M.* (1951), pp. 26–35.

———, and Leuilliot, Paul. "Les Élections à Mulhouse en 1869," *Revue d'Alsace* 99 (1960): 104–28.

Braun, Jean. "Les Débuts du chemin de fer en Alsace." In *Deux Siècles d'Alsace française: 1648, 1789, 1848.* Strasbourg, Paris, 1948, pp. 315–350.

Brocard, Charles. "Le Parti socialiste en Alsace-Lorraine." *Revue politique et parlementaire* 64 (1910): 56–63.

Bronner, Fritz. *Die Verfassungsbestrebungen des Landesausschusses für Elsass-Lothringen, 1875–1911.* Heidelberg, 1926.

Brück, Heinrich. *Die Kulturkampfbewegung in Deutschland.* 2 vols. Münster, 1905.

Buchner, Rudolf. "Die deutsche patriotische Dichtung vom Kriegsbeginn 1870 über Frankreich und die Elsässische Frage." *Historische Zeitschrift* 206 (1968): 327–36.

Casper, Paul. "August Bebel und Elsass-Lothringen," *Cahiers alsaciens* 2 (1913): 327–36.

Cerf, Barry. *Alsace-Lorraine Since 1870.* New York, 1919.

Cetty. Heinrich. *Un Alsacien. Vie et oeuvres de Charles Grad.* Colmar, 1892.

———. *La Famille ouvrière en Alsace.* Rixheim, 1883.

Chantriot, Émile. *La Lorraine sous l'occupation allemande, mars 1871– septembre 1873.* Nancy, Paris, Strasbourg, 1922.

Chapman, Guy. *The Third Republic of France: The First Phase, 1871–1894.* New York, 1962.

Church, Leslie F. *The Story of Alsace-Lorraine.* London, 1915.

Claretie, Jules. *Cinq ans après: L'Alsace et la Lorraine depuis l'annexion.* Paris, 1876.

"Clericus." "Bischof Zorn von Bulach." *Elsass-Lothringen. Heimatstimmen* 3 (1925): 75–83.

Contamine, Henry. "La Place forte de Metz de 1866 à 1914." *Annales de l'Est,* 4th series, 2 (1934): 341–361.

Curtius, Friedrich. "Ein Wort zu Alexander von Hohenlohes Memoiren." *Hochland* 23 (1925–26): 612–16.

Dehn, Paul. *Die kaiserliche Tabaksmanufaktur in Strassburg als Vorläuferin eines deutschen Tabaksmonopols.* Berlin, 1880.

Delahache, Georges. *Alsace-Lorraine. La Carte au liseré vert.* Paris, 1911.

———. *L'Exode.* Paris, 1914.

Delpech, Joseph. "La Dette publique et les dettes locales de l'Alsace et de la Lorraine depuis 1870." *Revue politique et parlementaire* 107 (1921).

Deux Siècles d'Alsace française: 1648, 1798, 1848. Strasbourg, Paris, 1948.

Didio, Henri. *L'église catholique en Alsace depuis l'annexion, 1871–1889.* Lille, 1889.

Dieffenbach, Ferdinand. *Elsass-Lothringen und der Freihandel.* Strasbourg, 1877.

Dominicus, Alexander. "Die deutsche Verwaltung in Elsass-Lothringen, 1871– 1918." *Elsass-Lothringisches Jahrbuch,* 8 (1929): 311–329.

———. *Strassburgs deutsche Bürgermeister Back und Schwander, 1873–1918.* Frankfurt a.M., 1939.

Dresch, J. "L'Opinion de Théodore Fontane sur la France de 1870 et la question d'Alsace." *Revue bleue,* 19 October 1912, pp. 496–98.

Duhem, Jules. *La question d'Alsace-Lorraine de 1871 à 1914.* Paris, 1917.

Dumont, Albert. *L'Administration et la propagande prussiennes en Alsace.* Paris, 1871.

Eccard, Frédéric. *L'Alsace sous la domination allemande*. Paris, 1919.

Elmerhoff, Daniel. "Ausnahmgesetze für Elsass-Lothringen?" *Elsass-Lothringische Kulturfragen* 3 (1913): 265–75.

Elstein, G. *L'Alsace-Lorraine sous la domination allemande*. Paris, 1877.

Elwitt, Sanford H. "Politics and Social Classes in the Loire: The Triumph of Republican Order, 1869–1873." *French Historical Studies* 6 (1969): 93–112.

"E. N." "Elsass-Lothringen und das deutsche Heer." *Elsässische Kulturfragen* 2 (1912): 477–85.

Engerand, Fernand. *L'Allemagne et le fer: Les Frontières Lorraines et la force allemande*. Paris, 1916.

"F. E." "Le Bilan des élections à la second chambre." *Cahiers alsaciens* 1 (1912): 16–25.

Fischback, Gustave. *Le siège et bombardement de Strasbourg*. Paris, 1971.

Fischer, Wilhelm. *Manteuffel in Elsass-Lothringen und seine Verdeutschungspolitik*. Basel, 1885.

Florent-Matter, Eugène. *L'Alsace-Lorraine pendant la guerre*. Paris, Nancy, 1918.

———. *Les Alsaciens-Lorrains contre l'Allemagne*. Paris, 1918.

Gailly de Taurines, Charles. "La Protestation de l'Alsace-Lorraine en 1874." *Revue des deux mondes* 45 (1918): 77–100, 302–29.

Galien, Paul. *Ephémérides alsaciennes de l'année terrible, 14 juillet 1870–mars 1871*. Colmar, 1910.

Gall, Lothar. "Zur Frage der Annexion von Elsass und Lothringen 1870." *Historische Zeitschrift* 206 (1968): 265–326.

Galli, Henri. *Gambetta et l'Alsace-Lorraine*. Paris, 1911.

Gerber, Philippe. *La Condition de l'Alsace-Lorraine dans l'empire allemand*. Lille, 1906.

Germain, Heinrich. "Die natürlichen Grundlagen der lothringischen Eisenindustrie und die Verfassung vor 1870," *Jahrbuch der Gesellschaft für lothringische Geschichte und Altertumskunde*, 24 (1912): 341–448.

———. "Die Lage der Eisenindustrie-Arbeiter Lothringens," *Jahrbuch der Gesellschaft für lothringische Geschichte und Altertumskunde*, 23 (1911): 447–72.

Gley, W. "Zur Bevölkerungsentwicklung in Elsass-Lothringen." *Elsass-Lothringisches Jahrbuch*, 12 (1933): 317–28.

Goldschmidt, Hans. *Bismarck und die Friedensunterhändler 1871*. Berlin and Leipzig, 1929.

Gradmann, Wilhelm. *Die politischen Ideen Edwin von Manteuffels und ihre Auswirkungen in seiner Laufbahn*. Düsseldorf, 1932.

Great Britain, Foreign Office Historical Section, *Alsace-Lorraine*. London, 1920.

Grumbach, Salomon. *Das Schicksal Elsass-Lothringens*. Neuchâtel, 1915.

Grunberg, Paul. *Zur elsässischen Lage und Frage*. Strasbourg, 1909.

Guerber, Victor. *Sozialismus der Erzfeind steht vor der Thüre*. Strasbourg, 1891.

Hachenberger, Herbert. *Bismarck und Elsass-Lothringen.* Jena, 1932.

Haehling, Gaston. "Le Rhin sous la révolution et l'empire." In *Deux Siècles d'Alsace française: 1648, 1789, 1848.* Strasbourg, Paris, 1948.

Hammant, N. "Les petits Séminaires d'Alsace-Lorraine sous le régime allemand." *Revue écclesiastique de Metz* 34–37 (1927–1931).

Harelle, Paul. "Réflections sur les élections lorraines," *Cahiers alsaciens* 1 (1912): 26–34.

Hartshorne, Richard. "The Franco-German Boundary of 1871." *World Politics* 2 (1950): 209–250.

Hauviller, Ernest. "Silhouettes et croquis alsaciens suggérés par les mémoires et les souvenirs des Princes Clovis et Alexandre de Hohenlohe." *Revue d'Alsace,* 80 (1933): 33–45, 161–77.

Hazen, Charles Downer. *Alsace-Lorraine Under German Rule.* New York, 1917.

Heffter, Heinrich. *Die deutsche Selbstverwaltung im 19. Jahrhundert.* Stuttgart, 1950.

Helmer, Paul Albert. *Alsace Under German Rule.* London, 1915.

Hepp, Eugène. *Du Droit d'option des Alsaciens-Lorrains pour la nationalité française.* Paris, 1872.

———. *L'Alsace-Lorraine et l'empire germanique.* Paris, 1881.

———. "L'Alsace-Lorraine sous le régime allemand." *Revue des deux mondes* 26 (1878): 448–73.

Herkner, Heinrich. *Die oberelsässische Baumwollindustrie und ihre Arbeiter.* Strasbourg, 1887.

Historique des élections à l'Assemblée National dans le département du Bas-Rhin. 1871.

Hochschild, Ernst. "Der Diktaturparagraph in Elsass-Lothringen." *Elsass-Lothringisches Jahrbuch,* 4 (1925): 149–66.

Hollyday, Frederic B. M. *Bismarck's Rival: A Political Biography of General and Admiral Albrecht von Stosch.* Durham, N. C., 1960.

Howard, Burt Estes. "Alsace-Lorraine and its Relation to the German Empire." *Political Science Quarterly* 21 (1906): 447–74.

L'Huillier, Fernand. "Les grands Courants de l'opinion publique en Alsace sous la révolution, le Consulat, et l'empire." In *Deux Siècles d'Alsace française: 1648, 1789, 1848.* Strasbourg, Paris, 1948.

"L'Intérêt de l'Alsace-Lorraine et l'incident Wetterlé." *Cahiers alsaciens* 2 (1913): 65–69.

Jacob, Karl. *Bismarck und die Erwerbung Elsass-Lothringens, 1870–71.* Strasbourg, 1905.

Kahan-Rebecq, Marie-Madeleine. "Importance de la classe ouvrière alsacienne en 1848." In *Deux Siècles d'Alsace française: 1648, 1789, 1848.* Strasbourg, Paris, 1948.

Kapp, Wilhelm. "Die Aera Mandel." *Elsass-Lothringen. Heimatstimmen* 3 (1925): 18–23.

———. "Elsass-Lothringen und die Aera Hohenlohe-Schillingsfürst." *Elsass-Lothringen. Heimatstimmen* 3 (1925): 114–21.

————. "Karl Hauss." *Elsass-Lothringen. Heimatstimmen* 3 (1925): 68–75.

————. "Der Nationalistenbund." *Mitteilungen der Elsass-Lothringischen Vereinigung* 1 (1911): 1–12.

————. "Parteiprobleme in Elsass-Lothringen." *Elsässische Kulturfragen* 2 (1912): 306–12.

————. "Die Wahlen." *Mitteilungen der Elsass-Lothringischen Vereinigung* 1 (1911): 57–62.

Kärnbach, M. "Die staatsrechtliche Entwicklung Elsass-Lothringens 1871–1879 im Spiegel der deutschen Reichspolitik," *Jahrbuch der Elsass-Lothringischen Wissenschaftlichen Gesellschaft zu Strassburg,* 5 (1932): 16–44; 6 (1933): 144–197.

Keck, Karl Heinrich. *Das Leben des General-Feldmarschalls Edwin von Manteuffel.* Bielefeld and Leipzig, 1890.

Kent, George O. *Arnim and Bismarck.* Oxford, 1968.

Kiener, Jean. *Rapport de M. Kiener sur le tissage et les importations temporaires.* Colmar, 1884.

Kitchen, Martin. *The German Officer Corps, 1890–1914.* Oxford, 1968.

Klein, Felix. *L'Evêque de Metz. Vie de Mgr. Dupont des Loges, 1804–1886.* Paris, 1899.

————. "Metz et son évêque après l'annexion." *Le Correspondant* 160 (1889): 209–32, 617–45.

Koechlin, Edouard. *Admissions temporaires des tissus écrus: Rapport de M. Edouard Koechlin.* Mulhouse, 1867.

Koenig, Friedrich. "Der Elsass-Lothringische Partikularismus." *Elsässische Kulturfragen,* 1 (1911): 110–17.

————. "Die parteipolitischen Verhältnisse Lothringens." *Elsässische Kulturfragen* 2 (1912): 486–96.

Koerner, Gustav. *Die norddeutsche Publizistik und die Annexionsfragen im Jahre 1870.* Hanover, 1907.

Kolb, Eberhard. "Bismarck und das Aufkommen der Annexionsforderung 1870." *Historische Zeitschrift* 209 (1969): 318–56.

Krieger, Anton. *Die Textilindustrie von Mülhausen i. E. in den letzten 20 Jahren, sowie die soziale Lage ihrer Arbeiter.* Kreuznach, 1911.

Lalance, Auguste. *La Crise de l'industrie cotonnière.* Mulhouse, 1879.

Lange, Raymond. "La Vie ouvrière alsacienne: Mulhouse et ses institutions sociales." *Revue des sciences politiques,* 28 (1912): 75–87, 428–41.

Laufenburger, Henry. *Cours d'Economie alsacienne,* vol. 1: *Les Bases matérielles, morales et juridiques.* Paris, 1930.

————, and Pflimlin, Pierre. *Cours d'Economie alsacienne,* vol. 2: *L'Industrie de Mulhouse.* Paris, 1932.

Laufenburger, Henry. "Die weltwirtschaftliche Stellung des Elsass." *Weltwirtschaftliches Archiv,* 35 (1932): 233–49.

"La Leçon de Graffenstaden." *Cahiers alsaciens* 1 (1912): 173–81.

Lepsius, Ernst R. *Nationalitätswechsel und Optionsrecht der Elsass-Lothringer nach den deutsch-französischen Friedensverträgen des Jahres 1871.* Halle, 1912.

Leuilliot, Paul. *L'Alsace au début du XIXe siècle*. 3 vols. Paris, 1959–1960.

────. "L'Opposition libérale en Alsace à la fin de la Restauration." In *Deux Siècles d'Alsace française, 1648, 1789, 1848*. Strasbourg, Paris, 1948.

────. "Politique et réligion: Les élections alsaciennes de 1869," *Revue d'Alsace* 100 (1961): 67–101.

Lévy, Paul. "La Lutte pour l'allemand en Alsace et en Lorraine de 1870 à 1918, d'apres des documents officiels," *Mercure de France* 154 (1922): 95–115.

Lévy, Robert. *Histoire économique de l'industrie cotonnière en Alsace: Étude de sociologie descriptive*. Paris, 1912.

Lipgens, Walter. "Bismarck, die öffentliche Meinung und die Annexion von Elsass und Lothringen 1870." *Historische Zeitschrift* 199 (1964): 31–112.

────. "Bismarck und die Frage der Annexion 1870. Eine Erwiderung," *Historische Zeitschrift* 206 (1968): 586–617.

Löning, Edgar. *Die Verwaltung des General-Gouvernments im Elsass*. Strasbourg, 1874.

────. "L'Administration du Government-Général de l'Alsace durant la guerre de 1870–1871." *Revue de droit international et de législation comparée* 4 (1872): 622–50; 5 (1873): 69–136.

Lothar, E. "Die deutsche Sozialdemokratie und Elsass-Lothringen," *Questions d'Alsace-Lorraine*, July 1918, pp. 5–20.

Mai, Joachim. *Die preussische-deutsche Polenpolitik, 1885 bis 1887: Eine Studie zur Herausbildung des Imperialismus in Deutschland*. Berlin, 1962.

Marx, L. H. *Denkschrift über die Nothwendigkeit der Einstellung des Betriebs der kaiserlichen Tabaksmanufaktur zu Strassburg*. Strasbourg, 1875.

Matter, Paul. "Les Tentatives de colonisation allemande en Alsace-Lorraine," *Revue des sciences politiques* 43 (1920): 184–96.

Mémoir concernant le maintien de la manufacture des tabacs de Strasbourg. Strasbourg, 1871.

Meyer, Eugen. *Das Deutschtum in Elsass-Lothringen*. Münster, 1929.

Meyer, Heinrich. *Wiederaufbau des Mittelstandes in Elsass-Lothringen*. Strasbourg, 1918.

Michaelis, Otto. "Die evangelische Kirche in Elsass-Lothringen 1870–1918." *Süddeutsche Monatshefte* 29 (1931): 196–99.

────. *Grenzlandkirche: Eine Evangelische Kirchengeschichte Elsass-Lothringens, 1870–1918*. Essen, 1934.

Mitscher, Georg. *Elsass-Lothringen unter deutscher Verwaltung*. Berlin, 1874.

Morizet, G. *Histoire de Lorraine*. Paris, 1926.

Morsey, Rudolf. *Die oberste Reichsverwaltung unter Bismarck, 1867–1890*. Münster, 1957.

Mossman, Xavier. *Un Industriel alsacien. Vie de F. Engel-Dollfus*. Mulhouse, 1886.

Muller, Paul. *La Révolution de 1848 en Alsace*. Paris, 1912.

Nadelhoffer, Emil. "Elsass-Lothringen und die Wehrvorlage." *Elsass-Lothringische Kulturfragen* 3 (1913): 259–64.

Nystrom, Anton. *Elsass-Lothringen und die Möglichkeit einer deutsch-französischen Allianz.* Berlin, 1904.

Oualid, W. "L'Avenir des exportations alsaciennes," *L'Alsace française* 5 (1923): 33–35, 133–35, 248–50, 368–71, 467–70.

———. "Les Etrangers en Alsace et en Lorraine." *L'Alsace française* 5 (1923): 552–54.

Parisot, Robert. *Histoire de Lorraine.* 3 vols. Paris, 1924.

Un Patriote alsacien. *Les Prussiens en Alsace.* Paris, 1874.

Penzler, Johannes. *Graf Wilhelm Bismarck; ein Lebensbild.* Berlin, 1902.

Pfister, Christian. *La Limite de la langue française et de la langue allemande en Alsace-Lorraine: considérations historiques.* Paris, Nancy, 1890.

———. *Pages alsaciennes.* Paris, 1927.

Phillipson, Coleman. *Alsace-Lorraine: Past, Present, and Future.* London, 1918.

Platzhoff, Walter. "Bismarck und die Annexion Elsass-Lothringens." *Elsass-Lothringisches Jahrbuch,* 3 (1924): 1–9.

———. "Die elsass-lothringische Frage in der russischen Politik von 1870 bis 1917." *Elsass-Lothringisches Jahrbuch,* 8 (1929): 359–69.

———. "Die elsass-lothringische Frage im Weltkrieg und im Versailler Frieden." *Elsass-Lothringisches Jahrbuch,* 13 (1934): 283–98.

Ponteil, Félix. *L'Opposition politique à Strasbourg sous la monarchie de juillet, 1830–1848.* Paris, 1932.

———. "En manière de conclusion: L'Alsace en 1848." In *Deux Siècles d'Alsace française: 1648, 1789, 1848.* Strasbourg, Paris, 1948.

Preiss, Jacques. *Figures d'Alsace-Lorraine.* Paris, 1913.

du Prel, Maximilian Freiherr. *Elsass-Lothringen: seine Vergangenheit, seine Zukunft.* Strasbourg, 1877.

———. *Die deutsche Verwaltung in Elsass-Lothringen, 1870–1879.* Strasbourg, 1879.

Puttkamer, Alberta von. *Die Aera Manteuffel. Federzeichnungen aus Elsass-Lothringen.* Stuttgart and Leipzig, n.d.

Rappolstein, Alfred von. *L'Alsace-Lorraine, 1870–1884.* Basel, 1884.

Rasch, Gustav. *Die Prussien in Elsass-Lothringen.* Braunschweig, 1874.

Redslob, Robert. "Le Changement de régime en Alsace-Lorraine après la défaite allemande." *Revue politique et parlementaire* 104 (1920): 387–99.

Régamey, Jeanne and Fréderic. *L'Alsace au lendemain de la conquête.* Paris, 1911.

Renouard, Pierre. *L'Alsace-Lorraine: sa situation juridique dans l'empire allemand, 1870–1918.* Paris, 1919.

Reumont, H. "Die parteipolitische Entwicklung in Lothringen," *Lothringen und seine Hauptstadt: Festschrift zur 60. Generalversammlung der Katholiken Deutschlands in Metz, 1913.* Ed. A. Kuppel. Metz, 1913.

Reuss, Rodolph. *Histoire d'Alsace.* 14th ed. Paris, 1918.

Ritter, Gerhard. *Staatskunst und Kriegshandwerk: Das Problem des "Militarismus" in Deutschland.* 4 vols. Munich, 1954–68.

Ritter, G. Erwin. *Die elsass-lothringische Presse im letzten Drittel des 19. Jahrhunderts.* Strasbourg, 1934.

Rossé, J., et al. *Das Elsass von 1870 bis 1932.* 4 vols. Colmar, 1936.

Sachse, Arnold. "Erinnerungen aus der elsass-lothringischen Schulverwaltung." *Elsass-Lothringisches Jahrbuch,* 6 (1927): 207–40.

———. "Die Kirchenpolitik des Statthalters Freiherrn von Manteuffel." *Elsass-Lothringisches Jahrbuch,* 5 (1926): 146–71.

———. "Die Schulpolitik des Statthalters Freiherrn von Manteuffel." *Zeitschrift für die Geschichte des Oberrheins* 39 (1926): 557–70.

Sauvaire-Jourdan, F. "Un Conflit dans la métallurgie allemande." *Revue politique et parlementaire* 69 (1911), 250–261.

Sayous, André. "L'Evolution de Strasbourg entre les deux guerres, 1871–1914." *Annales d'histoire économique et sociale* 6 (1934): 1–19, 122–32.

Schafer, Dietrich. *Das Reichsland.* Berlin, 1917.

Scherer, Emil Clemens. "Der Katholizismus in der Reichslandepoche." *Süddeutsche Monatshefte* 29 (1931): 191–95.

Scheurer-Kestner, August. *Les Réprésentants de l'Alsace et de la Lorraine à l'Assemblée Nationale de Bordeaux.* Paris, 1887.

Schieder, Theodor. *Das deutsche Kaiserreich von 1871 als Nationalstaat.* Cologne, 1961.

Schlenker, Max. *Die wirtschaftliche Entwicklung Elsass-Lothringens 1871 bis 1918.* Vol. 1 of *Das Reichsland Elsass-Lothringen 1871–1918.* Edited by Georg Wolfram. Frankfurt a.M., 1931.

Schneider, August. "Geschichte der Rheinregulierung Strassburg-Sonderheim." *Elsass-Lothringisches Jahrbuch,* 2 (1923): 72–107.

Schneider, Johann. *Die elsässische Autonomistenpartei, 1871–1881.* Frankfurt a.M., 1933.

Schricker, August. *Elsass-Lothringen im Reichstag, vom Beginn der Ersten Legislatur-Periode bis zur Einführung der Reichsverfassung.* Strasbourg, 1873.

Schumacher, Hermann. *Die westdeutsche Eisenindustrie und die Moselkanalisierung.* Leipzig, 1910.

Schuré, Edouard. "L'Alsace française, 1871–1914." *Revue des deux mondes* 28 (1914): 435–454.

———. *L'Alsace et les prétentions prussiennes.* Geneva, 1871.

Schwander, Rudolf. "Elsass-Lothringen." *Süddeutsche Monatschefte* 29 (1931): 161–63.

Seydler, Wilhelm. *Fürst Chlodwig zu Hohenlohe-Schillingsfürst als Statthalter im Reichslande Elsass-Lothringen, 1885–1894.* Frankfurt a.M., 1929.

Sittler, L. "Die wirtschaftliche Entwicklung des Elsass von 1870–1932." *Elsass-Lothringen. Heimatstimmen* 14 (1936): 183–87.

Société Industrielle de Mulhouse. *Histoire documentaire de l'industrie de Mulhouse et de ses environs au XIXme siècle.* 2 vols. Mulhouse, 1902.

Société de Protection des Alsaciens et des Lorrains Demeurés Français. *De l'option pour la nationalité française.* Paris, 1872.

Sonnemann, Leopold. *Die Strassburger Tabaksmanufaktur und das Tabaksmonopol.* Manheim, 1880.

Souchon, Auguste. "Les Problèmes économiques qui vont naître du retour de l'Alsace-Lorraine à la France." *Journal des économistes* 60 (1918): 247–53.

Spahn, Martin. *Elsass–Lothringen.* Berlin, 1919.

Spitz, Alois. *Zur Lage und Stimmung in Elsass-Lothringen.* Strasbourg, 1894.

―――. *Der Sozialismus im Reichslande.* Trier, 1891.

Stadtler, Eduard. "Die Judenkrawalle von 1848 im Elsass." *Elsässische Monatsschrift für Geschichte und Volkskunde* 2 (1911): 673–86.

Staehling, Charles. *Histoire contemporaine de Strasbourg et de l'Alsace.* 2 vols. Nice, Nancy, 1884, 1887.

Stählin, Karl. *Elsass und Lothringen im Ablauf der europäischen Geschichte.* Munich and Berlin, n.d.

―――. *Geschichte Elsass-Lothringens.* Munich, Berlin, 1920.

Staub, A. *Die Baumwollen-Industrie und die Annexion von Elsass und Lothringen.* Berlin, 1870.

Stephany, Alfred. *Germanisation, Willkürregierung und Polizeiwirtschaft in Elsass-Lothringen.* Zurich, 1906.

Stollsteimer, Albert. *Die Stellungnahme der Frankfurter Zeitung zur Elsass-Lothringischen Verfassungsfrage, 1870–1879.* Pforzheim, 1929.

Stroh, Louis. *Les petites industries rurales en Alsace.* Agen, 1914.

Strohl, Henri. "L'Esprit républicain et démocratique dans l'église protestante de Colmar de 1648 à 1848." In *Deux Siècles d'Alsace française: 1648, 1789, 1848.* Strasbourg, Paris, 1948.

―――. *Le Protestantisme en Alsace.* Strasbourg, 1950.

Teutsch, Edouard. *Notes pour servir à l'histoire de l'annexion de l'Alsace-Lorraine.* Nancy, 1893.

Thiele, Ernst. "Die deutsche Regierung und das Konkordat im Elsass nach 1870." *Archiv für Elsässische Kirchengeschichte,* 2 (1927): 350–63.

Thisse, Emil. *Die Entwicklung der elsässischen Landwirtschaft in der zweiten Hälfte des 19. Jahrhunderts.* Berlin, 1911.

Toussaint, Maurice. *La Frontière linguistique en Lorraine: les fluctuations et la délimitation actuelle des langues française et germanique dans la Moselle.* Paris, 1955.

Treitschke, Heinrich von. *Germany, France, Russia, and Islam.* New York, 1915.

Uhlmann, Hans. *Die Entwicklung von Unternehmung und Betrieb in der deutschen Zigarren-Industrie unter besonderer Berücksichtigung der Tabaksteurung.* Halle, 1934.

Vidal de la Blache, Paul. "Exode et immigration en Alsace-Lorraine," *Revue des sciences politiques* 35 (1916): 308–18.

Vizetelly, Ernest A. *The True Story of Alsace-Lorraine.* New York, 1918.

Von Einem Elsässer. *Politisches Leben und politische Parteien in Elsass-Lothringen.* Berlin, 1899.

Wehler, Hans-Ulrich. "Elsass-Lothringen von 1870 bis 1918: Das 'Reichsland'

als politisch-staatsrechtliches Problem des zweiten deutschen Kaiserreichs."
Zeitschrift für die Geschichte des Oberrheins 109, n. s. 70 (1961), 133–99.

———. "Der Fall Zabern: Rückblick auf eine Verfassungskrise des wilhelminischen Kaiserreichs." *Die Welt als Geschichte* 23 (1963): 27–46.

———. *Sozialdemokratie und Nationalstaat.* Würzburg, 1962.

Wendel, Herman. *Elsass-Lothringen und die Sozialdemokratie.* Berlin, 1916.

Wentzke, Paul. "Drei Darstellungen elsass-lothringischer Geschichte." *Historische Zeitschrift* 125 (1922): 19–44.

———. *Der deutschen Einheit Schicksalsland: Elsass-Lothringen und das
Reich im neunzehnten und zwanzigsten Jahrhundert.* Munich, 1921.

———. "Zur Entstehungsgeschichte des Reichslandes Elsass-Lothringens,"
Süddeutsche Monatshefte 8 (1911): 607–26.

———. "Die alte Universität Strassburg, 1621–1793." *Elsass-Lothringisches
Jahrbuch,* 17 (1938): 37–112.

———, et al. *Elsass-Lothringen, 1871–1918.* Frankfurt a.M., 1938.

Wenzel, Wolfgang. *Elsass und Lothringen sind und bleiben unser.* Stuttgart,
1870.

Wesendonk, Otto-Günther von. *Darstellung und rechstpolitische Würdigung
der durch das Reichsgesetz vom 31. Mai 1911 in dem verfassungsrechtlichen
Verhältnis zwischen Elsass-Lothringen und dem Reich eingetretenen Veränderung.* Borna-Leipzig, 1913.

Wetterlé, Emile. *Les Coulisses du Reichstag: seize années de vie parlementaire
en Allemagne.* Paris, 1918.

———. *Parti catholique et coteries.* Colmar, 1893.

Windell, George G. *The Catholics and German Unity, 1866–1871.* Minne-
apolis, 1954.

Winterer, Landolin. *Arbeit und Religion: Ein kleiner sozialer Katechismus.*
Rixheim, 1897.

———. *Le Socialisme contemporaine.* Paris, 1901.

———. *Die Sozialdemokratie; Was sie lehrt und was sie will.* Rixheim, 1903.

"Die wirtschaftliche Entwicklung Elsass-Lothringens unter der deutschen
Verwaltung." *Elsässische Monatsschrift für Geschichte und Volkskunde*
2 (1911): 497–518.

Wolfram, Georg Karl. *Oberpräsident Eduard von Möller und die Elsass-
Lothringische Verfassungsfrage.* Berlin, 1925.

———, ed. *Verfassung und Verwaltung von Elsass-Lothringen, 1871–1918.*
Vol. 2 of *Das Reichsland Elsass-Lothringen, 1871–1918.* Berlin, 1937.

———, ed. *Wissenschaft, Kunst und Literatur in Elsass-Lothringen, 1871–
1918.* Vol. 3 of *Das Reichsland Elsass-Lothringen, 1871–1918.* Berlin, 1934.

Index